# Lionel Morris and the Red Baron

# Lionel Morris and the Red Baron

## Air War on the Somme

Jill Bush

The growing good of the world is partly dependent on unhistorical acts; and that things are not so ill with you and me as they might have been, is half owing to the number who lived faithfully a hidden life, and rest in unvisited tombs.

George Eliot

PEN & SWORD
HISTORY
AN IMPRINT OF PEN & SWORD BOOKS LTD.
YORKSHIRE - PHILADELPHIA

First published in Great Britain in 2019 by
Pen and Sword History
An imprint of
Pen & Sword Books Ltd
Yorkshire - Philadelphia

Hardback ISBN: 9781526742223
Paperback ISBN: 9781526765871

Typeset in INDIA By IMPEC e Solutions

Printed and bound in the UK by TJ International Ltd, Padstow, Cornwall

Pen & Sword Books Ltd incorporates the Imprints of Pen & Sword Books
Archaeology, Atlas, Aviation, Battleground, Discovery, Family History, History,
Maritime, Military, Naval, Politics, Railways, Select, Transport, True Crime,
Fiction, Frontline Books, Leo Cooper, Praetorian Press, Seaforth Publishing,
Wharncliffe and White Owl.

For a complete list of Pen & Sword titles please contact

PEN & SWORD BOOKS LIMITED
47 Church Street, Barnsley, South Yorkshire, S70 2AS, England
E-mail: enquiries@pen-and-sword.co.uk
Website: www.pen-and-sword.co.uk

or

PEN AND SWORD BOOKS
1950 Lawrence Rd, Havertown, PA 19083, USA
E-mail: Uspen-and-sword@casematepublishers.com
Website: www.penandswordbooks.com

To my father, for remembering
Aunt Lil's boy.

# Contents

# Foreword by Trevor Henshaw

Author, *The Sky Their Battlefield II: Air Fighting and Air Casualties of the Great War. British, Commonwealth and United States Air Services 1912 to 1919*

Jill Bush has written what I feel to be a unique and important book on the First Air War. Concerted and devoted research has enabled the author to glimpse right into the thoughts and hopes and experiences of a loved ancestor, who would be killed, high in the unforgiving sky above the Western Front in September 1916. Lionel Morris, whose young life she reveals so well, was just nineteen years old when he was shot down, along with his Observer Tom Rees, following an attack by Manfred von Richthofen, a German fighter pilot who would emerge with such remarkable fame and notoriety in the following years. So much is written about such men, but Lionel's own story, told so well here, perfectly explains how important each man's life was. He had trained devotedly, and after only a few months, found himself at the Front Line in France, with 11 Squadron RFC – a unit boasting Albert Ball and others, yet filled with mostly ordinary young men, who were also impassioned young patriots, to a man. For a few hours each day, each of these highly trained individuals faced a numbing challenge of duty and survival in the sky, just as in the evening these same comrades linked arms and sang, talked and laughed, and helped one another to carry on.

It is amazing that Lionel's personal diary of these days exists. It is such a precious thing, and is one reason why this book achieves something unique – we move, with Lionel's thoughts and narration right into this world, almost able to see it through his eyes. Often, it feels like a book about minutes and moments, rather than the great sweep of history: the mood and atmosphere of squadron life is superbly evoked. All those other resonances and voices the author has additionally brought in, from the papers and memoirs of those who were around him, work superbly. Her deep reading and research also ensures that the wider stories of Lionel's earlier life, and of the war are not just very factual and straightforward, but often quite enlightening.

Ultimately, however, it is a story about Lionel Morris. We catch sight of a young airman, in his final months – striving so hard now, on every patrol, to learn and become a better pilot, team member and adversary, in the hope of surviving, of course. Like all the others who would die, he should have had all his life ahead of him. This book, told with such conviction and flair, goes a long way to keeping his and others' memory alive and vivid and meaningful, to readers over a hundred years later.

Trevor Henshaw

# Introduction

My grandfather's first cousin Lionel Bertram Frank Morris was the pilot of the first aircraft to be officially shot down by the Red Baron, Manfred von Richthofen, on 17 September 1916. The day he died marked a turning point not just in the air war, but in the creation of its greatest legend: the German pilot who ended Morris's life turned out to be not just a lucky German airman, but someone who developed into a lethally skilful killer. For a period of nineteen months he became a nemesis for Britain's Royal Flying Corps (RFC), the predecessor of today's Royal Air Force.

Pilots of the Great War were exceptional men, displaying levels not just of immense courage, but also unbelievable technical ability and survival instincts that we, with our twenty-first-century horror of jeopardy, can't hope to understand. By any standards, Morris's ten months with the Royal Flying Corps were an adrenaline-fuelled flight of terror and exhilaration. He had no more than two shared victories himself (officially, five was the necessary total to be an ace) but his achievement was still impressive – mastering machines just as likely to kill their own crews as the enemy was one thing; being able to successfully manipulate them in combat was another. Those first two years of the war turned teenagers into virtuoso performers without the benefit of adequate time-served experience. Their learning curves were as steep as the climbs they made when they stood their aeroplanes on their tails to evade their attackers. It was a time of incredible progress made at the appalling expense of many lives; when gallantry still had a place in warfare, and wreaths were dropped over enemy lines to show respect for the airmen who fell.

This is not a book about Manfred von Richthofen; his appearance in Morris's life came with ballistic velocity right at the end of it and I have not attempted to relate a story that others with better qualifications have told. I *have* drawn heavily on the charismatic presence of Albert Ball because his training and subsequent squadron placements often ran on an irresistibly parallel course to Morris's.

Up until Morris's arrival in France in May 1916, when he decided to start keeping a diary, direct mentions of him in surviving records are limited. For me, with that diary, a window that had been only slightly ajar was all of a sudden banging open. It tore me from the reference books. His gleeful participation in a real-life boys' own adventure sprang out in vivid moments, and was a touching expression of a young man not yet traumatised by a monstrous conflict. It was an unselfconscious day-to-day narrative of the most significant test the Royal Flying Corps had yet faced in the war, and one which highlighted the chaos and comedy of an under-resourced service always three steps away from the critical mass needed to comprehensively beat the enemy. The abrupt end to the diary, seven weeks before the endgame with Richthofen, was in many ways a relief – any references to the horror of war are concise and unremarked on.

Thanks to his diary, and the circumstances of Morris's death, I have gone from angling for small glimpses of his early life to trawling rich detail from the summer of the Somme. To provide context and background to his story, I have included specific contemporaries and events that I hope will illustrate, in the absence of more personal material, the life and times he experienced.

Morris's tragedy was an ordinary one warped by the accretions of history. His end came two days after the second phase of the offensive had commenced, when the trees still standing on the Somme were losing their leaves, and Kitchener's army, having already absorbed a mighty blow, were endeavouring to make good what progress had been made. As the historian William Philpott has shown, the subtle role of semantics in the developing legend of catastrophe is often forgotten: the 'Battle' of the Somme was a series of linked actions towards a drawn-out conclusion. The arguments – about just how catastrophic it was – have kept the linguistic uncertainty endlessly relevant.[1]

My aim has been to create a narrative for a young man whose corporeal life was compressed and anonymous. I set out to write with few sources and some scrabblings of family memory. But they were enough to create a bizarre and intangible connection, and an itch I haven't been able to stop scratching since, despite my rational conviction that these feelings are illogical and even fraudulent when applied to long dead strangers. The tap root of family history is as invasive as a perennial weed. You can try and dig it out, but it will lurk perpetually just out of reach, twisting and indestructible.

Seaford, June 2018.

# Chapter 1

## South to North End

Lionel Morris's roots were in London, but his mother Lil Read was Dorset born and bred and he was not allowed to forget it.[1] His father Albert, previously a teenage sailor based just down the coast from Lil's home in Weymouth, was a pale boy with an exemplary character.[2] Having decided against a life on the ocean wave, he turned instead to the world of commerce with a desk-bound job as a merchant's clerk – essentially a Victorian administrative assistant but a world away from his family's working class origins.[3] Lil was a builder's daughter, one of seven children born in Melcombe Regis, an area of Weymouth most famous for having been one of the principal ports of England that brought in the plague. On 4 April 1896 at St John's Church in Weymouth, Lil and Albert were married, with Lil's younger sister Nellie (a bit of a live wire: sued for divorce on the grounds of adultery by two different husbands before the nineteen twenties were out), and her father James as witnesses.[4]

Albert and Lil moved to Stockwell in London and Lionel Morris made his first appearance in the records on Boxing Day, just eight months after his mother and father's marriage.[5] It seems uncharitable to think that Lil may have been pregnant at the time of her wedding, as the birth could have been premature, but he remained the Morris's only child. Moving the short distance from Stockwell to Balham, and settling in what is now Romany Road in present day Lambeth, the Morrises took their ten-month-old baby back to Dorset and had him baptised amongst his Read family, in the same Weymouth church in which his parents had married.[6] Four years later they were on the move once more, to the parish of St Michael and All Angels in Walthamstow, east London, and again the family ties were strong, with Lil's father

James present at the time of the 1901 census. Albert's job title was now more impressive: 'stock taker tobacconist'. Lil's county of birth was written as 'Dowsett', proving that the girl could be taken out of the west country, but still bamboozle the scribes with her accent.

Another four years later and the family had returned to south London, settling in Norbury. Morris attended at least two schools before the age of ten, one in Forest Gate and one in Streatham.[7] By 1908, he was at Winterbourne Road Board School in Thornton Heath, now closer to the family home.[8] The admissions register gives an instructive picture of the snakes and ladders mobility of the lower middle classes of Edwardian London. On the same page as Morris, three boys are 'removed' with no further details; others become errand boys, junior clerks and gardeners. Morris is one of three who win scholarships: one goes to technical college, and he and the memorably named Rembrandt Herring are set for Whitgift Middle School at North End, Croydon, where he started as a day pupil in the Michaelmas term of 1908.[9]

Morris's school years took place at a time of great changes to the education system, starting with the growth of local council-funded elementary schools in the late nineteenth century. There were increases in provision of secondary education: by 1907 academically able children from poorer backgrounds were receiving more help to continue into secondary schools – when previously their leaving age would have been thirteen. But it was a royal anniversary that enabled Morris to continue his education beyond the majority of boys of his class, and to progress to 'Big School' at Whitgift Grammar in September 1910.[10] In 1887 the Whitgift Foundation endowed awards in recognition of Queen Victoria's Golden Jubilee, a gift which still exists today at the school. He was up against boys already there, as well as others like himself applying through open competition, sitting an examination including Latin, Mathematics, English and French. Only six places were offered per year. As a fourteen-year-old, Morris was entitled to sixteen pounds a year to cover his fees.[11] The success of their son's application to Whitgift was in line with the Morrises' status as an aspirant middle-class family. Lil and Albert, through fate or choice with no other children to support, must have rejoiced at such a pain-free advancement for their only son. Lil's older brother Ernest had also prospered as a watchmaker and jeweller in Kensington, but by contrast had five children to provide for.[12]

Headmaster Samuel Ogden Andrew had turned Whitgift into an exceptional school. An inspection of 1912 reported changes of 'so striking a character that it is difficult to believe that this is the same institution that was reported on in 1903', with standards high enough to 'fully entitle it to a place among the leading Secondary Schools in the country.'[13] The Whitgift values of loyalty and service, enshrined in its motto *Vincit qui patitur* ('He who perseveres, conquers'), together with an acceptance of both physical and mental hardships were impressed even more strongly on a scholarship boy like Morris, who had less reason than many to feel entitled to his Whitgift education.

*

By 1913 the possibility of a European conflict was growing, and Whitgift's Officers' Training Corps (OTC) was at the centre of the school lives of many of its boys. For teenagers safe in the home counties, war games were a source of both motivation and *ennui*; the practical skills of drilling and shooting a welcome alternative to the less exciting and uncomfortable necessities of roughing it like a proper soldier. The military service enshrined in the British public school system since the Boer War was streamlined as war loomed. A shortage of officer material was addressed by the remodelling of volunteer school corps: these Junior Divisions aimed at producing a consistent standard of rudimentary military instruction, and a good supply of new officers.

After a few years in the OTC, with the qualification of a Certificate 'A', those willing and able were directly handpicked for a commission in the services. Local loyalties were strong, and many Whitgift boys ended up as reservists in the 1st Queen's Regiment.[14] A rare photograph of the Whitgift Officers' Training Corps in 1911 (which is likely to include an unidentified fourteen-year-old Morris) shows forty or so boys outside the Junior School. The back row are in round-collared civvies, the rest in uniform; with the smallest at the front sitting cross-legged in wound puttees. On their cap badges is the lamb of the Queen's Regiment, an insignia that followed many Whitgift OTC cadets to their gravestones. A wishful search of the forty or so boys pictured focuses in on one, eighth from the right in the second row. He stares straight at the camera with a friendly open expression, squinting slightly into the sun. His face is angular, his ears are neat and he almost smiles. There's no proof, though, that it's Morris.

The school's official history remarks of the Corps that by October 1914 'it was only those few who, being old enough, were quite unfit that had not joined.'[15] In his novel of public school life, *Stalky and Co*, Rudyard Kipling (later to lose his only son in France) wrote 'We've got to get into the army – or get out, haven't we?... All the rest's flumdiddle.'[16] But there were no clues that Morris wanted to join the Army before the war, despite the direct route to a promising military career that must have been attractive to his upwardly mobile family. The only non-administrative glimpse of him at school is a brief, workmanlike appearance in the Junior XV Football (Rugby) team in 1911 – sport of course being the other great *raison d'etre* of public schools.[17] With that sole entry in the Whitgift annals of competitive glory, he left the school in December 1913.[18] A leaving age of sixteen was not uncommon and he does not appear in any matriculation lists for university. Perhaps Lil pressed him into her service – in 1911 she seemed to show more ambition than her husband and was listed as the manager of a china and glass shop whilst Albert was still a clerk.[19]

With the end of peace on 4 August 1914, Morris's quiet corner of suburbia was finally overtaken by world events. In Croydon, guards from the City of London Volunteers appeared overnight, ready to defend all the modern conveniences of peacetime (such as railways and power hubs) that Surrey had taken for granted.[20] It would take more than the portents of conflict to stop the rise of the Morrises: the tobacco industry was about to become one of the great victors of the First World War; the comfort of the humble weed sought both at home and in the trenches. Albert's career choice had proved a wise one.

By 1915, the Morrises had moved to Rotherfield Road in Carshalton; at that time a village between Croydon and Sutton at the source of the

River Wandle, whose ponds created a semi-rural atmosphere enhanced by market gardening and lavender fields. The creep of urban industry was as yet confined to several watermills and a sinister lack of trout in the Wandle.[21] It was on the London to the south coast, as well as the West Croydon to Sutton, train line. There was plenty of local character in the village – Morris would have been familiar with the eighteenth-century gallows beam still suspended between two old lime trees, from a time when the village was known chiefly for its trout and walnuts.[22] Three tobacconists were listed in the village in 1915, none of them bearing Albert's name, although like today's newsagents, core business would not have been confined to supplying the smokers of Surrey and there is no mention of a self-titled premises in the street directories.[23] By the time the Morrises had moved to Carshalton, the public hall where roller skating was enjoyed by the locals had been converted into a twentieth-century leisure convenience and renamed *The Picture Palace*.[24]

The christening of their new home *Merle Bank*, spoke volumes for their social ambition: they had escaped the grimy streets of Norbury for the watercress meadows of Carshalton. Rotherfield Road was outside the old village, but the Morrises had stepped up. From a busy street within sight and sound of the railway, they were now still conveniently close to the station, but the owners of a spacious new villa with desirable rurality.

Belgian refugees arriving in this green and pleasant village in autumn 1914 were welcomed by a community already mourning nine dead servicemen.[25] On Boxing Day of the same year, Morris turned eighteen, the minimum age for enlistment. By the following March the privations of war were coming home to the locals and the cost of living had risen by twenty-five per cent, forcing the council to award bonuses to their lower paid employees.[26] Conviction in the belief that the war would be over soon was waning, and at a meeting held to discuss the ramifications of such expense, one councillor finally voiced the unthinkable: "'Supposing," said he, "the war lasted another six months!"'[27]

Less than two months later Lionel Morris enlisted.

## Chapter 2

# Goodbye, Good Luck, God Bless You

Berkhamsted Common on a bright spring afternoon is a pretty and peaceful woodland spot, high above the Hertfordshire town, the haunt of deer and rich in birdlife. Unsurprising, then, that a crass effort by a local landowner to appropriate it for his own private use in 1866 was resisted with spirit and a landmark court case which eventually gave the public right of way. But for many years, strange features in the chalk ridge made it a dangerous place for careless wanderers: deep grooves in the earth were capable of causing nasty injuries to those unlucky enough to fall into them. By the turn of the twenty-first century the furrows were shallower and less of a trap for the unwary, and it took a frosty morning with the sun in the right place for the tell-tale scars on the landscape to reveal themselves. These marks were all that remained of a vast operation that had taken over Berkhamsted in the First World War – nearly seven miles of trenches, dug by the cadets of the Inns of Court (IOC) Officers' Training Corps.

Today some of them have been restored, with interpretation boards to explain their significance. Perhaps because of the softening effects of nature, the excavations remain evocative, their meanders and dogleg bends illuminated by shafts of sunlight between the trees. It's a good playground for children now, and muntjac graze around the banks of the cuttings. But the physical scars on the landscape haven't gone away in over a century, and show with graphic purpose just what the war to end all wars was all about for the men that fought in it.

It was to Berkhamsted that Lionel Morris went to learn to become a soldier.

*

In the spring of 1915, Surrey was attempting to carry on as normal. Croydon busied itself: organising presents for the troops, hiring special constables to cover for its policemen away on active service, and admonishing fearful citizens who were hoarding food.[1] Conscription was yet to be enforced but the white feathers were fluttering all over Britain. In Carshalton as early as October 1914, a local man, Mr H.V. Piers, took it upon himself to design a card to be placed in the windows of houses of families whose men had signed up, on which the words 'A Carshalton man from this house is now serving in His Majesty's Forces' was surrounded by the legend 'Not at Home'. The reverse held details of names and regiments. Ostensibly designed to keep the community informed of local lads who had already enlisted (and less brutal than the ill-conceived Order of the White Feather, which was attempting to galvanise the nation's women into shaming those young men not yet in uniform) Mr Piers's ulterior motive was nonetheless to encourage those eligible and still at home to join up. The proliferation of cards in homes all over the district must have been a painful sight to many of those who had, for whatever reason, not entered the forces.[2]

On 7 May 1915, anxiety rose to a new level after the sinking of the *Lusitania*; an event which may well have finally pushed Morris into the Army. The Cunard liner, returning to Liverpool from New York, carried an overwhelmingly American list of passengers, a load of war material, and a death sentence on its head, following official German government warnings in US newspapers. The loss of nearly 1,200 lives caused a knee-jerk reaction in Britain that sent recruitment lists soaring. The Parliamentary Recruitment Committee wasted no time in exploiting the propaganda opportunity, and lurid posters appeared, exhorting those previously unmoved by the war to take up the sword of justice on behalf of the innocent victims of the tragedy. Anti-German feeling reached terrifying heights for some of those remaining German nationals in Britain, many of whom had long been integrated members of local communities. Riots broke out in London targeting German businesses as well as pitching the odd unfortunate foreigner into a maelstrom of mob-induced hatred.[3] Croydon held its breath for four days and sent part-time special constables onto the streets as a precaution against copycat disturbances and looting. Although local newspapers restrained themselves from pinpointing the *Lusitania* as the catalyst for civil unrest, ominous mobs were reported loitering around premises owned by German-born shopkeepers, and the odd window was smashed by the disgruntled and inebriated under a guise of patriotism.[4]

In the same week, the highly influential Bryce report exaggerated genuine German atrocities against the Belgians. The general text of the report was sober and objective. But terrifying tales from narrators made unreliable by the horror of war were included in an appendix, causing sharp intakes of breath all over the world. *The Essex Newsman* reported that a bomb landing harmlessly in a Southend garden following a Zeppelin raid brought a chilling message written in blue pencil on cardboard: 'You English. We have come and will come again soon – kill or cure – German.'[5]

The British Army in 1915 was undergoing the most profound changes in its history, straining to absorb thousands of men, and May saw one of the largest expansion of volunteers that year, as the upper age limit of enlistment was raised from thirty-eight to forty. The regulars of the old army had been joined by the Territorial Force, but the number of old soldiers returning to do their bit was getting smaller and opinions differed as to how useful they were to a twentieth-century army. Ex-pats and retirees with wide life experience were welcomed as officers in many cases, but they were equally often ridiculed as 'Gorgeous Wrecks', from the GR initials on their armbands identifying the sovereign George V. By mid-1915 the rate of attrition on the Western Front had decimated the supply of officers, and the traditional training grounds of Sandhurst and Woolwich could not produce adequate numbers of replacements. The rush of volunteers who had signed up in 1914 was also drying up. A shortage of officer material following the early battles of the war was a headache for those concerned to keep a superior class of subaltern, and the scale of numbers now required was a rude shock. University and school OTCs provided the next logical pool of recruits. The direct route to a commission picked off the most promising of boys from the more illustrious public schools, and it took protests to the War Office from less well known educational establishments, frustrated at hierarchical protocol in the face of such national need, before admission was permitted from a much wider field. In answer to pointed criticisms of exclusion, the War Office, responding to a request for the definition of a public school, gave a definitive response: 'a school open to the public'.[6] Suitable officer material was too often rapidly absorbed in the ranks because of the lack of training organisations.

The Inns of Court Officers' Training Corps was an ancient militia with a history stretching back to the time of the Armada, 'practically unknown outside a limited circle', according to its leader and first historian Colonel Francis Errington. Traditionally cadets came exclusively from the legal profession. Their adopted nickname of 'The Devil's Own' was a label apparently bestowed on them, not by King George III as an oft-repeated legend suggests, but by their own Colonel, who proudly had relayed the nickname to the King himself at a review of troops in Hyde Park in 1806.[7] Lord Haldane, whose extensive Army reforms helped to mould a generation of boy soldiers, was fulsome in his praise of the model of the Inns of Court OTC, calling it 'one of the very pivots upon which the Army organisation acted.'[8]

In 1915 an advertising campaign began to get the message out that it was now unnecessary to be a lawyer to join the Inns of Court OTC. Targeting transport hubs, theatres and schools, it stretched all the way to the colonies; recruitment officers sometimes travelling to port cities like Liverpool. In the three months between March and June of 1915, recruiting had nearly doubled. At its peak, the Selection Committee was interviewing 1,200 candidates a day and producing eighty officers a week by the summer of 1915.[9]

Posters went up all over Croydon exhorting young men to join the war effort. One of them used the image of faithful female dependents gazing steadfastly at lines of departing soldiers with the headline 'Women of Britain Say Go!' Morris finally made up his mind. On 13 May 1915, at the age of nearly eighteen and a half, he went up to Lincoln's Inn, the HQ of the Inns of Court OTC in London, and took the irrecoverable step of signing his Attestation papers – the beginning of the legal process of enlistment. He was prodded and examined by doctors to ascertain his physical fitness. Like his father before him, his character also passed the test, with a terse but satisfactory 'VG' noted in the medical report. Within four days he was approved and appointed as a private. The attestation form has 'Territorial Army' stamped on it – something of a red herring for Morris, whose objective was a commission via the Inns of Court OTC.[10] Territorial soldiers could waive their right to serve solely at home by signing the Imperial Service Obligation form, but Morris would have known what the implications of becoming an officer were, and that he was signing up to fight overseas. His route to the war was shared by thousands of officers – but with that crucial delay in enlistment which perhaps says more about how he (and possibly his parents) had really appreciated the difference between playing at soldiers at school, and signing up for a real and deadly conflict.

When Morris received his introduction to grown-up soldiering with the Inns of Court OTC at Berkhamsted, he earned a shilling a day as a cadet, with an allowance of 2d for kit and 1/9 for rations.[11] He undertook boundless marching, field exercises, map reading, lecture attendance and trench digging. Local landowner Lord Brownlow provided the space for the rapidly expanding Corps, which had outgrown the precincts of Lincoln's Inn. Kitchener's Field (as it remains, now the home of Berkhamsted Cricket Club) named after the Secretary of War, was the heart of the operation. In the summer of 1915 row upon row of pale tents began to 'spring up with the suddenness of mushrooms' on adjacent land.[12] The site, near Berkhamsted Castle, was conveniently close to the railway station, providing room for drill, while large marquees hosted lectures and catering.

Sacrificing quality for quantity made the War Office's increasing demands uncomfortable for the Corps. Their answer to converting to mass production was to distill what they considered to be the most crucial attribute for an officer: his character. This they believed was achieved principally through discipline and by the example of their own trainers, who were to encourage both enthusiasm and the stimulation of an *esprit de corps*. Experienced officers were expected to be able to mould raw recruits and to distinguish 'between the real and the improveable wrong-un'.[13] Many of these training officers were torn between the need for their experience and skill at home, and the desire to be on the front line themselves. A crude proposal to solve this problem was to replace them with wounded officers who had been sent back to Blighty. Wisely, this suggestion was vetoed by Errington with the support of the War Office.[14]

On 3 June 1915, Whitgift's school magazine noted Private L.B.F. Morris's arrival with the Inns of Court Officer's Training Corps.[15] His company commander was Sir Frederic Kenyon, erstwhile Director of the British Museum, and one of those officers yearning for a more active role in the war.[16] Every Friday and Saturday morning the recruits spent an hour drilling. Parades were nerve-wracking ordeals even for the hardest-working cadet. One trainee who was to follow Morris into the Royal Flying Corps, and arrived at Berkhamsted just a few months after him, provides a timeless portrait of the belligerent Sergeant Major: 'he got me taped unfortunately for moving my head when at 'shion and enquired if I was looking down the line for my long lost friend or what.'[17] Colonel Errington gave his own endorsement of Regimental Sergeant Major Burns of the Scots Guards: 'Immaculate in appearance, with every detail of army life at his fingers' end, this RSM was also an excellent lecturer, and I believe one of the best speakers at the Army temperance meetings.'[18] Lieutenant T.S. Wynne of the Suffolk Regiment described his more intimidating qualities: 'His was the voice which spread desolation all over the parade ground. His eye always seemed to light on us cowering in the rear ranks and spotted a chilled hand straying into a greatcoat pocket.'[19] Kenyon was clear about what the recruits needed to know: 'They were never allowed to forget that they were learning to be privates so that they might learn to be officers.'[20]

Morris was 'at home' for the entire length of his training.[21] A lack of accommodation was a growing pain for the Inns of Court Officer's Training Corps, and it was not unheard of for new entrants in the summer of 1915 to commute from their homes to Berkhamsted after an initial fortnight of drilling at Lincoln's Inn.[22] Travelling from Croydon to Hertfordshire by train even today is still a haul at nearly two hours; although for Morris, returning to the comfort of his own bed at *Merle Bank* must have been preferable to roughing it under canvas in Kitchener's Field. The initially vexing question of accommodation was lampooned in the Corps's magazine *The Hades Herald* (proceeds of which were given to British PoWs and the RSPCA's fund for wounded horses). 'Bedridden' is written in diary form and its humour is still effectively droll today: 'July 12th, 1915. Disquieting rumours to the effect that the epidemic of Billetitis, hitherto confined to the north of King's Road, shows signs of spreading.' Cadets would have recognised the cheerful fortitude shown by the character of Private Montease:

> Maid came to bedroom door with some cough lozenges which she asked me to take to the new billet. Took them. Private Montease thanked me, but said he didn't mind coughing. Said it was an heirloom; Montease cough, known in the highest circles all over Scotland since the time of Young Pretender.[23]

A particularly miserable part of training that Colonel Errington himself admitted was of limited value over and above fitness and the instilling of discipline, was the digging of trenches: 'Trench life and trench routine cannot be taught under ordinary training conditions, and a week in France or up the Salient taught more than months of playing at it at home can do.'[24] The back-breaking lesson the cadets learned in the trenches was one of gloomy recognition when they finally arrived on the Western Front, as the soil of northern France shared the same viscous combination of clay and flint that they had struggled with in Hertfordshire. In a real theatre of war rain quickly turned them into intolerable and sometimes lethal channels of mud and water. Errington pointed out that such labour was nevertheless a reminder of how the men who would be under the cadet's command would experience orders: 'It is good for every man to have some experience of what a heavy job of digging feels like, and the carrying of tools on the march.'[25]

Locals got used to swarms of young men all over the countryside, with every geographical feature, from woods to rivers and commons, utilised to prepare the boys for warfare. Night operations tested their powers of vigilance and stamina. Boredom thresholds were tested as the long dark hours were spent watching and waiting.

Smartness was a constant struggle; Errington noted that 'baths were a difficulty for some time' and helpful locals who provided billets had to expect 'the entry at all times of the night of mud-covered men'.[26] For a period, long-suffering neighbours of the OTC were spared the shattering reports of guns going off as there were so few weapons available and even fewer places where the cadets could safely shoot. Until February 1915 they had to be transported to Middlesex to practice at a pre-war training site.

A 'miniature range' was hastily assembled at Berkhamsted, and it was not until July 1916 that a dedicated new building was ready for cadets, now finally able to work out how to handle guns in practice rather than just having to use their imaginations. Developments in the tools of war reached the IOC cadets slowly and painfully. One enterprising officer happened to meet the inventor of the Lewis gun and had the benefit of a couple of days of tuition before the weapon became generally available for use by the Regular Army.[27] It must have sat like a rare and exotic bird amongst the more arcane weapons of the Inns of Court.

Morris took a little over two months at Berkhamsted to ready himself for a commission and he requested service in the infantry on his application form. As he was under twenty-one, his father signed the form.[28] His almost seamless progression to the Inns of Court OTC and soon-to-be-confirmed subaltern status with his home county's regiment, suggested his time at Whitgift had sown the seeds of duty. He now made a six-year commitment, with six months of full time training, and demonstrated he was willing to fight abroad.

The Special Reserves had a long history as a form of county militia, but became an anachronism and were reformed in 1908 to provide an additional trained supply of soldiers for home defence. The ongoing emergency of war turned the Special Reserves into a vital supply of draft replacements for the rapidly diminishing regular force: most counties formed a Third Battalion Special Reserve, allowing men to be trained whilst also protecting Britain's vulnerable coasts. It was a natural place for young men like Morris to try out military life. He joined a varied contingent of officers: some had been abroad and unable to enlist previously, some were older and didn't want to wait until conscription forced them into the Army.

Berkhamsted's camps were visited regularly by regimental colonels scouting for talent, and on 19 August 1915, Morris was granted a commission as a probationary second lieutenant with the Queen's Royal West Surrey Regiment (QRWS).[29] Despite his ambition, undoubted ability and bravery, he was never to be promoted beyond this lowliest of subaltern posts.

Morris moved east to his new battalion. His destination was coastal Kent, where the British war effort was being funnelled to France.

*Chapter 3*

# The Mutton Lancers

In the mid-1920s, as the shell holes began to fill up on the Western Front, the Queen's Royal West Surrey regiment (also known as 'the Queen's' or 'the Surreys') were still toiling for the Empire in Utter Pradesh. A regimental legend says that in the heat of the northern Indian sun of Allahabad, the soldiers marched past the wife of the brigadier, Mrs Coame Stewart. Mrs Stewart turned to Major A.N.S. Roberts, veteran of the North-West Frontier, and enquired as to why the regiment were using a German melody to accompany their ceremonial manoeuvres.[1]

Many regimental melodies have opaque pan-European origins and the answer may lie, perversely enough, continents away, in seventeenth-century Africa. It also explains why the Queen's would have appealed to Morris not only as his local regiment, but as an infantry unit second only to the Royal Scots Foot in age and prestige. Charles II's bride in 1662 was of the Portuguese royal house of Braganza, and her dowry brought Tangier (indispensable due to its position at the gate of the Mediterranean) under the yoke of the British. Constantly harassed by the Moors, the territory needed a garrison, and the force raised stayed for nearly twenty years, returning home forever linked with Catherine as the Queen's Regiment. The in-breeding that had occurred in royal households may hold a clue as to why the Brigadier's wife had recognised the tune. Mittel European and Latinate families had intermingled over the centuries, not just in blood, but also in culture and tradition. The *Braganza* tune adopted by the regiment was similar to the melody of the Portuguese national anthem, composed by none less than the Portuguese king himself, but the ubiquitous composer Anon still officially receives the credit and provides a host of intriguing genesis theories.[2]

The Surreys continued globetrotting over the next couple of centuries, taking part in the Peninsular War and the Wars of the Spanish Succession, as well as returning to garrison duties in Gibraltar, suffering decimation by disease in the Caribbean and fighting in South Africa, Afghanistan, Ireland and India. One of their finest moments came (fittingly enough) in Portugal, marching over the Pyrenees and constantly fending off attack after attack, under the command of a soldier of some reputation known as the Duke of Wellington.

In one of the two photos of Morris still existing, the lamb insignia of the Queen's Royal West Surrey Regiment that earned them the nickname of 'The Mutton Lancers' is clearly visible on his shoulder. The origins of this are as uncertain as the regimental marching tune, but may again lean towards the figure of Catherine of Braganza, who was on occasion portrayed in paintings with a lamb. The Surreys' Lamb carries a flag representing resurrection but the overwhelming symbolism is of sacrifice. Nowhere was this more appropriate for the regiment than in France in 1914: as part of the British Expeditionary Force, the 1st Battalion alone had lost 956 out of 988 men by the end of November.[3]

As a newly commissioned officer (described on the Special Reserve Commission certificate as 'Our trusty and beloved') Morris's behaviour was under scrutiny.[4] Avoiding the stigma of conscription as a volunteer, he was less under suspicion than some of the 'temporary gentlemen' who came after him, but there were standards to be upheld. Some, such as avoiding drunkenness or being seen walking 'about with one of the opposite sex with whom you would not care for your colonel or men to see you with', were understandable, but others such as reading too much betrayed the Army's need to avoid dangerously independent thinkers.[5]

The Special Reserve of the Third Battalion was collecting ready men in preparation for sending them to France, and on 19 August 1915 Morris was ordered to report to them at Fort Bridgewood on the outskirts of Rochester.[6]

The new recruits weren't just there to train. Bridgewood was one of a ring of defensive forts built in the nineteenth century to protect the naval dockyards at Chatham, and the outbreak of war gave them a renewed significance. One of the battalion's companies had been stationed there since November 1914, and its officers were housed at Chatham Lower Barracks as recruiting expanded.[7] Airship raids were making the previously distant dangers of war a present and terrifying threat on the south coast. For a country that had considered its shores inviolable for centuries, and at a time when parents were separated from their children on active service, the realisation that home was no longer safe was profound and appalling. 'Darkness and Composure' was recommended by the authorities.[8] Attempts at blackout created their own anxieties: people stumbled around on moonless nights or were dazed by flashlights pointed carelessly into the murk.[9] Lights left on were there by necessity. But there were always those who thought it was all about them: objecting to being illuminated when their neighbours weren't. In July 1915 *Flight* reported some trouble with 'Air Raidism': 'One had his house newly painted and the light helped to single out his abode as an especially fine mark for Zeppeliners.' Fines ensued for flouting the restrictions and any malice the airships might have shown towards such high standards of exterior decoration was avoided.[10]

Road maintenance was neglected and potholes tripped up pedestrians.[11] In 1915 a dark clear night meant the likelihood of airships: later a full moon would bring the Gotha bombers. Nights of watching and waiting produced 'a general clenching of the teeth… We were all astronomers of a kind in those days.'[12] Only when it rained did people feel safe. But relying on the lunar calendar became reckless when the raiders became bolder and began to attack in daylight.[13]

The sense of unease was not confined to the general public. That the British armed forces were out of their depth was reflected in the DIY instructions sent to Morris: 'You should provide yourself with bedding and kit… and should join in uniform, but if your uniform is not ready, in plain clothes.'[14] The Surreys' new recruits were expected to make do and march. Building up distances from a few miles to all-day slogs, with packs full of lead pieces to simulate ammunition (nicknamed 'Kitchener's Chocolate'), these gruelling exercises were designed to reinforce discipline as well as fitness, and were frequently accompanied by desultory singing to alleviate boredom. The standard of Tommy's musical rigour in 1915 was disappointing:

> The men liked to sing but, in that respect, they certainly did *not* come up to the best standards. The singing was usually spasmodic and none too good. If they had taken the trouble to learn the words of songs, and not merely fragments of choruses, singing on the march would have been far more inspiring. It was surprising what a large proportion of men could continue to sing contentedly with the beat on the wrong foot, or even attempted to march to rag-time![15]

\*

By the end of the summer, Morris had begun dreaming of a more glamorous theatre of war than messing about in trenches. On 24 September, a Surreys' medical report pronounced him fit for general service. On the same day he wrote from Chatham to the battalion adjutant to request a 'Government course of instruction with the "Royal Flying Corps"'. The self-conscious use of quotation marks is touching: as if he wasn't entirely convinced the service existed.[16]

Morris, the low-achieving sportsman of Whitgift, couldn't ride a horse, as his application for temporary commission showed, and any helpful connections he might have had were not preserved in his records. He was also, by modern standards, on the diminutive side at five feet six and three-quarter inches, according to his enlistment medical report, although he himself added a whole extra inch on his transfer application.[17] His 'physical development' was good and his eyesight fine.[18] What he also had going for him was his public school education and his extra-curricular proficiencies. In his transfer request, he supplied his age, height and weight, and then neatly listed the competencies he thought appropriate for flying. The fourth and sixth items provided perhaps the best clue as to why he felt equipped for the change:

(4) My knowledge of motor mechanics is good.

(5) My knowledge of map-reading and Field Sketching is good.

(6) I have a good knowledge of elementary mechanics (statics, Hydrostatics and Dynamics).

(7) I am conversant in the French and German languages.[19]

It is likely that Morris's route to the skies involved a clammy-palmed visit to the Whitehall home of the War Office, where the Directorate of Military Aeronautics sifted through thousands of applicants keen to avoid the trenches. Other hopefuls recorded rudimentary questioning (which often involved establishing common acquaintances from public schools) and an uncomplicated medical which looked for problems of balance by energetically revolving candidates in a chair and then asking them to walk in a straight line. Other tests included candidates raising a tuning fork whilst not being unduly bothered by a large clapper suddenly erupting close by, and distinguishing between variously shaded yarns as a check for colour blindness.[20] As late as March 1916, *Flight* was reporting studies from France published in *The Lancet*, which had observed authoritatively: 'What is essential for a good pilot is a combination in one person of resistance to fatigue, emotional passivity, and very rapid motor reaction.'[21]

Morris's request for transfer was granted quickly. He was ordered to 'join at Norwich, on the 8th November, for instruction in aviation' under the General Officer Commanding Second Brigade. He was told to 'take camp equipment' with him.[22] The whiff of canvas that followed him from the tented town of the Inns of Court OTC at Berkhamsted was still strong. About a month and a half after his application, his flying training had begun with No. 9 Reserve Squadron at Mousehold Heath.[23]

The tobacconist's boy was ready to spread his wings.

*Chapter 4*

# This Flying Business

The Royal Flying Corps that Morris was to join was a long way from the RAF as we know it today. In 1915 he was in it to serve the Army.

Only six years had passed since Blériot had crossed the Channel. Aeroplanes themselves had existed in barely functional form for less than ten. Leonardo da Vinci had failed to crack the mystery of flight back in the sixteenth century, and another four hundred years passed before others with more understanding and better toolkits were able to. It was then all the more extraordinary when early aircraft designers finally overcame the setbacks of nearly half a millennia, and put men in flying machines that worked. The Industrial Age had contributed power and mechanisation but before the war even the pioneers had limited success. The catalyst for astonishing design improvements was the biggest global armed conflict in history thus far.

Divisions between the Navy and the Army were reflected in the incessant debate about how aviation was to fit into Britain's military organisation. The RFC formed in 1912 out of a small Air Battalion of the Royal Engineers and was tied to both services – with the result that (as is normal in British military tradition) the two often fell out over it. The Army's priority was the RFC's reconnaissance function, while the Navy's was defensive support.

Britain's application of aviation lagged behind that of its Continental allies as well as its rivals. 'Air' in the particular imaginations of the generals had been useful for a birds-eye view of the battlefields. In 1914, the RFC was dysfunctionally stretched between the Army and the Navy, with a woefully inadequate supply chain for its technical and infrastructure needs. The Royal Naval Air Service (RNAS) was attached to the Navy the following year, leaving the RFC as the Army's aviation wing. Resources remained constrained, with the RNAS enjoying much more freedom than the RFC, which had the restriction of pre-war contracts with the Royal Aircraft Factory. The eventual leader of the British Expeditionary Force, General Douglas Haig, had been made aware of the difference 'Air' could make after peace-time manoeuvres in East Anglia. Haig's 'Red' Army, a well-oiled machine compared to their improvised 'Blue' Army opponents, was defeated with the help of accurate aircraft reconnaissance, championed on the day by Major Hugh Trenchard, whose intervention with the suggestion of sending revised orders by aircraft saved the day for the 'Blue' Army.[1] Haig was left with, if not respect, curiosity, for the new technology.

When peace finally fractured in 1914, Trenchard was obliged to marshal his own war effort from a desk in leafy Hampshire. Appointed commander of the RFC's military wing and based at Farnborough, it was Trenchard's senior, Brigadier-General Sir David Henderson, who took to the field in France as commander, leaving behind Major Sir Sefton Brancker, Deputy Director of Military Aeronautics, as chief quartermaster, with the thankless responsibility of resourcing the RFC. The trio of Henderson, Trenchard, and Brancker worked together effectively for the first few years of the war. The odd man out in senior command was Major Frederick Sykes, whose Machiavellian ways and aloof manner put him in direct conflict with many, including the bluff and straightforward Trenchard.

As the RFC flexed to adapt to its wartime responsibilities, a complicated game of musical chairs shuffled its top officers. Henderson was recalled to Britain by Lord Kitchener in 1915 to resume his pre-war role of Director of Military Aeronautics, and Trenchard was finally given the opportunity to do what he most wanted to do: lead the RFC on the Western Front.

Devon-born Trenchard had been unlikely material for a military commander, struggling at school and failing entrance exams for the Navy and for Woolwich officer training. But his organisational skills and love of sporting competition finally gave him career momentum after a third attempt at a commission finally won him a place with the Royal Scots Fusiliers. Poor health seems to have been the greatest impediment to his advancement in the Army. A period of service in India was brought to an end by a hernia operation. He had barely survived the Second Boer War after a bullet wound to the chest, when a lengthy recuperation in England was followed by service in Nigeria; and then another serious illness sent him back to Blighty. At the age of nearly forty in 1912, he paid for flying lessons after an Army friend-turned-pilot had filled his head with airborne possibilities. Trenchard won his wings at Brooklands Aerodrome in Surrey, enabling him to join the first military flying course at the Central Flying School (CFC). Although he was an undistinguished pilot, his Army experience was useful to the School's commanding officer, Godfrey Paine, and a quick appointment as Adjutant followed. In the environment of improvised expansion at the CFC, Trenchard's organising energy found a perfect home and his rise continued inexorably. The word 'martinet' is most commonly applied to this irascible, awkward man, and there is no doubt he struck fear into most. But for those who understood him and were able to help him channel his formidable drive (like his suave and unlikely sidekick, Maurice Baring) he was a towering figure who galvanised the floundering service and brought it successfully through a world war to earn its independence as the Royal Air Force in 1918. It was then also Trenchard, through sheer hard work and bloody-mindedness, who pulled it, in a slimline but sustainable form, through the twenties – when it was most at risk from Navy and Army encroachments, and the efforts of an indifferent government to get rid of it. Trenchard took over the RFC in 1915, just as it was finding its feet in a war that had been slow to recognise its unique potential.

Good draughtsmanship was a skill that aeroplane designers needed, but the flying officers themselves were soon proving that even a basic facility for sketching was invaluable. Pencil drawn reconnaissance at the Battle of Mons was a crude but powerful demonstration that here was an exceptional new handmaiden of war that could be developed as the conflict went on.

The observation skills of the RFC had also proved crucial in the lead up to the 'Miracle of the Marne'. The battle that saved Paris from the German advance and brought to an end the previously unsinkable Schlieffen Plan was helped in no small measure by the ability of RFC pilots to spot watering horses in great numbers. Believing the French were beaten, the Germans had changed direction and the discovery of their cavalry's position betrayed an over-confidence that the Allies were able to exploit. Von Kluck's army, instead of chasing the British retreat, were moving south past the French capital, leaving their right flank exposed to a fierce counter-attack by the French Sixth Army.

By the Battle of Neuve Chapelle in March 1915, Haig, then a Corps commander, had been convinced of the crucial difference that the RFC could make. He was prepared to delay action if the weather stopped them flying and put his faith in their ability to upset enemy communications by means of tactical bombing. A mutually beneficial working relationship with the RFC First Wing commander had been established early in the war, summed up by Haig's irritable response to a general who disturbed a conversation in late 1914: 'Don't interrupt, I am listening to Trenchard describing Air.'[2] But despite the fruitful personal ties, inter-service rivalries were long established and brought out the worst in the generals as well as the politicians.

It is easy to forget, through finest hour nostalgia, what an impossibility the Royal Air Force must have seemed in the territorial atmosphere of the British military in the early years of the war. Fractious relationships weren't just a British problem. Maurice Baring attended a War Office meeting with a British general tasked with keeping hold of Italian aviation:

> He said one thing which stuck in my mind, and which made me laugh a good deal internally, although I kept an absolutely grave countenance. He said 'What I am going to tell you will be absolutely unintelligible and unthinkable to you as Englishmen, but I regret to say that here in Italy, it is a fact that there exists a certain want of harmony, a certain, occasional, shall I say, friction, between the military and naval branches of our Flying Service.' We murmured 'impossible'.[3]

Crucially, however, both Haig and Kitchener were far-sighted enough to give the new technology not only their blessing, but active sponsorship. Haig's belief in cavalry power has often been judged to have been outdated, but it has also been argued (by Gary Sheffield) that his over-enthusiasm for new technology led to tactical blunders in France; the most famous of these being the failure of the first tanks in the Battle of the Somme.[4] Luckily for the Flying Corps, despite mechanical inconstancy and haphazard planning, Haig's faith in airpower turned out to be one of his less controversial legacies.

*

Legend has it that unconventional types were attracted to the RFC: those who were thought by their senior officers to have been too eccentric or reckless for the Army or Navy. Lofty ideals of serving king and country aside, there was also the excitement and association of glamour that the new service had, and the accompanying advantages of this for young men were highlighted as a joke in *Flight* magazine in 1916: '"So Rita married that aviator fellow after all. Was it a love match?" "Yes; Rita loves aeroplanes."'[5] The glamour was not always entirely associated with just the gentlemen fliers: 'There is rivalry between the Government Departments as to which can boast the most beautiful corps of shorthand writers and typists. I think the palm, or the apple, or the biscuit, would be given to the girls of the Flying Corps.'[6]

The members of the young Corps enjoyed a more informal atmosphere than their land or sea based contemporaries. Trenchard, bringing together pilots from both the Army and the Navy in the pre-war RFC, had been at pains to neutralise tensions between them, by placing less emphasis on custom and traditions in what his biographer Andrew Doyle called a 'massive indifference to his pupils' parent services.'[7]

Relatives or family friends in the Flying Corps willing to provide good references were useful for gaining entry. Morris's future commanding officer in No. 11 Squadron, Major Thomas Hubbard, was happy to pull strings for an old friend whose cousin wanted to join the RFC in 1915. Hubbard took a relaxed approach to nepotism: 'He seems a very desirable person and as he is at GHQ is easily get-at-able... I hope you will get him for us out of the kindness of your heart. You owe that to me for nagging me – when keeping discreetly out of range – about generals.'[8]

Those able to handle a petulant horse could also handle an aeroplane. A gentlemanly mien and a practical physical nature were also welcomed. The nomenclature of squadrons in the developing RFC reflected the Corps' rapid growth. Early in the war, Reserve Squadrons (RS) were simply training squadrons – and initially included the careful addition of the word 'Aeroplane' in their designations, (RAS). After the 'Aeroplane' became understandably unnecessary, the name was simplified in January 1916.[9] Reserve Squadrons had nothing to do with a non-reserve front line squadron of the same number.

Prior to 1918, RFC military wing members were assigned to army brigades, and if an officer transferred from the regular army to the RFC to become a pilot, he would often still wear his regimental uniform with the addition of an RFC badge and wings. The golden ticket for Flying Corps entry early in the war was indeed a 'ticket', officially from the Fédération Aéronautique International, of which the Royal Aeronautical Club (RAeC) was a founder member in 1905. A middle-class boy like Morris, despite his good fortune and brains, did not have the private means necessary for such an expensive qualification, but the £75 fee was now a mortgage being paid by the War Office. There was a proviso: new pilots had to finish the war, if they survived it, or repay the money – plus the cost of their uniform. It is likely that as a direct transfer from the Army, and coming from a family unable to financially support such an expensive apprenticeship, Morris would have reclaimed part of his flying training fees.[10] A ticket was effectively a pilot's licence, but the criteria for success in the 1910s hadn't developed beyond repeated figures of eight, and landing and height tests. Brigadier Higgins of Second Brigade, RFC, complained to the Directorate of Military Aeronautics: 'the only purpose of the RAC certificate is to show that the pilot has a certain amount of confidence in himself.'[11]

By December 1915, the Royal Aero Club had assented to a War Office request that the number of figures of eight be reduced from five to two, as all flying activity on aerodromes had to be postponed whilst certification tests were in progress.[12] This corner-cutting, accepted for the period of the war at military schools, produced some anxiety. Colonel Charles Burke, who was to succeed Paine as commander of the Central Flying School, felt any pilot who could fly a Bristol Scout aeroplane was good enough to get his ticket and expressed his concerns that the instructors were not being given any indication of how to improve their methods, or how much time they had to whip the novice pilots into shape. He was also horrified at the suggestion that pilots were expected to fly in the dark after just fifteen hours solo: 'I think this is a grave mistake. I have suggested fifty hours flying after graduation, and then systematic training for night flying.'[13]

For an officer at the forefront of RFC training, witnessing disasters on an almost daily basis, his caution was entirely understandable. Others emphasised the need for autonomy for the instructors: a suggestion that any novices insufficiently keen should be removed was given a marginal note by the commander of Seventh Wing, Lieutenant Colonel Hugh Dowding: 'Yes, but a "thruster" should be given a good deal more law than his more prudent bretheren.'[14]

In October 1914 the Royal Flying Corps took over an old cavalry ground on Mousehold Heath in Norwich dating from the Napoleonic Wars. The suitability of the site for aircraft was quickly recognised by enterprising local manufacturers Boulton and Paul. They had transformed themselves from ironmongers (making, amongst other things, huts for Captain Scott's luckless final polar expedition) to producers of pioneering aeronautics – a mutually beneficial arrangement with the Army for a company who had been wondering how they would survive when the war shrunk their markets for glasshouses and garden tools.[15] Initially called on to make habitable and watertight pre-war buildings for the RFC, Boulton and Paul's patriotic eagerness led to an unexpected request for help with making sixty FE2b aircraft – a not entirely unreasonable assumption considering the basic materials of primitive biplanes, and the company's expertise in fitting motor engines in boats.[16]

The War Office had already begun to turn Thetford into the centre of military aerial operations in Norfolk, discounting Mousehold as too small as a result of out-of-date maps that showed land use restricted by small holdings that were no longer there. Boulton and Paul took advantage of a pre-arranged visit and invited Army officials to inspect the site, convincing them that all stages of production, including assembly and testing, would be possible in Norwich with the minimum of landscaping effort. Local motor engineer Stanley S. Howes, whose premises were nearby, was brought in to share skills and production. Construction began of buildings on the Thorpe side of Salhouse Road, providing a new home for the RFC's School of Flying Instruction.[17]

Boulton and Paul's initiative was rewarded when the War Office sent Sir David Henderson as guest of honour for a gala celebration on the day that the first FE2b was due to make its debut. The disappointment of its failure to take to the air due to a faulty engine (practically the only part not made in Norwich) was lightened by Henderson's tactful request to the Mousehold Commanding Officer:

> ...who very kindly sent up all the machines he had into the air, to give a show to the spectators, a very fine exhibition he gave; our poor old FE2b was wheeled round for general inspection, the pilots and guests partaking of tea and light refreshments in a marquee provided for the purpose. Mr Paul kindly bought up some magnums of 'jump' wherewith to christen our offspring, and on being assured we could not be held responsible for what we call in Norfolk a 'feeasso' allowed the bottles to be broached.[18]

When the FE2b finally proved airworthy and was delivered to Farnborough the following week, all was well. One of Boulton and Paul's managers, William H. ffiske, recorded the comments of a civilian passenger on the new aeroplane: 'Arrived to scheduled time, never want to travel motor car or train again, aeroplane every time.' The FE2b may have been impressive in its performance, but it was not luxurious: the review continued with ffiske's observation that the passenger 'like most of the pilots I have met, admits the aeroplane has its uses, but that the corner seat of a "Smoker" in a railway train is more comfortable.'[19]

*Flight* noted the new aeroplane and its manufacturer, asking its readers to trust in their expressed opinion (which, with war-time discretion, they were unable to provide additional details of) that, despite the metaphorical and literal hiccups surrounding the new aeroplanes, the new venture would prove a great success.[20]

The FE2bs were soon on their way to active service. Now they just needed more pilots to fly them.

*Chapter 5*

# How to Fly a Plane and
# Other Horror Stories

By the time Morris arrived at Mousehold, work on a new Riverside Lane premises was well underway. For an air-mad adolescent on his first RFC posting, Mousehold was a thrilling home, humming with industry and at the cutting edge of aircraft production. A new generation of fighter planes were onsite, including two that Morris was to become very familiar with, the Vickers FB5 and the FE2b. The physical sensations of flying, the numbing cold, the smell of heated castor oil and the din of the engine became second nature to him at Mousehold.

Another trainee pilot who arrived in Norwich just weeks before Morris was Second Lieutenant Albert Ball. Ball is one of the great icons of Britain's first air war, a source of such pride and awe that Second World War pilots were reputedly reminded of his exploits: 'He must fall/Remember Ball!'[1] Although the similarity of career destinations of the two men are striking, their circumstances were quite different. Ball was born in Nottingham four months before Morris and had been working for an engineering company before war came. He joined the Sherwood Foresters, going on to secondment with the North Midlands Divisional Cycle Company. After his unit was moved to Middlesex, Ball had learnt to fly privately in the summer of 1915, using up all hours of the day that the Army didn't need him, travelling on his Harley Davidson to Hendon Aerodrome for lessons. On his transfer to No. 9 Reserve Squadron, RFC, he was initially put up at the Royal Hotel in Norwich, but a downgrade to a less than satisfactory private billet was enough for him to request a third accommodation option.[2] He had the advantage of private wealth well beyond Morris, whose father was a respectable but hardly high-earning tobacconist, rather than a director of the Austin Motor Company and a former Lord Mayor.

The dangerous reality of the trainee's airborne dreams began to dawn not long after their arrival in Norwich. Plenty of books and websites on the development of the RFC insist that to be a trainee airman in the early part of the war was a more lethal business than actually flying around the Front, and the power of the blunt statistic is irresistible. Debate on just who has the definitive figures is a favourite subject amongst experts, and the absence of reliable records thwarts historians, but the black-humoured nickname the RFC gained of the 'suicide club' was certainly apt on an empiric level.[3] Great caution and expertise was required to get the early machines up and down again in one piece. A range of mechanical, navigational and physical skills were necessary – the kind of accomplishments that were not always associated with such teenagers. Levels of technical understanding in novice pilots depended as much on their curiosity as any official syllabus, with no consistent curriculum at this stage of the war. The range of subjects covered included understanding how an engine worked and the mechanics of flight, as well as how different parts of the plane functioned to keep it in the air. Practical application of this knowledge in potentially life or death situations seemed to have been less important than purely remembering it.[4] The priority was to get the men in the air.

The inadequacy of training and the unreliability of the aeroplanes made Mousehold a febrile environment. A popular instruction manual of the time attempted to explain, in a jocular fashion, some of the contending factors that made flight tricky at *any* time:

> The Angle of Incidence would have two Angles and two Cambers in one, which was manifestly absurd; the Surface insisted upon no thickness whatever, and would not hear of such things as Spars and Ribs; and the Thrust objected to anything at all likely to produce Drift, and very nearly wiped the whole thing off the Blackboard.[5]

A lack of organisational initiative to disseminate crucial knowledge compounded the dangers – getting an aeroplane out of a spin to avoid a catastrophic stall was a bit of mystery for the first couple of years of the war, even to those who managed it accidentally. Thoughtful pilots were working it out for themselves and the Royal Aircraft Factory at Farnborough were conducting experiments, but until 1917 no one thought to tell the instructors, or explain how to deliberately apply a spin in combat.[6] Nor were parachutes made available as an alternative to going down in a flaming aeroplane. The technology was developing but it was crude, and speculation suggests that the generals used this as a justification for the slow acceptance of the parachute as a vital piece of equipment.[7]

Both Ball and Morris trained initially in a Maurice Farman, a peculiar stick insect of a plane. Basic ingredients for aircraft-building included wood, cloth and a lot of wires; while the Farman came in two varieties. The Longhorn name given to the earlier version was explained by the protuberance at the front (like a cross between a sledge and a pair of cattle horns) which aided landings. The Shorthorn, reserved for those that had got their ticket, had this removed, but remained distinctive with the rumbling sound it made on arrival and departure, earning it the name 'Rumpety'.[8] A lethally small margin of safety, between full speed (approximately 66 miles per hour) and stalling, had to be observed to prevent disaster. A glide had to be achieved at just the right speed to avoid crashing. In the absence of brakes, a magneto switch turned the engine off momentarily to aid landing, but it didn't stop the fuel supply continuing: a light-fingered approach to resuming power through the switch was crucial to avoid the whole thing going up in flames.

The only way to get a feel for the machine was for a trainee to reach for the controls with their arms around the instructor – their feet being of little use as they were nowhere near the rudder. Communication was effortful, shouting being the main method (after first kicking the back of the trainee's seat in front to ensure attention). Standing up was also a bad idea in case drag made the engine choke. Any winds over five miles an hour would ground the aircraft; flying was mostly done in early mornings and evenings in benign conditions. Woe betide unlucky pilots aloft miles from an aerodrome when a gale threatened to brew.

The quality of the instructors themselves varied tremendously. Standards had been laid down but due to the exigencies of war it seems they were simply not followed stringently enough.[9] When Morris was learning how to fly it was not uncommon for another pilot who had barely got his own ticket to be asked straightaway to begin instructing new pupils. The reasons for this were not complex: the result of the incredible speed with which the RFC had to expand, and a lack of available skilled personnel as the war haemorrhaged experienced crew. The decent (and only) thing to do was to keep preparing new recruits despite the accident rates.

Subtler but no less present perils existed for trainees under more experienced instructors. Pilots who had survived active combat at the Front suffered great psychological stress, which in many led to agitation and nervousness. Few with authority were willing or able to see that sending them up in volatile machines (with pupils who could be cocky, or nervous, enough to threaten their lives all over again) would do nothing for their mental states. Fears of dying needlessly on home soil after suffering and surviving deep trauma in France could lead to a failure of nerve – with instructors at risk of taking the new boys down with them.[10] Pilots were reported on occasion to have had control of a plane in the air for as little as fifty minutes before an instructor had deemed them fit to fly solo.[11] For some instructors, it was a way of minimising accidents – by spending as little time as possible flying with the beginners.[12] In the heat of war, justifications were made for the failures of the training system, but the motivation of the anguished instructors is not difficult to recognise in hindsight, as aviation historian Michael Skeet observed:

> No pilot, having survived six months of wrenching front-line duty, wanted to be killed by a clumsy pupil. Though few wrote about it in those terms, there's something

viciously Darwinian in the sink-or-swim approach of RFC training.[13]

Not for nothing were the trainees known as 'Huns'. The late autumn and early winter of 1915, when Morris began his training, could hardly have been a worse time to learn to fly. The season itself was against him and created its own tension as bad weather held up training. Ball wrote to his parents in early November: 'It rains and blows and seems as if it never will do anything else. I do hope that it will soon clear up, for we are doing no flying. All we get is a lecture about four times each day, the rest of the time we have to slack or read.' The inactivity seemed to have brought out the worst in some of his fellow trainees: 'A few of the chaps are getting sent back on Monday for slacking and playing the fool.'[14]

The German Air Force cut swathes through the RFC during the 'Fokker scourge' of 1915 and early 1916. Dutch aviation pioneer Anthony Fokker had invented a machine gun interrupter mechanism, enabling bullets to be shot through the propeller of a plane, without danger of them hitting the blades and ricocheting back into the nacelle of the aircraft. Whilst RFC pilots struggled with conventional machine guns that had to be aimed wide of the propellor, Allied death rates in the air had soared.

The method of co-opting private flying schools for new pilots was not working and many arriving in France were then sent home for more training.[15] Squadron commanding officers became increasingly concerned about the ill-prepared young men who had been sent to them, and communications between the Air Ministry at home and RFC leadership in France were often fraught. Major Cogan of No. 7 Squadron in France sent a report to Second Brigade HQ regarding a pilot who claimed to have had twenty-six hours experience of a BE2c before leaving England: 'He is one of the worst pilots I have ever seen. He crashed two machines in the same day, one getting off and one landing. He has just crashed another on landing. I do not allow him to take a passenger and he is quite useless to me, as a pilot.'[16] Trenchard himself sent many letters of complaint about the raw pilots being sent out to France in the months just before Morris was posted there, writing in April 1916 of one unfortunate pilot who confessed (to the General Officer Commanding himself) that because he had never been in combat, he had no idea how to change an ammunition drum.[17]

Newly arrived on active service, some would be introduced to aircraft they had never flown before, clueless as to how to use a machine gun and ignorant of wireless equipment, how to communicate with artillery, how to navigate and, most pathetically, considering their vulnerabilities, how to use the machines they flew in for combat purposes.[18] Spirits needed to be kept high during training, despite the constant presence of ambulances (nicknamed Hungry Lizzies) that haunted the aerodromes, taking away the dead and injured. Morris appears to have come through the process unscathed: there are no records of accidents involving him that survive at the National Archives in London.

He had enough confidence in his abilities to refuse a request for trainee pilots to switch to the role of observer, so that they could be sent to France earlier. Observers were the equivalent of air gunners in the next war, but in 1915 they were sometimes damned as incompetent fliers. The unique value to the Flying Corps of effective observers was recognised as far back as 1913 by Major Charles Burke, who wrote in a report recommending the establishment of a new station at Montrose that 'training in observation can be roughly divided into: (A) seeing (B) recognising what is seen, and (C) reporting it correctly. Experience seems to show that most Officers find (A) easy, (B) difficult and (C) very difficult.'[19]

In April 1916, Brigadier Ashmore of Fourth Brigade had made his views clear about the dangers of observers with initiative:

A French observer 'deduced' from his observation that an attack was coming in a particular direction. The business of observers is to tell what they see, not to make deductions. Squadrons should cooperate closely with the Intelligence branch of their Corps or Army, but they must not encroach on its work.[20]

Coming from the man who later founded the Royal Observer Corps, this seems a little counter-productive, but the line between smart thinking and misplaced confidence was a thin one.

On 25 January 1916 in Norwich, Morris got his RAeS 'ticket', paying one pound and one shilling to collect his aviator's certificate. The occasion provided one of only two verified photographs of him that survive.[21] One of four pilots who have made the grade on that particular page of the RAeS record book, he has a placid, half-smiling expression, and looks every inch the young nineteen-year old he was, in his Surreys' uniform. Not one of the three new pilots with him on that page of the RAeS book was to survive the war.[22]

There were a couple of weeks for Morris to celebrate his achievement before he left the bustling hangars of Mousehold, with its poisonous smell of propellor varnish, behind. On Valentine's Day 1916 he returned to the home counties and reported to No. 19 Reserve Squadron (RS) at Hounslow in Middlesex.[23] There was much still to learn, but now he was amongst the real first of the few on home soil. Britain's shores were being threatened in a new and terrifying way and, not for the last time, Morris was in at the beginning of a key development of the air war. A hasty reorganisation of London's defences was taking place, and No. 19 RS were under the flight path of the Zeppelins.

*Chapter 6*

# Bringing Down the Whales

As the government grappled with the need to protect the capital against the airships, Morris joined the squadron that was the RFC's brave but insufficient response to it.

No. 19 Reserve Squadron's aerodromes served a wide geographical area ringing London, and he could have been sent to any of them. Centre of No. 19's training operations as well its HQ, the RFC's aerodrome at Hounslow Heath was in a district brisk with manufacture of all sorts. The military, long established in the town, were diversifying to meet the needs of a twentieth century war: the Army Service Corps were training drivers and growing their own food at nearby Osterley Park.[1] In 1830 William Cobbett had described the surroundings as 'a sample of all that is bad in soil and villainous in look'.[2] Flying into or out of the small airfield that was eventually to become the colossus of Heathrow Airport provoked a strong sense of danger for pilots taking off and landing, surrounded as it was with wires, and the added hazard of a high brick wall. But any aerodrome so close to London was an enviable posting.

The opportunity of being close to the attractions and connections of the capital, together with the convenience of flying over such a familiar cityscape, made it especially welcome for new pilots whose navigation skills were still limited.[3] For Morris (a Londoner only recently transplanted to the suburbs of Surrey) to be able to gaze down in such privileged circumstances over the city he had spent all but the smallest part of his eighteen years living in, must have been a particular thrill.

The arms of No. 19 Reserve Squadron were stretching around a very big circle, and the danger of enemy air raids loomed large. The first bombs to hit the capital had fallen in May 1915, five months after the Kaiser had finally overcome his qualms about targeting the city which was home to a significant part of his extended family, and consented to the possible destruction of historical and cultural treasures that could appal the rest of the world. Dirigibles were developed by several different companies, but Count Ferdinand von Zeppelin's name had stuck. Some airships were framed with wood, others with aluminium; all were known generically by the name of the German pioneer.

Practical flight training to supply the squadrons in France was paramount. But the loss of life from enemy air raids added political pressure to the RFC – even though it was not officially their job to deal with the airships.[4] For Sir David Henderson, at the coal face of RFC home command in the autumn of 1915, the problem of the raids was a political as well as a national dilemma. Henderson's army boss Lord Kitchener was in a difficult situation. The Government and the public found it hard to understand why the Army was reluctant to commit the resources of the RFC at home when the RNAS, who were nominally responsible, did not seem to be coping with it. At the same time, the Secretary for War was feeling the pressure to better equip the Army in France with aerial support. Kitchener apparently passed this pressure on to Henderson, who had to suffer his commander's frustration on the matter for several months to come.[5] The Navy was in charge of defence at home, but negotiations were ongoing for the Army via the War Office to take over. The Army's priority for the RFC was reconnaissance at the front, and any dilution of that effort was difficult, both logistically and financially.

Arguments over which of the various branches of the armed services would keep the wolves from the door had raged since before the airships had first attacked. In June 1915, the value of 'Air' had become clear, and Mr Joynson Hicks, a Conservative backbencher, confidently asserted that 'the Air Service, as far as the men are concerned, is absolutely perfect.' Despite this apparent perfection, however, Hicks followed his statement by calling for more support for the 'aeroplanists' and urged David Lloyd George as Minister of Munitions, to 'let them have their money' in order to guard home shores more effectively.[6]

In February 1916, inland defence was finally transferred to the War Office – with the RNAS put in charge of coastal and sea protection.[7] It would take time to put these changes into place; meanwhile the competitive rivalry between the War Office and the Navy continued and RFC pilots readied themselves to show what they could do.

Anti-aircraft guns began to appear in the capital; haphazardly placed to the passer-by, but carefully arranged in bands around the city. The daddy of them all, a 75mm monster rushed in from France, was given its own wheeled transport, ready to head straight for the action.[8] Admiral Sir Percy Scott (who had put noses out of joint in the Navy whilst energetically improving its efficiency) was given the job of organising guns for the protection of the capital; plans eventually coalescing as the London Air Defence Area (LADA). Scott was anxious about the vulnerability of munitions production hubs around London, and warned that sending all the best pilots to France would backfire catastrophically: 'this policy should be reconsidered before Woolwich Arsenal is destroyed, and not afterwards.'[9]

Airfields in Essex at Hainault Farm, Sutton's Farm, (later RAF Hornchurch and a key Battle of Britain base) and Joyce Green near Dartford in Kent were requisitioned to provide extra liminal protection to the east and south of London. Existing aerodromes at Chingford, Croydon, Northolt, Wimbledon Common, Farningham, Hendon and Hounslow covered the rest of the capital's perimeter. Searchlights, guns, and night flying pilots were distributed amongst them, and each were given a pair of BE2 aircraft. Sutton's Farm and Hainault were designated Temporary Landing Grounds I and II. Sheep and haystacks were cleared, and officers billeted nearby in a flurry of preparations that fizzled out to nothing over the late autumn and early winter. With moonlight blowing their cover, and weather conditions unsuitable for night-time raids, the Zeppelins stayed at home. The prospect of their return the following spring kept Hainault and Sutton's Farm under War Office control but the bar at the White Hart Hotel in Hornchurch went quiet until the New Year.[10]

The necessity for more specialised offensive skills was beginning to influence the structure and purpose of individual squadrons. Morris may well have expected to follow Albert Ball to the Central Flying School in Wiltshire in February 1916, after he had completed initial instruction in Norwich. The CFS had been the usual place for a new pilot to refine and polish his skills, but units like No. 19 RS now tried to integrate advanced training within a squadron being prepared for front line action. Offensive readiness was crucial for new pilots posted to the aerodromes around the capital. Morris's placement with No. 19 RS, followed as it was by his membership of No. 39 Squadron, is perhaps the biggest clue as to where his strengths lay. His stint, just over two months with the unit, was typical in terms of its duration. The absorption of new fliers continued until the squadron held enough pilots to divide into two – one half going overseas and the remainder forming a new separate unit.[11]

Training approaches were changing. Previously, pilots learnt in several different types of aeroplane; now more time was given for them to get to know a particular aircraft properly. Service squadrons like No. 19 RS tried to facilitate this new strategy. Their medley of machines would have been broadly familiar to Morris, including the FE2b and the Vickers FB5, as well as the BE2cs, the 'Stability Jane' workhorses of the RFC, equally loved and hated for their reliability and lugubriousness.[12]

The necessity for more night flying capability created disagreements about which aircraft were most suitable. The BE2c had a reputation for staying true to the horizon, but was only stable when the rudder was effectively controlled, causing accidents for inexperienced or distracted pilots. The FE2bs were suggested as a safer alternative on nights of adequate moonlight. Robust landing gear, on four or two wheels, was less arguable, although in any circumstances a skilled pilot was crucial.[13] No matter how good the innovations were, as long as the training of pilots was so haphazard, the new service was in danger of taking one step forward and two steps back. And neither aircraft was capable of gaining height quickly enough for offensive advantage against the airships.

On the night of 31 January 1916, just over two weeks before Morris joined No. 19 RS, a calamitous series of events showed how difficult a proposition airships were for the RFC whilst resources were stretched so thinly. During a raid by nine German naval airships on the Midlands and Suffolk, during which seventy people were killed, a lethal combination of bad weather, inadequate weapons and a lack of night flying experience led to the loss of six RFC aircraft and two flight commanders.[14] One airship landed in the sea after being attacked by the Dutch as it flew home, and there was further controversy when its helpless crew were left to die by a British merchant navy vessel nearby. Its captain, baulking at the risk of seizing sixteen enemy prisoners, was haunted by his failure of nerve for the rest of his life, and a desperate last message in a bottle from the German commander washed up on the coast of Norway a few months later.[15] This disastrous night was witnessed by Second Lieutenant Arthur Travers Harris, a pilot who was to join No. 19 RS soon afterwards.[16] Harris became better known decades later as 'Bomber' Harris, forever associated with the controversial destruction of cities like Dresden in the Second World War. Harris was one of those extraordinary figures who emerged from the cradle of British military flying in the Great War, going on to become a giant of the RAF in the Second World War. In early 1916 he was at the beginning of his flying career, achieving his RAeS ticket just under three months before Morris.[17] Both were young and inexperienced pilots thrown into a hastily arranged home defence strategy that was operating under unprecedented strain.

Harris described the mortal wounding of one of the officers on the luckless night of 31 January:

> I was waiting at the end of the flare path to take off after Captain Penn-Gaskell, when he crashed and was killed. Colonel Mitchell, the C.O., came and stopped me on the grounds that the weather was unfit for flying, which was indeed true.[18]

Penn-Gaskell had learned to fly in 1912 and was one of the original RFC officers to cross the Channel on the outbreak of war two years later. He lost his life that night in 1916 testing conditions for the more vulnerable and unseasoned men. In the murky weather, his aircraft hit a tree and then the ground, bursting into flames. Two of the ground crew at Northolt risked their lives by pulling him out before the bombs his BE2C carried exploded, but he had already been terribly wounded and his end, coming four days later, made for quietly sobering conversations among the pilots who could have been in his place.[19] Penn-Gaskell's end illustrated how the 'bright golden fingers' (a description given to the Zeppelins by D.H. Lawrence) were proving so difficult for the hamstrung RFC.[20]

Within days of the 31 January raid, No. 19 RS Squadron was created as the primary unit for London's air security, with their commanding officer Lieutenant Colonel T.C.R. Higgins given strategic control of all of the capital's aerodromes a day later.[21] At the top of his operational to do list was the provision of more night flying pilots.

Arthur Harris experienced the determined attempts of the squadron to make do in the absence of adequate training. He displayed a Micawberish optimism in the following exchange with No. 19 RS's adjutant – a conversation which must have had a horrible familiarity to the pilots continually obliged to put their lives on the line: 'He looked at me rather quizzically and asked if I could fly in the dark. To which I replied that I couldn't fly in the daylight, so maybe I could in the dark.'[22]

The particular challenge of night flying had been recognised as far back as August 1915. Godfrey Paine at the Central Flying School had used no less strong a word than 'criminal' to describe the practice of sending unprepared pilots up at night.[23] Landing grounds weren't adequately lit. Wingtip flares, meant to guide returning pilots, temporarily blinded them instead. Temperamental aircraft were expected to work for both training duties and active home service. Higgins explained the problem: 'Officers under instruction ill-treated the engines and upset the true-ing of the machines so that it was impossible to expect pilots to fly at night in the machines which had been used for instructional purposes by day, even though they were still serviceable.'[24] Competent pilots were now given even more responsibility; combining daytime instruction duties with death-defying night-time flying. And each home defence detachment was expected to undertake the 'finishing' of lately graduated, or almost graduated, pilots.[25]

What constituted a 'competent' pilot at this time is not clear. One of Morris's contemporaries in both Nos. 19 RS and 39 squadrons was New Zealander Lieutenant Alfred de Bathe Brandon, one of the first RFC pilots to approach an airship at anything like firing range – a brave act he apparently achieved after just thirty hours of solo flying experience.[26] Getting a BE2c high enough to have any chance of spotting a Zeppelin put Brandon in an unusually advantageous position, as they were mostly too slow to reach such altitude in time.

Morris's later debut on the Western Front came in a faster Vickers FB5 two seater. These were fighter planes with thoroughbred natures, more agile and powerful, and pilots flying them were given longer to learn how to handle them effectively in combat.[27] Ambidextrous qualities were helpful for operating guns whilst flying: an excited pilot spotting an airship, employed all four limbs (and teeth if necessary) juggling ammunition, controls and excess clothing. Inexperienced and cack-handed pilots would lose their maps to their wind, and a fly-away glove could wreck a propellor.

Morris's new squadron was operating with a great sense of urgency. As late as July 1916, the necessity of initiative was still being emphasised to officers and NCOs joining No. 19 RS:

> Owing to a lack of instructors, it is up to you to learn as much as you can without waiting to be told. Every officer should actually know how to do the following: fill up tanks, clean a machine and engine, start up an engine in each type of machine he is on. Sooner or later he will be glad of having done so in a forced landing with no help in reach.[28]

In the event of such forced landings, the owner of the land had to be found, and any damage to property promptly reported on a special form to the Squadron Office. Discipline was reinforced as a point of honour: 'Loafing about is not only a gross waste of time, but is most

unbefitting for an officer. The mechanics frequently require help…
Ignorance of an order is never accepted as an excuse.'[29]

On the same day Morris was appointed to No. 19 RS, the Cabinet
sanctioned key improvements to early warning systems.[30] Centres were
set up in London, York and Edinburgh to coordinate information about
incoming threats. It was in the nick of time. German attacks, on both
coastal targets as well as the capital itself, had resumed, and questions
were asked in Parliament following an ineffectual response to a daylight
raid on Kent.[31] The combined work of both the RNAS and the RFC
also failed to stop a further action by German seaplanes, killing one
person and injuring dozens in Suffolk and Kent, on 20 February.[32]
At the beginning of March 1916, additional BE2c aircraft were
provided specifically for home defence action and on 25 March, a
new Thirteenth Wing was created in London for the RFC, under the
command of Lieutenant Colonel Felton Holt.[33] A one page memo
from the Directorate of Military Aeronautics gave Holt a breakdown
of his resources (not all of which were immediately available to him),
including six FE2bs at Hainault Farm, with the provision there of four
Night Pilots, two pilot pupils and two observer pupils.[34]

A week later, on 31 March 1916, home defence squadrons had a
night of great drama. Twenty-four sorties were launched in a terrifying
week of intensive air attacks on England and Scotland. Gales the
previous night brought down telegraph and telephone wires, and as
Holt assessed uncertain reports coming in to Room 242 of the War
Office-requisitioned Carter's Hotel in London, he made a quick
decision as to how many planes he could send up immediately, and how
many should be held in reserve in case of greater numbers of airships
arriving later. At 9.00 pm thirteen Night Pilots took off, but conditions
were later to become dangerously misty. A mixture of weapons went
up with them: explosive Ranken darts, designed to rip the skin of a
Zeppelin, plus sixteen-pound bombs and incendiaries.[35]

The airships made their way over East Anglia, expelling explosives
over military and civilian targets as they went, but their navigation
was unreliable. At around 9.00 pm one of them, *L15*, blundered into
No. 19 RS's home turf to the east and south of London. Few of the

squadron's pilots, except Brandon and Lieutenant Claude Ridley from Joyce Green, were reported to have come close to it. One was surrounded by anti-aircraft fire, another side-slipped in ground mist during take-off and was killed, and a third couldn't see where he was landing and ended up in a pond at Sutton's Farm.[36] Three machines were put completely out of action and forty-eight civilians were killed by enemy bombs from the airships.

Brandon's detailed account of his actions has an atmosphere of Moby Dick about it – his eerie description of *L15* sliding in and out of the darkness, re-appearing suddenly as though about to collide with him, and his frantic gloved fumblings for bombs and darts, illustrates the fear and excitement of a fleeting encounter in which he believed he had fatally compromised the airship.

The AA guns at Purfleet were more likely to have done their worst for *L15*. Losing height, she drifted over the treacherous sands of Foulness and out to the Thames Estuary, finally coming to grief as her frame broke in half at Knock Deep, about twenty miles north of Margate on the Kent coast. All but one of her crew (previously responsible for killing seventeen people in the West End of London) survived, picked up by an armed fishing boat. The airship captain, Joachim Breithaupt, kept a silence on her history, claiming 'higher military aims' than the killing of women and children.[37]

For all the panicked muddle and weather-related chaos of the RFC's response, the emphatic dispatch of *L15* was a reassuring step forward in the fight against the airships; thanks to the actions of Brandon and Ridley and the improved protection of AA gun power and searchlights. *The Times* reported with some relief:

> Just as gunfire is a protective measure, so are aeroplanes when boldly and skillfully handled; and it is a combination of the two methods, together with the development of searchlights, which will someday make it far more difficult for Zeppelins to raid our shores.[38]

Holt's pilots vented their frustrations the day after the raid, but their concerns about confusing flares, friendly fire, the difficulty of attacking airships from above and the absence of observers to share the tasks of navigating and flying (whilst also keeping a lookout for hostile machines) were carefully noted.[39] Despite ongoing handicaps due to inexperience and ineffective weapons, slowly but surely, improvements in patrol performances continued.

Against this background of painful but steady progress, Morris's apprenticeship was drawing to a close and soon he was on his way to a new posting with No. 39: his first operational job in a brand-new squadron which became synonymous with home defence in the First World War.

*Chapter 7*

# A Torch in the London Night

The sixteenth of April 1916 was a red-letter day for Morris. He earned his wings and officially became a fully-fledged RFC pilot.[1]

One of his original cloth wings badge survives a century later, embroidered with silk threads in colours still surprisingly vivid. A swift was used as the model – a bird that famously sleeps on the wing – and a fitting mascot for an air service on standby in the dark against night-time raiders. The badge was designed in 1912 by Sir David Henderson and his deputy Frederick Sykes, and the spidery letters 'RFC', have a distinctly gothic look, centred in a green laurel wreath surmounted by a crown, with finely stitched gold and yellow feathers fanning out on either side.[2] Fragments of thread fray around the backing cloth, tracing its original location on Morris's uniform.

The badges would often appear above the left breast of flying officers' uniforms before their new status had been officially confirmed in the *London Gazette*. Despite official disapproval of this practice, proud young pilots prepared the addition to their uniforms in advance. One contemporary of Morris's, William Fry, noted a liquid celebration after the squadron commanding officer had finally granted the trainees their wings – followed the next morning by a brace of swiftly badged fliers appearing at breakfast.[3]

The list of newly qualified pilots gazetted on the same day as Morris includes a Captain David Benjamin Gray, one of the men whose flying career was to be significantly abbreviated, but not ended completely, following the events of 17 September.[4] Gray is not a well-known figure in the annals of the RFC today; he nevertheless represents exactly the kind of singular character that any study of the early fliers throws up again and again – a man whose own adventures give Captain Biggles a run for his money.

Born in Assam in India in 1884, and older than many of his RFC contemporaries, Gray was short, moustachioed, a stickler for sartorial smartness, and dark-skinned enough to be mistaken for a native of the sub-continent. He transferred to the RFC from the Indian Army, and was nicknamed the 'Munshi' – Munshi being the Hindi word for teacher, and a nod to his fluency in French, German, Russian and several Asian dialects.[5] The two men met at ground school in Norwich. Their careers followed similar lines, with Gray joining No. 39 RS on the same day as Morris. Spending the next six weeks being shunted from unit to unit, Gray was sent to No. 1 Squadron in Hampshire, before embarking for France in early May 1916 with No. 60 Squadron, again a posting of just over a fortnight. On 25 May, six days after Morris, Gray arrived at No. 11 Squadron's aerodrome near Arras. He became a close colleague of Morris's, his friend as well as his senior officer, and a mentor who trusted him professionally.[6]

Morris and Gray were original members of No. 39 Squadron, formed out of the nucleus of No. 19 RS at Hounslow on 15 April.[7] The new unit's commanding officer was the familiar figure of Major Higgins, based with Holt's 18th Wing Brigade staff in the comfortable surroundings of Carter's Hotel in London. The scattered detachments that had made up No. 19 RS's bases were rationalised and later concentrated at three locations – Hounslow (as before, HQ and centre of training operations) together with Hainault and Sutton's Farms, the two landing grounds requisitioned the year before. Three flights of six aircraft were planned for each, with Joyce Green (where Gray had also trained briefly with No. 10 Reserve Squadron) and Farningham available as additional aerodromes for the squadron.[8]

Preparing new pilots and compulsory night flying were still crucial functions. Higgins had his work cut out whipping the new squadron into shape at such a dangerous time. Further airship raids followed the 31 March attack – and although strong winds and the strengthened bastions of London's gun emplacements and searchlights had saved the capital from their attentions, over thirty more people were killed.[9]

The propaganda victory of *L15*'s demise had not reassured an increasingly nervous public – and warnings were deliberately muted to avoid disruption to the nation's domestic war effort. Especially vulnerable to false alarms that held up vital distribution systems, were the railway networks.[10] *Punch* made light of the public's frustrations:

> Tradesman (at the basement door): 'Are you insuring against Zeppelins for the New Year?'

> Householder: 'Well, I'm thinking of it, as I remember reading in the last raid how they dropped seventeen bombs in one area. I wonder they don't get hit, standing still all that time in the air.'[11]

No. 39's badge was (and still is) a winged bomb; its motto *Die noctuque* meaning 'by day and night'. In 1916 they had an onerous, and very public, responsibility on their shoulders:

> It was at home, in the dark skies over London, that the people waited to see their ordeal avenged. If our gunners and airmen were to knock down Zepps now that things were better organised, it must be where it would be seen by the greatest number, a torch in the frightened London night.[12]

Arthur Harris was soon to be made a flight commander with No. 39. Ginger, as he was then known to his colleagues, was developing into one of the most promising officers of the squadron. His was a self-sufficient approach to learning a skill for which no training had been provided. An initial night flight with No. 19 RS had not been a complete disaster – he claimed to have come closer than any of the other patrol pilots to a practice target, albeit only to lose it again. He also managed to land safely, despite barely knowing 'what country I was in, let alone where the ruddy aerodrome was' and earned the praise of Penn-Gaskell's replacement at Northolt. But it was a salutary experience for Harris, who then took it upon himself to fly a BE2 repeatedly at twilight, staying up longer every time, until he felt comfortable being airborne and landing in the dark. Within weeks he was instigating similar training at Sutton's Farm, despite his own relative dearth of flying hours.[13]

There were other memorable personalities around No. 39 – a flight sergeant whose panacea for any technical difficulties was always: 'Git me an 'ammer!', and the blissfully calm Muriel Huskin, one of many visitors to Sutton's Farm, drawn to the excitement of the aerodrome every weekend, but content to sit knitting whilst all around her busied themselves with more important work.[14] As a good-looking young man engaged in such dashing work, Morris would have experienced the same kind of attention as the most famous member of No. 39. William Leefe Robinson, known as Billy, Robby or Robin to his friends – no one in the RFC seems to have done anything so dull as to use their given names – had also been a member of No. 19 RS. He was later to earn a Victoria Cross as the first pilot to bring an airship down over Britain. Leefe Robinson's landmark achievement was an act guaranteed to provoke hero-worship, and several months before, he had enjoyed the *cachet* that being a member of the RFC gave him: 'It is really quite amusing to go into a hotel or café, and people turn round and nudge one another, and you often hear, "Royal Flying Corps", "Flying man," etc. etc., in awed whispers and, "Oh, what a nice flying boy" and so on from the coarser class of female.'[15] Coarser females aside, it was a seductive atmosphere that must have gone to the heads of a few callow youths, and Leefe Robinson's report to his mother (also written before his career-defining achievement) about the tiresome nature of all those young women has the unmistakeable ring of protesting just a *little* too much:

> Wherever I land I have a simply ripping time… you are immediately surrounded by people offering you cars, lunch, tea, bed and Lord knows what. Of course if you are wise you generally pick out the grounds of a country house… Talk about autograph books and cameras. By god I was positively sick of seeing my own signature.[16]

It was a brave girl who took on a flier, as *Flight's* attempt at humour in January 1916 showed: "'It was very romantic," said the friend. "He proposed to her in an aeroplane." "Yes?" murmured the listener encouragingly. "And she accepted him in the hospital.'" [17]

By the beginning of October 1916, No. 39 was to produce two other 'Zepp Wreckers': Wulstan Tempest and Frederick Sowery. An iconic postcard showing the squadron's three most successful musketeers linking arms and smiling broadly, adorned the scrapbooks of a generation. The *joi de vivre* of these early days was particularly poignant in Leefe Robinson's case. Shot down in France by 1917, by a pilot with Richthofen's Flying Circus, his fame as an airship destroyer had a bitter legacy. He would become a prisoner of war at Holzminden: persecuted for his achievements and suffering solitary confinement. His spirit survived strongly enough for him to attempt escape several times (as was the obligation for captured officers) but his health had been fatally compromised and he was killed by influenza at home, less than a month after repatriation at the age of twenty-three.

The squadron's off-duty pleasures were naturally appreciated all the more by crews whose nocturnal obligations had less allure than any they may have had to local ladies. Pilots on standby for anti-airship patrols mostly slept fitfully in chilly hangars on the airfields, awaiting War Office instructions. With a two-hour limit on flying times due to the limited capacity of the BE2c's petrol tank, two pilots were needed on any given night – one to take off ninety minutes after the first, allowing time to reach enough height to see enemy craft. Each identified airship was given a non-threatening British first name (girls' names for naval airships, boys' for military ones) such as Mary or George, to lighten the tension spreading to the stations reporting on their progress all over the UK.[18] Attempts from the ground to let the Night Pilots know where an airship had been spotted were laborious: rockets were fired towards them initially, followed by giant fabric markers in the shape of a 'T', visible from between 14 and 17,000 feet.[19]

With cockpits open to the night cold, pilots chose between protecting themselves in bulky clothing, or staying unencumbered enough to be able to respond quickly should they come across an airship. Motoring clothes had been the model for flying gear, but despite the buffer of three-quarter-length leather coats, gauntlets and goggles, pre-1917 pilots were cruelly exposed to the elements and bought their own extra protective clothing from enterprising private companies. Like early Channel swimmers, their faces were slicked with primitive emollient to offset the abrasive effects of very low temperatures on thin skin. The appearance of a fully togged-up flier may have alarmed small children:

> The face would then be smeared with whale-oil, surrounded by a balaclava helmet and covered with a non-absorbent face mask, ideally of Nuchwang dog-skin from China. If dog-skin was unavailable, the mask would be wolverine fur, favoured anyway by the Canadian flyers since breath would not freeze on it. The triplex goggles, which covered the single gap in the mask (32s 6d over a London shop counter) were of fur lined moulded sponge-rubber with sage-green-tinted glasses to absorb ultra-violet rays. Various preparations would finally be rubbed on to the glass to counter fogging below ten degrees Fahrenheit and frosting at minus ten, with perhaps a touch of ointment on the lips, though pilots philosophically accepted the fact that all lips cracked at altitude whatever specifics were used. Fully dressed, the flight would walk together to the CO's hut stumping as noisily and heavily as lunar astronauts.[20]

Patrolling empty skies with only the dim lights of their instruments for company, their senses were heightened: as their eyes strained in the darkness, with fear and adrenalin kicking in, some began seeing things. One naval pilot, who at no time had come any closer than sixty miles to a Zeppelin, gave a convincing description of 'something like a railway carriage with the blinds down', and another's reported sighting brought forth a frank response from a sceptical, but not entirely unsympathetic, Rear Admiral: 'Night flying must be most difficult and dangerous, and require considerable nerve and pluck, but this airman seems to have been gifted with a more than usually vivid imagination.'[21]

In April 1916, the political situation in Ireland leading to the Easter Rising was coming to a head. The German government sought to worsen the crisis by launching the distraction of a naval bombardment on Lowestoft, whilst they spirited the Irish nationalist leader Roger Casement back to County Kerry from his exile in Berlin. A nervous British government linked intelligence of these events to a return visit over four nights by German Navy and Army airships on 24–27 April, but the raids had limited success – again kept away from London by strong winds, but nonetheless doing some damage in East Anglia and frightening one old lady to death.[22] Arthur Harris went up in search of them, equipped with new incendiary bullets which he hoped would be an effective weapon. As one of the airships loomed over him, he opened fire, but his gun jammed. William Leefe Robinson was equally thwarted: sent up fifteen minutes later than Harris but unable to get the height advantage he needed for accurate fire and suffering no less than five gun jams.[23]

Despite these missed opportunities, the barking of the AA guns and the intensified searchlights were enough to harry the hostile aircraft away and give their commanders food for thought about the success of any further missions. Eight of No. 39's Night Pilots had been on patrol and Higgins received almost unanimous complaints about the crude and confusing flare path at Hainault Farm. Bombs were dropping as close as a mile away, and the telephone line to the War Office had been put out of action.[24] Harris was one of the pilots whose description of events from the air had insisted that something more mysterious had also occurred:

> At a point between Leyton and East and West Ham – where the Zeppelin was first caught by the searchlights – a very brilliant green flare flashed intermittently… I noticed the Zeppelin immediately turned in the direction of this light, and steered a course over it, which would have taken it straight over Woolwich. Before reaching the river, however, it turned due East, and it was shortly after this that I attacked it. I have not the least doubt that these lights were signals; they could not have been mistaken for anything else.[25]

Paranoia about the enemy within was understandable in a period when the airships had created a 'new shape of fear'.[26] Whatever it was that Arthur Harris and his No. 39 colleagues had actually seen remains unknown.[27] Something similar happened to another Mousehold trainee pilot, Archibald James, who went to the police after spotting 'a very powerful light which flashed up a quite long, probably twenty or thirty letter signal' whilst sitting in the observer's seat on a moonlit night flight over the east of Norwich in the autumn of 1915. James and his pilot knew the Germans may well be in the vicinity: 'Norwich was in a line frequently taken by Zeppelins going to bomb the London area,' and they were instantly suspicious of the light coming from a suburban back garden: 'It occurred to us both that of course this was somebody signalling to, I suppose, Zeppelins, which they had mistaken the noise of our engine for.' Poring over a large map of Norwich with the police, James and his pilot were unable to pin down exactly where the incident had occurred in relation to the many crossroads they had flown over, and enquiries came to a dead end.[28]

May was quieter for No. 39. The RNAS dealt with further incursions, and Higgins had time to reflect on the tactics and experience of the new unit. More efficient anti-airship innovations were being developed, including the Pomeroy bullet, the first 5,000 of which were reported to have been produced by the wife of its inventor from a room in the heights of Adastral House.[29] The RFC had been promised the strength of ten squadrons to deal with the airships, but pressure on the British Army to relieve the French at Verdun (by launching a new offensive in northern France) had reduced that to eight in May 1916.[30] Committing too much effort at home would be helpful for the enemy.

*

On 17 May, at Savy-Berlette, near Arras in France, Albert Ball recorded the recent losses of No. 11 Squadron, RFC: 'Yesterday we lost six machines... So far only one of our machines has been done in today. This makes seven in two days.'[31] One of the casualties was Second Lieutenant Morden Mowat, downed by the German ace

Max Immelman. Immelman's success in No. 11's sphere of operations was a significant burden for the British squadron. Arrangements to fill the empty chairs in the officers' mess were made without delay. Replacement aircrew had to be welcomed, introduced, and settled in. Everyone was kept busy.

The day afterwards, Lionel Morris left England for the war on the Western Front, taking with him a small, brown-covered notebook. On the inside first page he wrote: 'LBF Morris, No 11 Squadron 3rd Brigade in the Field. Vickers Fighter, 160 FE2b, Nieuport Scout, Bristol do'.[32] In this diary, which he kept for just over three months, the particular struggles of No. 11's Battle of the Somme were recorded in his unsensational prose.

*Chapter 8*

# Field Notes from France

The RAF Museum at Hendon holds innumerable objects in its archives, from full size aeroplanes to medals. It has even boasted a cake in its café made to an original recipe of Albert Ball's family, giving us literally a taste of the Great War period. In a quiet space at the top of the building is its reading room, where the studious or just curious can pore over myriad items. One such item tucked away is Morris's personal diary. It is a small A5 size notebook, with a brown cover and the inscription 'Mrs L Morris' on the front. These ego documents, as they are now described, inform our imagination about the First World War.

It is not a well-known memoir (not surprising given Morris's anonymity) and it has only been cited a handful of times in specialist histories. None of the luminaries of No. 11 Squadron are mentioned. Lionel Morris was the quiet man of a unit packed with past and future legends, and his undramatic, often prosaic prose, confirms that he was just doing his job. The handwriting is generally legible and his manner is straightforward, his sense of humour dry. He doesn't seem to have been a romantic and didn't waste time convincing himself of the validity of war. Many of the colleagues he mentions in the diary died, like him, before the winter of 1916.

But the power of the diary lies in the occasional shock of names and phrases ingrained in our national consciousness amongst the comments on the awful weather and the banality of waiting for action; reminders that here was a young man in the thick of one of the most notoriously bloody battles of history. 'Arras' and 'Vimy' and, most sinisterly, 'gas attack' jump out of the pages. There are very few overt hints of the undoubted stress and fear which must have enveloped him on occasion.

Whether that was down to the conditioning of the era, a reluctance to externalise those feelings by writing them down, or simply because his high-spirited enjoyment of the job had yet to be affected is difficult to tell, but it was certainly the norm and fits with the tenor of the time.

\*

Arriving in Boulogne from the Folkestone boat train just before lunch on 18 May 1916, Morris's confidence in the smooth running of the British war effort in France was not boosted when he got to the Officers' Club: 'Found everything upside down, luggage everywhere.'[1] The next day, after a morning wandering around Boulogne, he finally made his way to his new base at Savy in the Pas de Calais: 'Wretched slow train stopped at every station... Got there 1.15 after a very dusty ride with a missing engine.'[2] Savy was a hamlet around nine miles northwest of Arras, with an aerodrome that was home to No. 13 as well as No. 11 Squadron.

No. 11 was a unit with a good claim to be the first true fighter squadron of the Royal Flying Corps. Born three months after the war had started, it arrived on the Western Front at the end of July 1915 with a swarm of Vickers FB5s (also known as the Gunbus) aircraft.[3] Two-seaters for the dual purpose of fighting and observation were still omnipresent before people like Albert Ball in nippy and agile single-seaters like the Nieuport (or the Bristol Scout, the first British plane to be fitted with interrupter gear[4]) proved that another pair of hands and eyes weren't always needed to bring down enemy planes. No. 11's crews were also expected to perform reconnaissance in all its forms, including photography and, sometimes, with the aid of wireless, co-operating with the French Army.[5]

The squadron's base in May 1916 was in a rural location shared with ongoing French agriculture. Rats were everywhere, providing a gruesome entertainment for off-duty officers. Fiercely competitive hunts were held, during which the men were locked in a pig sty with nothing but a walking stick to slaughter the rodents. Challengers were not allowed out until all the rats were dead.[6] The nearest village was Aubigny-en-Artois, a place of ghosts for anyone with half an imagination. No less than five casualty clearing stations buried their dead there, and the wounded of many salients, including Vimy Ridge, passed through. In early 1916, when the French Air Force handed their aerodrome at Savy over to the RFC, it was an unsophisticated place, put together on a needs-must basis, and challenging for pilots both on the ground and landing, as even Albert Ball found out.[7] From the village of Savy, through which the river Scarpe, scarcely bigger than a stream, trickled, the road climbed gently towards the corner of a large field. A pretty young woman, believed to be the local miller's daughter, often lingered at the top of the small lane leading up to the aerodrome entrance, observing the comings and goings of the aeroplanes.[8] A small copse obscured some of the aerodrome buildings; further ahead on the right, a triangular assortment of huts and hangars were revealed, lining two sides of the field. On the third side was a hedge with a large gap, through which aeroplanes taxied, and a landing ground beyond stretched up north west towards the neighbouring village of Villers-Brûlin. A walk back down into the village as far as Mayor Dorge's château, requisitioned for accommodation for some officers, took around five minutes. A further fifteen led south to the less palatial officers' billets, the church and the railway station.[9] One of Morris's No. 11 Squadron colleagues, Second Lieutenant Lyle Buntine, noted the reconnaissance necessary to avoid getting lost: '[I] have just walked down from the aerodrome about a quarter of a mile away. It is not a very easy road to find at night either, as the path goes along a winding railway embankment, over a bridge and through a small wood.'[10]

On arrival at Savy, Morris reported to No. 11's commanding officer, Major Thomas O'Brien 'Mother' Hubbard. Thirty-four years old, fair-haired, with a stutter and a gentle manner, Hubbard was already steeped in the history of aviation in Britain. Honorary Secretary of the RAeS from 1908 to 1912, when he became one of the original RFC officers, he had enthused a younger generation (no doubt including some of his current squadron charges) with *The Boy's Book of Aeroplanes*, published in 1912.[11] Hubbard's equable personality made him popular with the often nervous young men already scarred by combat. Albert Ball, who reported to him just a few weeks before Morris, had expected home leave after active service of three months in France. But his spirit had been noted, and he was moved from two-seater BEs with No. 13 Squadron to No. 11, where he was recommended to Hubbard for flying the single-seater Nieuport Scout. No. 11's Adjutant, Second Lieutenant Archibald Insall, related Hubbard's positive effect on Ball: 'I found A. B. in confab with the C.O. He was in high spirits, and I could see that [Hubbard] had won another heart.'[12]

The appearance of Hubbard's rooms at Savy owed much to the amiable negotiations that had taken place with their previous occupants.[13] The whole northern sector of the Western Front was plastered over the walls in a cartographic display that left visitors in no doubt about the immense geographical challenge the RFC were absorbed in.[14] The vastness of the skies demanded a relentless offensive effort from Allied aircrew: to pursue daily, obstruct, and frustrate the enemy over the lines; never giving them a moment's peace or allowing them the opportunity to consider that if they were to use similar tactics in superior machines, they could beat the RFC at their own game.

Taking over an existing aerodrome had at least spared the RFC some potentially delicate discussions with the local landowner – although ultimately the land could be requisitioned anyway. Sugar beet was the ubiquitous crop in the area, providing an unpromising surface for delicate early aeroplanes: British ace Major James McCudden wrote of a whole squadron turning out for an afternoon's square bashing to flatten the roots.[15] A proportion of the rent paid to the owners acted as insurance cover in the event of damage.[16] Morris, as a new member of B Flight, was billeted in a farmhouse in the village. He was pleasantly surprised by his new quarters: 'a small room at the top of a private house with quite a nice garden. Very nice woman with two small children. Got all my kit stuffed in and was allotted servant.'[17]

Morris was happy to fit in with his local hosts, and made no mention of the cockroaches and mosquitoes that plagued other officers.[18] Albert Ball was more comfortable on his own in a tent on the aerodrome – replaced in time with a hut and a garden created around it as a refuge from the stresses of fighting.[19] The men of No. 11 were generous and welcoming. Ball wrote of his colleagues: 'I have struck a topping lot of chaps in this squadron, and they look after me.'[20] He shared small luxuries with his fellow officers: 'Now my tent is full of chaps wishing to hear the gramophone.'[21]

Morris described his new base briefly: 'Fine aerodrome... We have a large hangar for each flight.'[22] A small but cheerful black and white neo-Tudor hut, complete with an attempt at a low picket fence and straggly shrubs, was nicknamed 'The Bungalow'.[23] Some huts on the aerodrome were used as workshops, another became a canteen, which Insall rated as unique on the Western Front at that time.[24] On sunny days, as the bombers and artillery machines of No. 13 Squadron returned to the landing field, officers and men stood in the gap to watch them, assessing the damage done to the machines flying over their heads, as Morris's contemporary William Fry noted: 'Bullet and shrapnel holes showed up against the sky, and we could often see how they had fared, some of them coming in like colanders.'[25]

On 20 May Morris made his flying debut with No. 11 in a Vickers Fighter. The FB5 Gunbus was a step up in engine and firepower and at last had a more effective defence, with a machine gun on a flexible mount for the observer in the front nacelle to use. It was still slow – so slow that the pilots nicknamed them 'Mossies'; not after the zippy insects, but because some wag suggested a little horticulture could develop on it at the sedate speeds it achieved.[26] Like all First World War aircraft, it was uncomfortable, with aircrew suffering creeping numbness of limbs in all seasons. Morris's first flight was adequate rather than impressive:

> Was temporarily allotted Vickers 5501. Went up for a trip first to try my hand. Misjudged my first landing so had to do a second circuit... Went up again and had a look at the country... My second landing was quite decent. Sat and watched the people landing the rest of the day. There is practically nothing to do when one is not flying.[27]

He was on his own during this maiden voyage. Observers were too precious to be put at risk from relatively untried Vickers Fighter pilots. Officers named 'Lieutenant Sandbags' appeared in logbooks – an ironic reference to a sack of earth that replaced a human passenger in the plane.[28] Inexperienced newcomers needed to be restrained from doing themselves and others any damage through excessive zeal. But it was essential for them to familiarise themselves with the terrain, including landmarks and advance landing-grounds, in case they were attacked and needed to find their way home.[29] A contemporary of Morris in No. 23 Squadron, Lieutenant Donald Macaskie, admitted in a letter to his parents he was struggling with orientation: 'It is awfully hard to find the aerodrome, as all the villages have trees round them, and they all look the same.'[30]

Having made it through his first day with the squadron without disaster, on the next Morris flew northeast from Savy to Arras and Vimy Ridge, skirting the front line for the first time, but reluctant to go too near.[31] After a week of practising on his own in the Gunbus, he was allowed to join an escort formation (a strategy of safety in numbers in response to the Fokker scourge) and registered the local town of Doullens, with its ancient citadel and distinctive belfry, and the rich agricultural area around Avesnes-le-Comte. On 24 May he had the first of many mishaps that punctuated his flying with alarming regularity. A stone hit the propeller of his aircraft on take off, severing three of the piano-like wires that braced the wings of the aeroplane: 'Was first getting off the ground when I heard a bang and turning round saw that there was a large hole in my top plane.'[32] The only option was to get down to the ground as quickly as possible and the machine was out of action for the rest of the day. Away from the mess, Albert Ball spent the evening at his hut, working late into the night, and building a frame for his 'cumbers', but for Morris, the descant of the guns continuing in the distance meant a sleepless night.[33]

\*

On Tuesday, 25 May, Morris reported: 'Am fairly settled down now. West for another practice flight in Vickers 5468, a C Flight machine.

Hear we are getting into Fes. [FE2bs]. Wonder if they will be better than the 120s.'[34]

The Allies' answer to their lack of machine gun interrupter/synchroniser gear had been to mount the engine and propeller at the back of the aeroplane. The FE2b variant about to arrive at Savy had two machine guns flexibly mounted on the nacelle. Providing the observer was brave enough to risk free movement without a safety harness – and willing to stand up with only the lower half of his legs protected (the nacelle side came up to about knee-height) – the guns had an improved arc of fire that gave these stable and comparatively simple to land machines an advantage that the RFC hadn't previously enjoyed.

The 120 horsepower Glasgow-built Beardmore engine that Morris referred to was to be replaced by a bigger 160 hp one – in the short term a mixed blessing as it turned out. What was gained in power was lost in reliability, as Morris was to discover, but he had still to convince Hubbard that he had enough skill to cope with the challenges of the doughty Vickers Fighter. On 27 May he wrote with understatement: 'Had rather an exciting time this morning. Went up in practice in 5501, got up to about 200 feet when the engine petered out and I was forced to land in a cornfield about 1½ miles from the aerodrome.'[35] The French-built 100 hp rotary Gnome Monosoupape engine was a highly-strung instrument that didn't allow pilots the luxury of throttling down; this all or nothing approach demanded skill and nerve, while gaining altitude was a sluggish business. Morris was now also over unfamiliar territory. Having managed to land without injury either to himself or the machine despite the engine failure, he was lucky as a new flier to have his own squadron technicians close at hand. One pilot had been reported as having over thirty forced landings (although luckily all on the right side of the lines), and they were a fact of life. For Morris, the major difficulty was taking off again once the engine had been fixed: 'After some time some mechanics came out and after about an hour got the engine to run again. Found it rather difficult to get off and only just cleared a belt of trees. Got back safely though.'[36]

His attempt to spend the next day productively was a partial success: 'Sat outside the tent and watched other people landing. Also had a snooze.'[3] But during the last two days of May, the war finally became a reality for him: 'large German shells bursting well behind our line, just north of Arras by Vimy Ridge. They sent up huge spouts of earth and stones which seemed to hang in the air quite a long time before they fell again.'[38] He was partnered with an observer for the first time on 31 May on a dawn patrol from 5.00 am to 7.00 am – an acknowledgement that he was now proficient enough for a passenger. It was an achievement he took pride in, describing his feelings in characteristic RFC vernacular: 'am rather bucked.'[39]

If any phrase serves to conjure up the character of Great War aviation, it is the dawn patrol. Every day along the length of the Fourth Army front, between the limits of the La Bassée Canal in the south, to Gommecourt in the north, the RFC's pilots looked for trouble, on both sides of the lines. It was a strategy that aimed to cow the enemy, as James McCudden had insisted: 'Nothing succeeds like boldness, and the Hun is usually taken aback when boldness is displayed.'[40] As a confidence trick it saved the life of many inexperienced men like Morris, who would have stood little chance against a skilful enemy in those first few weeks of active service. His diary entry for 31 May illustrated the striking contrasts of a RFC pilot's day; from the sheer freedom of flying on a beautiful morning in an empty sky, through to the momentous sights of the front line:

> A lovely morning, but very cold. Wrapped myself up jolly well and we started. It is lovely flying in the early morning, no bumps and beautifully fresh… Having climbed to about 3,000 feet we made off towards the lines which are very distinct in some places. Just two white or brown wavy lines in some places not more than 15–20 yards apart…The ground on each side is very torn and wasted and on Vimy Ridge for about a mile on either side there is not a single sign of vegetation, the earth is brown and covered with shell holes and huge mine craters, just as though it had a severe attack of smallpox. Our patrol extended between Souchez and Gommecourt and we flew quite close behind our own

lines and I could see demolished houses and small villages all the way along. It is common to see the way the trenches cut across tracks and railways. In one place they cross the railway at a deep cutting and one can see where this has been severely shelled and partially collapsed.[41]

Morris's usually acceptable grammar stumbled in his efforts to convey descriptively what he saw:

We flew right over Arras and I could see the effect of the shells there. The cathedral is a ruin and dozens of big houses but it is still in fairly decent condition. We crossed the line unwillingly and got archied. Not very mean though they are just like large balls of cotton wool suddenly appearing after a flash and a small report. By the end of two hours I was fully cold and was glad to turn our nose homewards and get back to breakfast.[42]

His dismissive reaction to this first encounter with anti-aircraft fire (the colloquial name Archie was from the line of a music hall song – 'Archibald, certainly not!' – adopted by airmen suffering its attentions) was confirmation of how secure the skies were for the RFC at that stage of the war, but there was plenty of time to reflect on the abrupt environmental adjustments every combat pilot had to get used to: 'The rest of the day I simply hung about the aerodrome.'[43]

The officers' mess was a small haven where the men gathered to relax and tell tales of the day's engagements, as one flight came in another left, and the constant normality of the gramophone blocked out the everyday tragedies that were occurring. Alcohol was to the men what castor oil was to the engines: a necessary lubricant, soothing stress alongside the distractions of card games, newspapers and talk of home. With many of No. 11's airmen coming from North America or Australasia, Morris's education was expanding far beyond the confines of his job: the international flavour of the squadron gave young men like him opportunities of friendship he would have been unlikely to experience without a war. As an early flier, Morris must have recognised more than most the possibilities and attractions of foreign travel once the whole dirty business was over.

*

The last week of the month was a triumph for No. 11, and on 29 May, Albert Ball scored a double success in his Nieuport Scout. Both spirits and nutrition were high: these second and third victories were joined by another, more modest achievement: Ball's first harvest of mustard and cress, shared with his fellow B Flight Officers.[44] The oscillation between excitement and *ennui* was evident again on 1 June when, despite being off-duty, Morris went up on a line patrol anyway, taking with him a new observer, Lieutenant Guy ('an awfully nice fellow') and watched the war on Vimy Ridge.[45]

When the first of No. 11's much anticipated FE2bs, with the improved 160 hp engines, arrived on Friday, 2 June, Morris was keen to have a go:

> Four came altogether… I asked the major if I could have a trip in one, he consented and I took Lieutenant Guy up with me for three quarters of an hour. They are jolly fine machines. Will do about 80 to 85 level and you can fly them hands off. It is quite comforting to feel that you have a decent engine behind you. They climb very well too, we got to 7,500 in 20 minutes, not bad. We could see the sea quite distinctly to the NW it was so clear.[46]

The more experienced eye of his commanding officer informed his own description of the new machines: 'the FE's fo'c'sle… likened to a Highland shooting-lodge, with room to spare for such pursuits as Swedish exercises on the part of the bored observer.'[47] These distinctive arthropod-like machines were already familiar in the skies above Northern France. Their ungainly design, with a heavy engine at the back, and a complicated tracery of struts and wires, contrasted with the stolid lines of the bathtub nacelle that accommodated the pilot and observer in separate compartments. The pilot's cockpit displayed the elementary tools of the First World War airman in a rudimentary combination of switch, gauge, valve and meter. There were the mechanical necessities of rudder bar and spade grip control column, and the timeless navigational basics of compass and map. A hand pump under the nacelle was operated on the ground before take-off to push oil to the engine. Everything was housed in an immaculately polished wooden setting, 'more like a piece of furniture than a war machine.[48] The pilot was afforded a modicum of comfort in a seat behind a tiny windscreen, with the engine's radiator to the rear, whilst, in the event of combat, the observer was obliged to hop up on a box to reach the guns; darting around the nacelle with no safety restraints – or clinging on with both arms and legs to the guns or the fuselage. Homeward flights in a limb-numbing crouch with a grimace against the wind once the work was over, were safer, but not much more pleasant.[49] The fatal flaw of this otherwise steady and surprisingly versatile aircraft was its blind spot. For all the manoeuvrability of its guns, the high sides and back of the nacelle made it difficult to see what was approaching from the rear.

Major Hubbard's confidence in Morris's growing abilities had been demonstrated when he had allowed him to take up one of the new FE2bs, but the squadron was still functioning with some relatively outdated aircraft. Back in March, HQ had increased the number of aeroplanes in all squadrons from twelve to sixteen on paper, but by the end of June, No. 11 had some oddities amongst the Nieuport Scouts and new FE2bs. Additional single-seaters with their pilots had arrived from units now operating with two-seaters.[50] There was a whole new flight of 'stream-lined' Vickers FB9s that Morris was to get to know.[51] The arrival of the 'Fees' was significant for him, not just in terms of a new technical challenge. Their superior performance compared to the Vickers biplanes made them the squadron's go-to machines for formation flying on offensive patrols, so his forays across the lines and his exposure to danger were increased. But it was back to the Vickers FB5 Gunbus and its flighty engine on 3 June. Lieutenant Floyd partnered him for a dawn patrol:

> I was therefore dragged out of bed at the unearthly hour of 3 am and got to the aerodrome about a quarter to four. We started at 4 but had not gone above 1,000 feet when the engine began missing badly and cutting out. We therefore came down again with all possible speed and landed. Found that the distributor was oily. Started off again at about half past and this time she was alright. We stopped up there for two hours but saw nothing in the way of enemy machines.[52]

Morale was high amongst the British squadrons. Commander of the Fourth Army General Rawlinson was deeply impressed by the efficiency of the Allied air operation: 'for the moment at any rate we have command of the air by day on the Fourth Army front. I cannot speak too highly of these young pilots, most of whom have come out recently from England.'[53]

The boldness was succeeding.

*Chapter 9*

# Waiting for A Scrap

The Arras region had some comforting echoes of home. The weather was similar, chalk was the predominant stone (making the roads well visible from the air) and the pastoral geography reflected the agricultural value of the land. The most striking feature was its relentless horizontal nature. Morris noted:

> The country around here is rather peculiar. It is quite flat as regards large hills, but is covered with small depressions and valleys which in some places make difficult landing. It is chiefly covered with crops, corn and sugar beet. Dotted all over the place at frequent intervals are small villages and woods. Generally where there is a wood there is a village but there are also some fairly large woods near Doullens. All the woods are clearly defined and form very good landmarks. We follow roads in the country in preference to railways for the latter are always bad and indistinct whereas the roads are generally well made and perfectly straight.[1]

The Somme river meandered to meet one its tributaries west of the waterlands that encircled the medieval town of Corbie. There it joined the Ancre, heading northwards to Albert; a town that in 1916 was home to the leaning Virgin Mary – left at a suspenseful angle to the top of the Basilica of Notre-Dame de Brebières after an inconclusive shell burst. The Allies chose to launch an offensive in an area noted for its tranquil beauty – but one which had been haunted by war since medieval times because of its strategic importance. Around 420,000 British lives alone were lost between July and November of 1916. The

French and British armies were geographically close to each other in this part of Northern France, but historians, including Peter Hart, have questioned why such a rural area, with so little in the way of modern transport infrastructure, was chosen: 'modernised solely to facilitate the prosecution of a battle that would eventually reduce much of it to mud, splinters and rubble.'[2]

The position of Arras, as a well-connected corridor through hills facing the elevated table-land of the German-held Douai, guaranteed the city a painful history in the First World War. Before the end of 1914, the city centre had already been pummelled by artillery. Captured by German cavalry in September and re-captured by the French the following month, it lay only around seven miles from the front line for most of the war. By July 1915 shellfire had decimated the beautiful medieval and Renaissance city that was the centre of the historic Artois region: 'Arras is still uninterred. She is the corpse of a city that waits for burial and day by day the German shells are trying to dig her grave.'[3]

The British Third Army had taken over an additional twenty miles of the front line in Artois to help the French committed to the battle for Verdun in the south. They inherited a wilderness of broken stone, displaced earth, vegetation and human remains. Subterranean struggles were later to commence at Vimy Ridge to the north east of Arras, with German and Allied tunnellers trying to out-mine each other in desperate attempts to win the most vital high ground in the region.

Morris was still untroubled by the enemy. A diversion on 3 June took him to the aircraft depot at Candas: a place with the same air of novelty as Boulton and Paul's hangars at home and full of the latest machines destined for the front. He returned an ailing Vickers Fighter, 'as the FEs are replacing them and most of them have done less than 100 hrs.'[4]

The arrival of the FE2bs was significant for him: their superior performance compared to the Vickers biplanes made them the squadron's go-to machines for formation flying on offensive patrols: so his forays across the lines were increased and his exposure to danger heightened. For now, though, the novelty was welcome:

> I took a fellow with me named Wyatt, observer in B Flight. They sent a tender from here about 2 hours before we started so as to be there when we arrived to bring us back. All the instruments were taken off so I had to fly by instinct… [Candas] is a very small aerodrome with a large number of sheds on two sides of it. I managed to get into it alright. Having delivered the machines we had a look round the sheds and saw all sorts of machines. Morane monoplanes, FE8s, De Havilland scouts, 2ds and 2es included.[5]

No. 2 Aircraft Depot at Candas was a combination of central stores and distribution centre. All new aircraft were issued from there, and machines too badly wrecked to be repaired within squadrons, were sent there. Its sister site was No. 1 at St Omer, from where RFC HQ had shipped out in favour of the village of Fienvillers in the lead up to the Somme offensive. Candas, north of Amiens, was out on a limb – all supplies arrived by sea at Boulogne, which had no direct railway connection with Doullens, the nearest town. No more than a month's worth of stores were kept there. In the event that the war may at any time change its course, the locations of aerodromes and their satellite buildings needed to be as mobile as possible.[6] Ferrying aircraft to Candas was a welcome break from the stress of patrols, allowing the pilots a chance to enjoy their flying.

*

The London papers in the mess were full of news of Ernest Shackleton's safe arrival in the Falkland Islands, after one of history's most incredible journeys. The aircrews of the Flying Corps in France had plenty of time to read them, as an iconic Western Front misery that plagued all sides without prejudice, reappeared on 3 June.

No account of the Battle of the Somme is complete without reference to the rain: an element as crucial to military success or failure as any industrial or human variable, and one that was gifted with its own RFC soubriquet, 'dud'. The chalk of the Somme area was bedded down beneath layers of viscously clay-clarted loam, picturesquely known as *Limons de Plateaux* (silt of uplands) by the French, but with a propensity to liquify in wet weather.[7] In 1916, and for the duration of the conflict, the rain took on mythical qualities. "'The fourth element of war" is how wounded men in the recent fighting in France describe the indescribable new ally of Germany – MUD.'[8]

Bad weather in the summer of 1916 could well have increased Morris's life expectancy, as instead of risking his life in the skies, he was grounded. But equally it stopped him from gaining crucial flying experience. Rain set in at Savy on Sunday, 4 June, and whilst artillery air work continued and ground staff toiled to keep the planes airworthy, Morris had the leisure for a little grumble: 'The weather has broken and is cold and miserable. Bridge has been tabooed so there is not much to do except sit about and read.'[9] At nearby Le Hameau, one of No. 23's pilots, Second Lieutenant Donald Macaskie, wrote home for a book of algebra problems and exercises and used one of two horses (available to officers for exercise) to visit Savy.[10] By Wednesday, 7 June, at teatime, Morris was on his way back to Candas, taking a passenger, Corporal Downes, 'just along for the ride.'[11] Forced to hang around for a return lift in the squadron car, Morris was treated to dinner in the Officers' Mess whilst the lowly Corporal stayed at the aerodrome. By the time they were ready to leave, the drizzle had returned. It was no respecter of rank: 'I found to my dismay that they had sent an open tender and that it was starting to rain. Suffice to say we had 2½ hours of the most miserable journey possible.'[12] Another two days of downpours continued: 'Weather something awful for June. Nothing doing.'[13] To compound the gloomy mood, news reached Savy of the death of Lord Kitchener, drowned along with 600 others off Scapa Flow in the Orkneys when the ship HMS *Hampshire* struck a German mine. Morris remained on stand-by for patrols. He found creative ways of readying himself for action: 'went to sleep in the observer's tent in front of a petrol flare which smoked us out eventually.'[14]

The Daylight Savings Bill of May 1916 (ushering in the concept of British Summer Time, and adopted by the Army in France a month later) was also a challenge to squadron sleepyheads, as Morris had found out on 12 June: 'I was on early patrol and had therefore to turn out at 4 instead of 5 am.'[15] He soon woke up:

> Went right over the line once and was just getting back again when I heard a terrific explosion just over our tail and felt the whole machine shake. This archie was followed by several more, more or less close. I shoved her nose down and did a deuce of a sideslip and managed to get away alright.[16]

The disdainful tone Morris used on 31 May to describe the 'not very mean' puffs of archie had disappeared in his first serious encounter with the enemy: 'I thought we were hit… but when we landed later I found that we had not been touched. A jolly narrow escape though.'[17] Anti-aircraft missiles were developing incendiary new habits: 'flaming onions' could set the fabric of a plane alight at 5,000 feet.

In addition to the dangers of anti-aircraft fire, flying through artillery tested reflexes as well as skills. Exploding shells in the path of an aeroplane forced the pilot to take evasive action by throwing the aircraft away from them. Not that direct hits were the only danger, as Norman Macmillan of No. 45 Squadron described: 'the hidden menace of their passage was presaged by the waves of air that made our aeroplanes dance like frightened horses.'[18] Other hazards were caused by natural fine weather phenomena, like the thermal bumps that played havoc with a badly rigged plane.

But for 13 June, there was a continuing theme of inaction: 'The weather has again sent a complete dud.'[19] And on the next day: 'Same as yesterday, only more so.'[20]

After nearly two months with the squadron, Morris received a 'nasty shock' on the evening of 15 June: 'It came out in orders that I was to be transferred to C Flight. I was frightfully fed up having been in B Flight for a month and got to know all the fellows and machines. Still can't be helped I suppose.'[21] Morris's lack of interest in recording his fellow flight members ensured a dignified absence of gossip in the diary. But the presence of another of B Flight's pilots had quickly created an impression in the squadron as a whole. Albert Ball kept a low profile at Savy whilst not in the air, haunting the hangars to watch the mechanics and working on his improvised shed and garden, but his growing confidence in combat was marking him out as an increasingly useful fighter pilot. Whatever Morris's thoughts on his soon-to-be-famous contemporary were, it was clear he was more concerned with his own change of comrades. By 8.30 the next morning he was in a new machine with a new colleague in C Flight – in a group of officers destined to be wiped off the strength of No. 11 Squadron in less than three months.[22]

\*

A report by Philip Gibbs of the Daily Telegraph caught the sinister mutation of the French landscape as the presence of the British Army increased in the summer of 1916:

> Along the roads towards the battlefields there was no movement of troops. For a few miles there were quiet fields, where cattle grazed, and where the wheat grew green and tall in the white mist. The larks were singing high in the first glinting sunshine of the day above the haze. And another kind of bird came soaring overhead. It was one of our monoplanes, which flew steadily towards the lines, a herald of the battle. In distant hollows there were masses of limber, and artillery horses hobbled in lines. The battle-line came into view, the long sweep of country stretching southwards to the Somme.[23]

The modestly populated nature of the land itself gave the Germans the upper hand. Morris had remarked on the woods and small villages that dotted the terrain of the Somme, providing the enemy with often small but very effective fortifications harbouring pockets of determined opposition that could eat up significant numbers of Allied soldiers. Within just a few weeks the Allies' bombardment was to send a thunderous warning of significant action ahead, and the RFC's penetrating offensive patrols were intended to stop enemy aeroplanes from observing the preparations for the battle as well as providing a show of strength. The plan for the Big Push was for the First, Second and Third Armies to support the Fourth Army's attack on a roughly fifteen-mile front to the north of the Somme. By diverting and diluting German defensive efforts in this way, it was hoped that the French offensive to the south of the river would be more effective. Haig and the French commander Joffre agreed to 29 June as the commencement date for a massive bombardment to precede the attack.

Morris had only to look out of the window of his billet on any particular day to guess what his participation in the clash of empires was destined to be. An 8.30 am line patrol on 16 June with Lieutenant Capel was curtailed by impenetrable clouds and mist and there was little flying for the rest of the day as the rain set in again.[24] Lieutenant Claude Gibson in one of No. 11's single seater Bristol Scouts came close to disaster around 6.00 pm when the engine failed immediately after take off. He was unhurt when the aeroplane crashed after banking to avoid a sunken lane, but the Bristol was put out of action for the meantime.[25]

Morris was concentrating on the mundane task of unpacking in his new quarters:

> I got all my things shifted into C Flight where I got a rather comfortable little bedroom leading off the mess. It is rather a cold cheerless place though but possesses a lovely gramophone and a good few records. Mess quite 20 minutes walk from the aerodrome but this may be an advantage as it will provide a little exercise. The flight hasn't really an O.C. [Officer Commanding] as Captain Pattinson has gone home to get a squadron. Chadwick is in command, a rather decent fellow. [26]

Captain Pattinson had already won the Military Cross and had been promoted to Officer Commanding No. 57 Squadron.[27] The day after Morris met him, Lieutenant Reginald Chadwick and Second Lieutenant Wedgwood reinforced No. 11 Squadron's aggressive reputation when they saw off an eight-strong enemy reconnaissance group.[28] Morris missed the action, rising at 4.00 am and walking from the mess to the aerodrome for a 5.00 am take off.[29] He was partnered with Corporal Morton on a line patrol from Souchez in the north to Gommecourt in the south, some thirty-three miles as the crow flies. There were no enemy to be seen: 'Got extremely bored by the time we came down.' He returned to the aerodrome, to sleep: 'the best part of the rest of the day.'[30] When hostile planes reappeared on 18 June, Morris described in sardonic terms the urgent keenness of No. 11 to engage the enemy:

> Reconnaissance of eight Huns came over and everyone rushed into the air to strafe them. I got up in FE 6357 (*Shanghai*) with Lieutenant Harvey of A Flight. We stopped up 1 hour 20 but saw no Huns. Kept chasing our own machines in hope of them being Huns. I don't think anyone bagged a Hun for directly they see us coming they make full speed for home.[31]

In the relative peace of Savy, his thoughts were still focused on his domestic arrangements on the ground: 'No patrols but have been busy shifting all my kit again, for we have shifted our mess from the farm to a large Château not five minutes walk from the aerodrome. No 13 Squadron used to have it but they have shifted into hutments by the aerodrome.'[32] Mayor Dorge's château was a much more convenient location for billets than the village and Morris was satisfied with his new home:[33]

> We have a fine room for a mess room, with large French windows, so plenty of light. There are plenty of rooms above the mess room but they are still troubled [sic] by No. 13, and when they clear out we shall have them. At present I have a tent in the orchard and am quite comfortable albeit rather

damp. The people too are awfully nice and do all they can for us. We also have a new Flight Commander, Captain Rough, whom I knew at Norwich. He was adjutant there and is quite a nice fellow.[34]

After a rare lie in with a 'nice cold bath' on 20 June and a uneventful line patrol with Lieutenant Wedgwood, Morris had time to talk to other officers and noted an air of growing expectancy in the squadron: 'Great rumours are abound of a large offensive slated for the end of this week and also that we shall be pretty busy during the time that it is on.'[35]

*

Sometime in late June, at the chateau of Querrieu, home to the Fourth Army HQ on the old Roman road between Albert and Amiens, a uniformed white-haired man with heavy-lidded eyes arrived. Fabian Ware was an Empire man of great capability and energy, who had already proved influential in the professions of education and journalism, holding the editorship of the *Morning Post* and a directorship with an international mining company. Like Frederic Kenyon, he was now too old to be a soldier, but was desperate to do something to help the war effort. An influential friend had pulled a few strings to get him to the Western Front, and in September 1914, he was given the command of a Red Cross mobile ambulance unit, clearing up in the aftermath of the Battle of Mons. Ware immediately saw that there was a lack of coordination for these most difficult, but crucial tasks, and began systematically organising the collection of information about casualties. Procedures were established for dealing with the bodies, and where they were to rest. From these small beginnings, with Ware's drive and foresight, arose the Graves Registration Commission (GRC), an organisation now known as the Commonwealth War Graves Commission (CWGC), whose presence is always found beside the dead of the First World War and innumerable subsequent conflicts all over the world. Ware's Corps Burial officers were nicknamed 'Cold Meat Specialists'. They undertook the grimmest of jobs, necessary not just for the cleansing of the battlefield, but for the morale of the surviving soldiers subjected to the ghastliest of reminders of the slaughter.

In the early summer of 1916, despite the experience gained during two years of bloodshed in France, the GRC were facing a daunting task, not least because they had little idea of the scale of the fighting yet to come:

> At the beginning of the Somme offensive last year I called at the Fourth Army HQ and saw General Hutton with regard to this question of burials. There was no organisation for the purpose of the time and I was satisfied after having discussed the matter with them that it was impossible to establish any proper organisation at that time in the middle of severe fighting. Subsequently the organisation of Corps Burial Officers was established.[36]

Whilst preparation for the dead was quietly arranged, the fields and lanes of the Somme flatlands were alive at night, with men moving up to the front lines for the next eleven days. Seven trains a day delivered three million artillery shells ready for action.[37] As neat stores of waiting ordnance began to pile up all over Picardy, the squadrons of the RFC went over the lines looking for guns, and movement of German troops. Thousands and thousands of aerial photographs were taken and interpreted, giving up to the trained eyes of intelligence officers the positions of German batteries for the British artillery to target. The progress of nocturnal wire-cutting parties, wielding heavy duty equipment to clear the way for Tommy into enemy trenches, was also monitored and noted by the RFC, and any topographical obstacles on the battlefield that might halt the hit and run of an Allied breakthrough were meticulously recorded.

No. 11 Squadron had continued to concentrate on looking for the enemy in the sky instead of on the ground. Their scouts were about to be given a terrestrial directive requiring outstanding courage. And the FE2bs and Gunbuses were soon to become familiar with more earthbound targets as the Third Army's attentions focused on needling the Germans where it would hurt. Something momentous was about to unfold, as Insall recorded:

> Around the aerodromes, there were tell-tale shifts of mood and response: it was to be seen in the way the staff of the Chocolate Shop in the rue des Trois Cailloux in Amiens greeted you, when you went in to shop for the mess, in the way that Madame Joséphine, round the corner in the Ruelle du Corps Nu Sans Tête, sparkled with it when she caught your eye from her desk in the long little restaurant.[38]

At home in England, the poet Edward Thomas scooped up a handful of soil to illustrate for a friend what he was fighting for.[39] In France, the same mud, dust and stone was exploding over the battlefields.

The Big Push was on its way.

*Chapter 10*

# Up and Down in Paris

For No. 11 Squadron, as well as for the benighted British Army as a whole, the Battle of the Somme was not a campaign of great success. That had nothing to do with the squadron's lack of endeavour or work ethic: it was simply a question of strategic resource allocation. Whilst the Fourth Army took on the burden of attack, No. 11 were with the Third; nipping at the enemy's ankles in the north to distract them from the Allies' primary effort in the south. The unit's involvement in the mainly ineffective Gommecourt offensive put them in a support role on 1 July 1916. But this satellite campaign provided many opportunities for the squadron to prove themselves. Episodes of the campaign were to go down in the RFC's history, providing a vivid narrative for the creation story of the Royal Air Force, which continued to inspire its members in the next war.

The appearance of Albert Ball in one of those moments guaranteed that Lionel Morris was elsewhere – the diary, though full of references to his day-to-day colleagues, barely acknowledges the scout pilots that often shadowed the FE2bs. But the approving mention of the inception of this next chapter in No. 11's history brings a rare connection between Morris and the big hitters of the squadron: 'They are fixing up our Nieuport Scouts with large incendiary rockets for destroying the Hun kite balloons so that they won't be able to spot our artillery. It is a neat idea, and I hope it comes off.'[1]

Kite balloons were a ubiquitous feature on both sides of the lines. These were the static eyes in the skies of both armies, nicknamed 'sausages' by the British, tethered to the ground and highly vulnerable to attack, but a vital source of constantly updated information that helped to position the fire of artillery accurately. To observe from a kite balloon was a bad job at the best of times: crews had less protection from the weather than the pilots and observers in aircraft, and fewer options in the event of attack, relying on the quick response of men on the ground to haul them out of the way as speedily as possible. Strong stomachs were necessary, as the wind could make conditions as uncomfortable as enemy action, and as target practice for long-range shells they were irresistible. A few days previously, a thunderstorm had wreaked havoc on British observation balloons, setting many loose from the ground. It was a ghastly experience for the crew of one of them: the observer's frost-bitten hands fumbled to destroy maps and photographs as they were blown towards the German lines. A change of wind direction pushed them back westwards, but their primitive parachutes had turned into malign octopi, wrenching a crewman out of the basket, tangling with the ropes of the balloon and dragging it upwards. Both men survived, traumatised and hypothermic.[2]

The destruction of the enemies' kite balloons was a central part of the RFC's pre-offensive tactics. It was a strategy that hadn't started well for No. 11 Squadron. Captain Herbert Ambrose Cooper was one of the elite band of pilots, like Ball, who had been trusted with flying the valuable single-seater Nieuport fighter. A New Zealander who had travelled across the world to gain his flying ticket privately at Hendon in January 1914, Cooper had then gone home again two months later. Not a character to be daunted by international travel in the pre-jet age, he promptly returned to England in July and joined the Royal Flying Corps on the day war was declared – allegedly the first Kiwi to join the service.[3]

Cooper came up with a quick fix to a visibility issue he had with the cavernous fuselage of a Vickers Bullet aircraft. Not being a man of great height, he had found the elevation of two cushions still insufficient for him to able to see where he was going. Insall's description of 'tip-toe flying' suggests the positive spirit that made Cooper a much-admired member of the squadron.[4] The resourceful Sergeant R.G. Foster was also a useful ally for Cooper in his drive to improve No. 11's fighting capacity, and he provided a solution to the lack of flexibility of a Lewis gun on Cooper's Nieuport Scout. If, in combat, there was a gun jam, or if the ammunition drum needed changing, the pilot had been obliged to stand up to sort it out. Various hinged devices to allay the problem had proved unsatisfactory. Sergeant Foster's gun mount fixed the gun to a semi-circular sliding track attached to the top of the nacelle – enabling it to be brought down within easy reach of the pilot. An unforeseen benefit of the mount was that it could also lift the gun above the propellor to fire upwards and forwards – an advantage which pilots like Ball were quick to exploit at a time when synchronised guns had yet to reach the RFC. Insall explained the genesis of the new mount in a 1929 magazine article: 'The "Foster" mounting originated in Cooper's brain and took first shape in Foster's workshop lorry. Any night in April 1916, Cooper and Foster could be found hard at work at their lathe, long after normal activities had ceased, and the result, when it appeared, aroused lively interest throughout the Royal Flying Corps.'[5] Foster's ingenious invention was taken to the Battersea Experimental Station for refinements, proving so successful that it was also later adopted by the French.[6]

Cooper was not to live to see the fruits of his mechanic's labours. His death came in a flying accident on 21 June, when his aircraft, equipped with Le Prieur incendiary rockets, took a fatal nose dive. Albert Ball's fitter, Flight Sergeant Joseph Lang was on the scene quickly, along with a doctor who, knowing there was no hope, 'put a needle into him, as much to say he was done.'[7] Cooper was buried in nearby Aubigny. Insall recorded mournfully: 'Poor little "Coops", he had flown into the ground the day before, and Mother Hubbard had lost perhaps his most skilful pilot.'[8] Trenchard was reluctant to blame the scarce and hard-won aircraft for the accident. 'I fancy he did not realise it altered the flying qualities of the machine slightly. The Nieuports are quite safe to fly, and even with the aerial torpedoes on they are quite safe and easy as you will realise they are a good deal heavier than they were before.'[9] But the loss of Captain Cooper had spooked some of the more cautious members of the squadron. One of the flight sergeants later recalled how intimidating the Nieuports could be even without the Le Prieur weapons: 'Several of our pilots that were flying FEs had tried to fly [Nieuports], and they were frightened of them, they really were.'[10]

The drizzling hours that Morris spent with the mechanics preparing his new 'bus' at the aerodrome marked the other extreme of life at Savy: 'Have been allotted a new machine at last, FE2b 6950, named *Newfoundland II*, so have been watching them getting her in order.'[11] The miserable weather had one good use: the engine manufacturer's manual recommended topping up the aircraft's radiator with rain water.[12] But for every aeroplane that was operational during the summer of 1916, at least twenty-five men were needed to ensure it kept flying.[13] Every single part had to be meticulously cleaned, oiled and adjusted, a straight-forward if time-consuming job in summer, but an endurance test for the frozen-fingered mechanics in the cold months of winter.[14]

FE2b 6950 had arrived at the aerodrome earlier in the month.[15] Its adopted name of *Newfoundland II* hinted not only at its geographical origin but also the tentacles of empire and a diaspora of sympathetic expatriates keen to do their bit to aid the war effort in Europe. Across the globe a request had been put out for donations to a fund set up with the aim of building an Imperial Air Flotilla. Like the later, and more well-known, Spitfire funds, the sums asked for were specific, and *Newfoundland II*, at a cost of £2,250, was named in recognition of the gift from this small, and at the time still British, colony.[16]

On 22 June, Morris took his new machine up for the first time, with Lieutenant Capel: 'Nothing in the way of Huns as usual.'[17] Later that day he noted an intensified tone of anticipation in the mess: 'Rumour has it (the) offensive is to start about June 26th. Shall see some fun I expect.'[18] The rumours spread quickly: the London *Telegraph* reported that restrictions on visits by relatives to wounded officers in France were to be put into force. For anxious families scanning the tiny type of the casualty lists for all categories of bad news, from the discreet 'Wounded' to the painfully specific 'Blown Into the Air', the implications were less difficult to read.[19]

The bombardment heralding the Big Push began on 24 June, drilling its way into the nerves of every single man, woman and creature near and beyond the Front. Morris was given a short reprieve:

> I was told to proceed to Paris immediately with Lieutenant Toone to fetch two 'stream-lined' Vickers back. Hurried off to pack a few things and we started off in the CO's car at about noon. Two hours lovely drive brought us to Abbeville station, where after much red-tape with the RTO [Rail Transport Officer] man, we caught the 2.35 to Paris via Amiens.[20]

This was a rare jolly, an opportunity to enjoy the countryside at length from the ground – but the novelties of the French capital were even more alluring. Lieutenant John Toone was *au fait* with the administrative formalities needed to complete the transfer of the Vickers FB9, and they took a taxi to Avenue de Montaigne. Just a few months younger than Morris, and a London boy like him (he had been born in New Mexico, returning with his British family to Wandsworth before the war[21]) Toone had joined No. 11 in March 1916 from the Royal Irish Rifles. Arriving at the Aviation Militaire, they found that there was no-one of sufficient authority around to sign the papers and that their collection aerodrome was some distance from Paris. It became obvious that there was not much hope of completing their journey that day and they were told to return at 7 am the next morning. This left them with a dilemma. There were no Huns likely to need chasing in central Paris and besides, they had no aircraft to do it in. Instead, they were left in the trying situation of being energetic young men free to do as they pleased in the City of Light for the whole evening.

They headed to the Hotel le Meurice, an establishment where the walls could tell a hundred stories. Opened in 1835 in the Rue de Rivoli, it was the grande-dame of Parisian hotels; its name a byword for comfort. Morris's sense of occasion relegated the hotel to a convenient place to have a quick 'wash and brush up', eager as he and Toone were to hit the town. A 'top-hole' dinner was followed by a walk through the Place de la Concorde and down the Champs Élysees to the Théâtre Marigny, a venerable Parisian public building, which would host hundreds of soldiers, sailors and airmen looking for entertainment during the war. After 'quite a good review', Morris reported that they had 'got to bed about 12.30.'[22] Many British officers had been overwhelmed by the exotic and sensual possibilities of the French capital. James McCudden wrote diplomatically in his memoir of a couple of colleagues 'getting lost' one afternoon whilst on leave in Paris – and of them failing to return until the following morning 'in a most dilapidated state'.[23] Perhaps Morris was mindful of where his diary would be returned to in the event of his death, and of his mother Lil's delicate sensibilities. Venereal disease was the elephant in the war room, with nearly 417,000 hospital admissions from Britain and her colonies.[24]

As Morris slept in a comfortable bed in Paris that night, the elemental barrage that marked the true start of the Battle of the Somme was attempting to wipe the Germans off the trench maps. A week of fire and fury commenced with the intention of destroying barbed wire entanglements, killing the enemy in the trenches and dugouts beyond, and flattening the villages and strongholds that the Germans held. It had been supposed to last only five days but the generals needed more intelligence. The RFC laboured in the dank weather to provide aerial observation but there was no certainty that the enemy wasn't still dangerous enough to scupper the whole effort.

For the Tommies, who weren't getting any more sleep than their German counterparts, exhaustion and fear were bolstered by excitement and the widely held belief that no serious resistance could survive such a concentration of offensive power. It was the biggest bombardment the world had yet seen: armageddon with the purpose not just of material and corporeal wipeout, but of a psychological defeat that would be the beginning of the end of the war. There were those whose heads were not turned by the almighty roar of confidence that the barrage gave out. Political pressures at home from governments recognising that there was no other choice in an industrial age than to embrace an attritional struggle, created great practical difficulties for the organisation of a war involving four British armies and three French ones. The French had been too bloodied at Verdun to trust their ally, but they could not do without their help and had been forced to give them a battle they would have rather led themselves. Neither was inaction an option.[25] Famously, there were also differences of opinion between Rawlinson (Fourth Army commander) and Haig, which were submerged by personal loyalties.[26] Kitchener's New Army were in waiting but the reliance on quantity over quality hid the fear of a battle coming too soon for Britain's underprepared volunteers arriving 'in good faith and bad boots.'[27]

*

On the morning of 25 June, Morris and Toone travelled by car to Villacoublay aerodrome on the outskirts of the French capital, a laboratory for all sorts of aircraft not only awaiting distribution, but being tested and pushed to the limits of 1916 technology: some successfully, others not. The 'stream-lined' Vickers FB9 7828 that Morris and Toone were there to collect was one of the less successful ones. This version of the FB5 Gunbus Morris was accustomed to have shorter and rounder wings, modified landing gear, a bigger nose and less rigging. It underperformed on the Western Front and was often a liability. As No. 11's squadron history related, 'their axles would snap at the smallest provocation.'[28]

    The pilots were loath to drag themselves away from the novelties of Villacoublay on a bright morning: 'The weather being most annoyingly fine, we had to start there and then. We left the ground at about 9.10 and after a final look at Paris from the air, reluctantly turned our noses in the direction of Candas.' Collecting new log books and refilling their fuel tanks at the depot, they were then back at Savy for lunch, 'the Major was quite bucked at our quick return.' Morris was rewarded for his efficiency by being sent straight up again: 'As if I hadn't had enough flying for one day, I was requested to take another old-type Vickers back to Candas.'[29]

In his absence, No. 11 had enjoyed an explosive success over a German kite balloon. One particular pilot had been keen to master the Nieuport, having already proved his robust approach in another squadron with other more staid aircraft, as Flight Sergeant Joseph Hellingoe recalled: 'Ball threw BE2s about as if they were scouts.'[30] Ball's flight mechanic Sergeant Lang recalled decades later what had happened whilst Morris was away:

> Ball said, 'We'll have another go.' We modified another Nieuport to fire Le Prieur rockets. These were fired electrically by the pilot, and pointing upwards for him to get high enough to get out of the machine-gun fire, or the anti-aircraft fire. Ball went up and got the hit first time. We could see the smoke and the flames ascending, the Jerries climbing out of the basket. Ball had been away for only ten minutes – another ten minutes he was back. When he returned, he jumped out of his machine, and danced about with joy; he was on top of the world. And we clapped and cheered; everybody on the aerodrome turned out, even the 13 Squadron. Wonderful feat.[31]

Fifteen of the twenty-three balloons targeted by the RFC were attacked, with five successfully put out of action that day, three the next.[32] Ball was lucky to be alive. Taking a hit to his engine from the enraged German artillery, he had limped home to Savy, barely clearing the treetops.[33] Morris missed most of the celebrations. Although the Commanding Officer had sent a car to Candas to pick him up, he didn't return to the aerodrome until 10.00 pm that evening. His assignment the next day was incompatible with a hangover; his dry sense of humour masking any sense of unease about its dangers:

> The great push is supposed to begin today[34] and so to sort of celebrate the occasion, they wanted us to drop some bombs on a railway junction near Vitry several miles over the Hun lines.[35]

The constant presence of racks of bombs under the lower wing of an FE2b held a disciplinary, as well as an offensive, challenge for pilots working directly with corps squadrons on reconnaissance and artillery cooperation duties. Bombs still in the armpits of returning machines were an invidious suggestion of cowardice and a failure to cross the line, although with bombing methods still experimental and haphazard, hitting a target was a bonus, rather than an expectation. The daily gathering of intelligence over the lines was at the heart of the British military effort on the Somme, and in this methodical and repetitive work the RFC crews were a visible source of reassurance or vexation, depending on which side you were on. Flights at extremely low levels were vulnerable to German anti-aircraft guns, not to mention anyone with a firearm who fancied taking a pot shot, but every day the pilots and observers risked their lives, knowing that if they did not do the work, someone else would have to. That the outcome of the war lay in their hands was made clear. Every day lost to bad weather could cost lives and threaten victory.

Morris's first experience of flying a bomb-carrying machine was a frustrating experience:

> There were five of us. We started off alright at 8 am and climbed steadily with eight 20lb bombs on up to 8,000 feet, on our own side of the lines of course, but when we got there we were hopelessly lost above a thick layer of clouds and our leader Captain Rough developed engine trouble so he fired a green light and we all came down again and landed successfully, bombs and all. Afterwards it turned out so hopelessly dud that we didn't try again but simply stood by for the rest of the day, awaiting an opportunity which didn't come.[36]

The experience of returning to the aerodrome still fully laden with bombs was as alarming as the prospect of dropping them over heavily defended territory.

One of No. 11's precious scout aeroplanes was out of action by the evening, after its throttle control suddenly seized up, causing the engine to fail and the aeroplane to turn over on landing. Lieutenant Claude Gibson, returning from a kite balloon attack, was unhurt, according to the casualty report, but 'every part of machine, complete with engine and instruments to be returned to 2 AD.' Only the Le Prieur bombsights were salvaged.[37] One of the new FE2bs was returned to the aerodrome by its pilot Second Lieutenant Guthrie Anderson after the engine cut out twice in the air.[38] Albert Ball recorded the unofficial litany of casualties in a letter home:

> We have been up to our eyes in work since I arrived. You see, we have only four Scout Pilots left, out of eight. Poor old Captain (Cooper) was killed on my machine during my leave. He had only just come back from leave. Lieutenant A's leg is smashed in five places. Lieutenant C is in bed, etc.[39]

Hubbard approached Morris later that day: 'The Major told me this evening that I was lent to "B" Flight to fly their "stream-lined" Vickers as there wasn't sufficient pilots in "B" Flight good enough so I was put down for first patrol at 5 am tomorrow.'[40]

Dawn patrol on 27 June was a familiar and slightly desperate tale of mechanical jeopardy combined with bad weather:

> I turned up at the Aerodrome only just in time, at 5 am this morning and the Major sent me up to find the height of the clouds. They were, I may say, 1,500 so the patrol was washed out. It is no good patrolling under the clouds if they are above 1,300 feet. In the afternoon the weather cleared a trifle and the Major asked me to do a patrol in a Vickers to see what was going on along the line. I took Lt. Capel and was getting my height nicely before going to the lines when the engine started missing badly and I had to come down again. I found that an ignition wire had broken thus cutting out one of the cylinders altogether. The Major said it was not worthwhile going up again, so that trip was washed out also.[41]

Albert Ball was on the 7.00 am patrol just after Morris's stint, but the weather failed to curb his marauding instincts. As a result of a peppering of anti-aircraft fire, his engine was hit and a bullet narrowly missed his leg.[42] The limited air reconnaissance intelligence reaching General Headquarters of the British Army on that day was enough to convince Haig that sufficient progress was being made with the bombardment to press ahead with the main attack. Many of the pilots of the RFC had another enforced day off on 28 June, as the rain continued and threatened to derail Haig's timetable. The development of weather forecasting was inching forwards, but the meteorologists relied on historical data collection as much as the latest technology. The first operational forecast for the Western Front didn't arrive until October 1916. It was no coincidence that the RFC played a hugely important role in the development of climatology – the early fliers, lucky enough to be the first people in the world to experience the clear blue above low clouds, were uniquely placed to further the new science from their aerial laboratories. Haig also capitalised on a less savoury use of RFC meteorologists, when Captain E. Gold was part of a team who advised on the most effective use of gas at the Battle of Loos.[43]

Morris had observed the die-straight Roman roads from the air. After days of rain and a constant pounding from streams of heavy vehicles, their surfaces were breaking up into potholes to match the spotted appearance of no-man's land, becoming dangerously impenetrable for the logistical preparation of the assault. Shell holes and trenches continued inexorably to fill with water. By 11.00 am on 28 June Rawlinson and Foch, commanding the French Sixth Army, had decided to postpone the attack until 1 July, the original date that the French had requested. The rest of that day was a washout for the RFC but the artillery thundered on for another two days to mitigate the lost deadline.

On 29 June Morris wrote: 'A very fine day. Had consequently a great deal of flying.'[44] His squadron colleagues Guthrie Anderson and Air Mechanic Gerald Bibby, came down in a field when their Vickers FB9 engine failed after an army patrol west of Aubigny-en-Artois. The aircraft landed on its nose, breaking the undercarriage and shunting the nacelle perilously close to them.[45] Morris's day was exhausting but less dramatic: a morning line patrol took him from Souchez to Hébuterne through skies empty of the enemy. During another in the afternoon he flew over the battlefield soon to become the focus of the energies and courage of the men of the Third Army. He noted briefly: 'Saw gas attack by Gommecourt, otherwise nothing doing.' Already weary, he ferried another old Vickers Gunbus 4565 to Candas in the evening and returned by car to Savy at 10.30 pm. 'Have done altogether about 6 hours flying today.'[46] On 30 June, his diary gave no hint of the events about to come: four lines reported more rain, cancelling his patrols, but he managed 'a little flying in the evening.'[47] He was fortunate to enjoy rest when the RFC was performing at the limits of its endurance. Ball flew in escort role on two bombing missions that day, and No. 21 Squadron's RE7s blew two big holes in railway sheds at Lille, returning the next morning to finish the job off.[48]

Down below, in the trenches with the Gloucester Regiment, the composer and poet Ivor Gurney had been impressed by the insouciant confidence of the flying service:

> A fleet of aeroplanes on reconnaissance has just returned from a dawdle over the German front lines… This is the ordinary manner of our aeroplanes at evening, who stroll over in the casual way that men use after dinner, smoking cigars and feeling pleased with themselves, not caring very much what the unimportant rest of the world think or do. A reassuring sight.[49]

That apparent confidence had been passed from the very top of the Flying Corps. Trenchard's grip on the job in hand, despite the overwhelming dangers to his men, was unshakeable. At forty-three years old in 1916, Trenchard was nearer in age to the men who served him than Haig, Rawlinson or Admiral Jellicoe were. His deep-set eyes and resonant voice added to a powerful personality and his manner and ubiquitous physical presence at the squadrons was reassuring, as RFC pilot Cecil Lewis, then with No. 3 Squadron, noted in his celebrated memoir *Sagittarius Rising*:

> On the eve of the offensive the General Officer Commanding, 'Boom' Trenchard, with his ADC, visited the squadron. Sitting on his shooting stick, he called us all up round him, gave us a bird's eye-view of the whole attack, and in his pleasant, masterful way congratulated us all on our work… 'Boom' infused men's enthusiasm without effort by a certain greatness of heart that made him not so much our superior in rank as in personality. When he left we were all sure that victory was certain, that the line would be broken, the cavalry put through, and the Allies sweep onto Berlin.'[50]

*

In the hours before dawn, the communication trenches leading to the front lines were alive with men wriggling and shuffling into position for the Big Push. Little rest was possible. Thousands of pencil-scratched letters to home were written: the Tommies waited and the poets amongst them contemplated, translated and recorded for the less articulate a new language of the anticipation of death, that gave a past tense to a battle yet to begin. Amongst the soldiers of the 1/5th Battalion of the London Rifle Regiment waiting to attack with the Third Army at Gommecourt was Rifleman Francis Wilton Ingram, an insurance clerk who lived close to the Morrises in Rotherfield Road.

Ingram went missing the next day.[51] There would be no telegram with similar news for Lil and Albert at *Merle Bank* whilst the summer of 1916 still held.

*Chapter 11*

# Z Day

First light on 1 July 1916 came just after ten to five in the morning, with mist and a little rain. Half an hour before the soldiers went over the top at 7.30 am, Morris was in the air in his Vickers FB9 7828 on a patrol with his observer Sergeant Glover:

> Had been patrolling for about half an hour and had turned north from Gommecourt towards Souchez, when we saw some specks on the Hun line coming towards Souchez. I turned the nose of the machine towards Souchez and we gradually saw that eleven machines were coming towards us all very high.[1]

There was an agonising wait as the aeroplanes became close enough for the British crew to identify them as friend or foe. Despite the numbers against them and the enemy's superior position in the sky, Morris and Glover's response was unequivocal, if not instinctive: 'After about five minutes we decided that they were eleven Huns. We were at 9,000 feet and the lowest Hun was at about 9,300, so we tackled him. One of the others came up and fired at us but after a few shots from us he sheered off and left us to deal with the first one.'[2]

It was a moment of reckoning for both men. Glover reacted with precise and deliberate control:

> The Hun opened fire at about 300 yards but Glover reserved his fire until we were within about 30 yards of him and then gave him a burst of about 10 shots. He then circled, we followed and got in two more bursts of tracer both of which

I saw were well into him. He then put his nose down and I saw some pieces of stuff fly off him. He went right down and disappeared through a bank of clouds.[3]

Even for RFC crew used to having the skies to themselves, it was a satisfying failure of nerve by the Germans, who despite such numerical strength, were wary of engaging in combat: 'We then had time to look around and I discovered that our engine was going badly and we couldn't climb at all and as the rest of the Huns were almost out of sight we decided to come home.'[4]

Relief turned to incredulity when they saw the damage that one German gun had managed to inflict on the Vickers:

When we got home we discovered that our machine had been hit in several places. There was a hole through the front of the nacelle and several through the planes, while the engine had gone dud owing to a cylinder having been hit. 'Archie' reported that the Hun we hit went right down and probably crashed. We were awfully bucked of course.[5]

This dramatic diary entry suggests that the patrol had brought first blood for Morris and Glover. But there appears to be no claim for a successful fight that day for No. 11.[6] Taken at face value, written for himself in his private diary in a matter of fact way, there's no reason to believe that Morris's account was exaggerated. The resolve he and Glover had shown in the face of such danger was an example of the everyday bravery that was expected of all RFC aircrew. Its rewards were limited in a physical sense but vital to the *esprit de corps*: to be able hold their heads high in the mess, knowing that they had been tested and not found wanting.

Every squadron was competitively motivated to achieve high victory scores as an affirmation of their fighting spirit. But British aerial victory claims remain contentious, reflecting a sporting approach to war riddled with moral and physical complexities, and often ignoring the valuable contributions made by non-fighter aircrew. During the

period that Morris was flying, a 'victory' was asserted if the pilot/
observer had brought down an enemy aircraft, either directly by arms
or indirectly by sending it out of control (or clearly stricken), forcing
it to land on either side of the lines. Sergeant Glover's report, once
Major Hubbard had signed it, would have gone to Wing HQ for the
Commander to decide on its merits. If it were allowed, it would then
be passed up to Brigade HQ. Several variables would affect its veracity:
because the RFC were continuously crossing the lines on offensive
patrols (and going well beyond on many occasions) any 'victories'
they may have scored came down in territory where there was little
chance of verification. With two-seater crews, establishing the number
of victories becomes even more difficult: it was clearly Glover who
had fired the shots, but squadrons differed in their recording methods.
Had it been confirmed (and sometimes a Commanding Officer would
grant a victory to bolster the confidence of inexperienced crews) No. 11
would have given the victory as a joint one shared by both pilot and
observer. This was peculiar to British aircrew. An unconfirmed Out of
Control claim for Morris and Glover on 1 July would not have been
accepted by any other nation in 1916 – other countries had their own
definitions of victory. The idea of a moral victory, with the conclusion
that an enemy aircraft was out of the fight for one day at least, still
held currency in the summer of 1916. In this case, perhaps Morris and
Glover were given reason on reflection not to make a claim; certainly
the evidence of the diary does not appear to have been enough for this
apparently triumphant experience to be confirmed.[7]

By the end of the war it was impossible to give entirely accurate
totals as the nature of aerial combats had changed so much. The 'lone
wolf' cliché of the ace, as applied to pilots like Albert Ball (who took to
the skies without any back-up and launched himself lethally at up to ten
German aircraft too stunned at his chutzpah to respond offensively)
was a combat strategy that looked increasingly irresponsible. Ball's
favourite tactic (which admirers likened to the Berserkers, the ancient
Nordic warriors who fought in a frenzied, hypnotic state) was to
appear to fly headlong at hostile machines that were forced to scatter.
He would then suddenly appear underneath one of them, in prime

position to pull his gun back and upwards, firing off a drum at a range other pilots would reject as suicidal. It showed an exceptional level of personal courage, but safety in numbers was becoming the guiding principle of military flying. One-to-one combats soon ballooned into fights between multiple aircraft, making it even more difficult to assign definite victories. The FE pilots' method of defence was to stick to each others tails closely in a circular movement, so that their blind spots would always be protected by another – a visually arresting ploy which gave a fight the appearance of 'two dogs attacking a hedgehog'.[8] This construction was difficult for a predator to find a way into if they were brave enough to get close. As the FEs were outclassed by German machines, the hedgehogs' sturdy defences became vulnerable. What could make the difference between life and death for these crews when faced with a supreme shark like Richthofen, was the kind of nerve that Glover had shown: stay together and the formation would have a reasonable chance of success; be spooked by a show of aggression, or foolish enough to break away and have a go on your own, then the odds would dramatically change to favour the enemy.

*

By the afternoon of 1 July, when Morris and Glover did another (this time entirely unmolested) patrol in an FE, the British attempt at a big push had come up against the immoveable force of the unbowed German Army at Gommecourt. The enemy thought to have been annihilated now emerged in some strength from dugouts too deep to be destroyed by the inadequate bombardment. Soldiers fell on barbed wire that in many cases was still impervious to invaders. The inexperienced volunteers were carrying between twenty-seven and thirty kilograms of kit (the equivalent of the weight of a husky dog) and knew well what they had been told to do – but not what they should do if it all went terribly wrong. The 46th Division, Midland men from battalions like the Sherwood Foresters (the regiment Ball had joined in 1914) snagged themselves on their own barbed wire as they attempted to leave their trenches, staggered through mud, and were blinded by a smokescreen intended to confuse the enemy. Unprotected by their own artillery (who were afraid of hitting them) against a fearsome German barrage, they were picked off by machine gun, or left to hide or die in shell holes in no man's land. There was nowhere on a mobile battlefield to lay trailing telephone wires. The Londoners of 56th Division (including Morris's old neighbour Francis Ingram) who had managed initial advances in some places well into the German lines, were reduced to frantically signalling for more bombs (grenades) in vain as they ran out of the means to sustain their progress.[9] On the point of eradication by German counter-attacks, each man tried to do whatever was necessary to stay alive: 'I hardly waited for the order, but it came, "Everyone for himself!"'[10] There was nothing for it except to run – straight into the waiting machine gun fire.

In the south, around Montauban and Mametz, there were successes for the British, and the experienced French forces managed a more sustained advance. For the RFC, whose observation work had been ceaseless, there were frustrations that the chaos of the failing offensive had hampered their support for the Army. Signalling from the ground had often been incomprehensible or deliberately muted to avoid exploitation by the enemy. Yet pilots and observers had consistently kept the skies clear of invaders. Morris and Glover had taken part in one of nine Third Army aerial combats that day, and had not been the only crew to face off a numerically superior enemy.[11] Their experience was repeated in a more celebrated (and confirmed) episode by ex No. 11 pilot and Military Cross winner Major Lionel Rees of No. 32 Squadron – whose solo intimidation of ten German aircraft (including the despatch of two of them despite being wounded in the leg) added a Victoria Cross to his cluster of medals.[12] RFC bombers attacked transportation routes all over the Somme area, and singled out the key objective of German-held Bapaume, for particular attention. No. 11's Lieutenant Robert Harvey was given a mention in the Third Army's War Diary for 'considerably damaging the railway line and siding at Boiry St Martin south of Arras.'[13] Many squadrons had spent six or more hours in the air, constantly attempting to gather intelligence from the ground for what was left of the beleaguered infantry, as well as relentlessly pursuing Germans in the air, before they had even crossed the lines. Trenchard, writing to Brancker on 2 July, took a statistically upbeat view of casualties for the day: 'Considering it is practically a bare 2% of the whole lot engaged and it's not as if they only went over the lines once as most of them did two or three trips, I think it is a very small percentage for pilots.'[14]

There is a canon of famous first-hand accounts for the RFC's experience of the first day of the Somme, examples of which are repeated in many books, but still convey in extraordinary and emotional terms the impact of their involvement on that unforgettable day. They range from an exhausted Albert Ball, writing to his mother in between flights: 'I am O.K., but oh! so fagged… Things are on full steam just now, 2.30 am until 9.30 pm',[15] to Maurice Baring's evocative capture of No. 60 Squadron's mixture of adrenaline and stress: 'I saw a lot of pilots hot from the fighting and in a high state of exhilaration as they had a grand day.'[16] And from Cecil Lewis, who had been warned to stay away from La Boiselle but felt compelled to bear witness to the monstrous mine that blew the biggest hole on the Western Front with a horrible curtain-raising grandeur: 'the earth heaved and flashed, a tremendous and magnificent column rose up into the sky. There was an ear-splitting roar, drowning all the guns, flinging the machine sideways in the repercussing air. The earthly column rose, higher and higher to almost four thousand feet. There it hung or seemed to hang, for a moment in the air, like the silhouette of some great cypress tree, then fell away in a widening cone of dust and debris.'[17]

At Savy, however, No. 11's war was staggering to a halt.

*Chapter 12*

# Hors de Combat

In the days following 1 July 1916, No. 11 Squadron was having its own battle with both new and old aircraft. There were regular minor catastrophes as well as grave operational losses.

Morris's FE2b suffered a thermometer failure that sent him home from a line patrol on 3 July.[1] Captain Murray and Second Lieutenant William Wyatt had a bad landing on 1 July, clipping the ground and writing off another FE2b,[2] and the streamlined Vickers that Morris had brought from Villacoublay tripped over itself and snapped an axle after landing on 3 July, its occupants Second Lieutenant Henry Turk and Corporal Parks unhurt according to the casualty report, despite the nacelle having 'crumpled up from nose to the Pilot's seat.'[3] A burst propellor put paid to another of the FE2bs on 5 July,[4] and two of the squadron's experienced members, Morris's flight leader Captain William Rough, with Captain Archibald Field, were forced to divert to No. 4's aerodrome at Baizieux for an emergency landing.[5] Battered by bullets during an army patrol, their perforated FE2b sustained enough damage to strike the aircraft off the unit's strength.[6] More chillingly, Morris's Parisian partner-in-pleasure John Toone, along with his observer Lieutenant Eric Harvey, was driven down behind enemy lines whilst on a photographic mission on 2 July, 'last seen near BAPAUME at 2.30 pm.' Both had been taken prisoner.[7]

A rare piece of good news came on 2 July when the persistent Albert Ball scored another double victory, destroying two German planes.[8] He followed that the day after by attacking a kite balloon. Troops on the ground hauled urgently at the ropes to bring the balloon down as Ball hurled a load of explosive darts; when they failed to make an impact he followed them up with a drum of Buckingham bullets within an extraordinary fifteen yard range. It was a brave attempt which didn't destroy the balloon, but put it out of action for a while.[9]

There was a homegrown aggravation for No. 11's exhausted ground crew to deal with when a cloudburst flooded one of the hangars.[10] The First World War had introduced the horrors of chemical warfare; on the ground squadron mechanics suffered a more mundane form of poisoning. No. 11 in particular gained the nickname of 'The Castor Oil Squadron', earned from constant exposure to the lubricant used in the Vickers Gunbuses. The mechanics suffered most holding the tail of a FB5: a faceful of noxious fumes had a speedy effect on the bowels, as Joseph Hellingoe pointed out: 'Nobody [was] constipated in this squadron believe me!'[11]

Morris flew another patrol on 6 July, this time with Wedgwood, but it was cut short by the failing engine of the FE2b.[12] On the same day another FE2b landed on a patch of soft ground after an army patrol, wiping out the undercarriage and breaking the nacelle, propellor and parts of the wings.[13] Lieutenant Ernest Leslie Foot (nicknamed 'Feet') ran out of fuel in sight of the landing field after a special patrol in his Bristol Scout.[14] Eighteen months older than Morris, Foot had been brought up in a small Sussex village and left his desk job at London Bridge railway station to join the Oxford and Bucks Light Infantry on the outbreak of war. He trained as an observer after leaving the trenches in 1915, and by February of 1916 had gained his pilot's wings.[15] Arriving at No. 11 in June, under the watchful eye of Major Hubbard, he turned into one of the squadron's most talented and confident fliers, making the transition from FE2bs to scout aircraft. Good-looking, with beetle brows and a discreet moustache, Foot was a pilot of natural ability who was admired by No. 11's other virtuoso, Albert Ball. The two became close friends.

On 7 July more dud weather set in. Morris wrote, 'We seem to have had practically no summer up til now.'[16] Looking at his diary for July 1916 it appears that his skill at bridge (despite the nominal daytime ban) must have been one of the few competencies he was *consistently* able to develop. He was unable to fly on eighteen out of the thirty-one days of that month: eleven of those cancellations were due to rain and low clouds and the rest as a result of problems with the new FE2bs, the mercurial streamlined Vickers, and the shortage of other serviceable aircraft or pilots. Morris's non-appearance in the lamentable list of Reports of Casualties to Personnel and Machines could be due to the fact that he was so rarely able to fly. The squadron was *hors de combat* for a full ten days according to the unit history, and Morris's diary relates the glum monotony mixed with quiet relief that sprang from his inability to get into the air.[17]

No. 11's stop-start week was brightened with the news that Ball's endeavours had won him the Military Cross. Officers and gentleman kept their minds on the job and he subsequently wrote home to chastise his mother for her suggestion that he be sent an autograph book, after Trenchard had arrived at Savy to offer his congratulations.[18] But the commander's policy, 'the best is the enemy of the good' (with the implication that there was no time to wait until the planets aligned and provided a perfect model of machine efficiency) did little to justify the deeply unsatisfactory chain of supply: for the crews and mechanics it was a daily headache.[19] Trenchard was steadfast in his optimism for the long-term result, but continued to badger Brancker at home over the dearth of dependable aircraft arriving in France: 'If it goes on like this now, God help us when we get the Huns on the run.'[20]

*

On 9 July Morris was in the air for six hours with Glover, encountering nothing more than one distant hostile aircraft, too far away to attack.[21] Captains William Rough and Archibald Field, having survived their mauling earlier in the week, suffered another burst FE2b propellor that nearly brought them to grief on a dawn patrol,[22] and an inauspicious note was struck in Morris's diary when he related news of two missing FE2b crews: 'The FEs did an offensive patrol to Douai and unfortunately two never returned. Speer and Macintyre.' The possibility of the enemy being responsible was not conceded: 'Engine trouble we surmise. The FEs are turning out very dud. The engines seem to go after about 5 hours flying.'[23]

The truth was less easy to swallow. Lieutenant Alfred Speer, flying with Wedgwood, had been brought down on a dawn patrol and most probably burnt to death.[24] Born in St Albans, Cambridge undergraduate Speer had come to the RFC from the Royal Artillery, earning his ticket at Norwich just a few weeks before Morris.[25] In his short career with the Flying Corps, he had come to the attention of Major Trenchard in April 1916, following a dicey take off at Candas that earned him a caution from the General Officer Commanding 'This officer went off at right angles to the wind and as a result nearly wrecked his machine in getting off. There was absolutely no reason why he could not have left the ground up wind.'[26] Speer had made up for it by hitting the railway at Courcelle on 1 July.[27] He was aged twenty-two.

Thirty-year old William Wedgwood had joined the RFC from the Durham Fortress Company of the Royal Engineers. A photograph was taken by the German officers who buried them at Neuville Vitasse, showing their joint grave marked by a propellor blade; with their gloves and helmets amongst the flowers.[28]

Another crew, Second Lieutenant David MacIntyre and his observer Lieutenant Hayden Floyd, had met a Fokker. Floyd died of his injuries a few days later; MacIntyre survived to languish in internment in Holland until the end of the war.[29] Albert Ball's reaction to the losses hinted at a similar hope to Morris's about what had happened to them all, but as an already seasoned fighter pilot, he would have suspected the likely reasons: 'All of our machines are going rotten just now and we keep losing a lot. Yesterday four of my best pals went off, and today one of our new chaps has gone over, so you can guess we are always having to get used to new faces.'[30] To another contemporary, William Fry, the lack of skill demonstrated by new pilots was not the critical issue: 'it was just a matter of luck – if enemy scouts were up, there were losses.'[31]

Morris's luck continued on 10 July: 'Have only done one patrol today. Still on stream-lined Vickers with Sgt. Glover. We were up from 9 am to half past eleven. We saw five Huns a good way over their own line and followed them to and fro for some time but they eventually cleared off.'[32] Boredom and resignation registered in the diary for the next few days:

> No flying again today. We have only four or five machines serviceable in the squadron. It transpires that the engines they have sent us out (160 Beardmore) have all got soft gudgeon pins[33] and their bearings are bedded in all wrong. Consequently they develop trouble after a few hours flying. We have to take each engine down in the squadron, overhaul it, and put it together again. This is going to take time.[34]

The ongoing state of the aircraft mirrored the rhythm of life at Savy, as it continued at a stuttering pace. Morris had another truncated patrol on 15 July due to an engine cutting out intermittently[35] and another two machines went out of action; Foot's Bristol Scout ran away with itself into a ditch and the unfortunate Lieutenants Buntine and Wyatt flew into a shed at Candas with a new FE2b.[36] By 20 July another two Bristol Scouts were out of action – one, piloted by new No. 11 recruit William Fry, rolled over into a cornfield on a practice flight.[37] The other was also crashed on a practice flight by a new pilot, whose arrival at No. 11 must have sometimes caused confusion in the mess: Second Lieutenant John F. Morris (sometimes known, perhaps for obvious reasons, as Fitzmorris) was a Scot who had come to the RFC from the Highland Light Infantry. He had won his wings just eight days before.[38] The damage done to him physically was not life threatening – a gashed chin and a sprained ankle – but someone (presumably Major Hubbard) amended his casualty report by crossing out the word 'severe' which had preceded 'shaking' in the list of his injuries.[39]

And yet still Lionel Morris continued to keep himself out of trouble. On 18 July he showed enthusiasm for the nuts and bolts of the aircraft, as well as his respect for the toiling ground crew: 'They are working day and night in shifts on the engines with the help of a couple of experts specially sent out.'[40] But Savy was a dull place, and distractions were hard to find beyond upsets between the chickens on the streets. Old folk watched the world go by from their front steps, and women flirted with British soldiers in bar doorways, but it was a place that the war seemed to have mostly forgotten, bar the farmyard billet boards announcing the presence of an army amongst the livestock.[41]

Morris wrote on 19 July: 'I went on patrol at 10.00 with a fellow named Harris. He is attached for a few days from 8 Squadron and supposed to go back tomorrow. An awfully decent fellow. He has been flying [BE2s] and doing artillery work so it was a pleasant change for him to fly in an FE and he says he likes it much better.'[42] No. 8 Squadron had reported on the chaos following the attack on Gommecourt. Harris and Morris clearly hit it off as the next three days of diary entries were cheerful. A kindred spirit enlivens work and play and they were fortunate enough to enjoy time off together when the sun put in an appearance on 20 July.[43] They set off for a walk before a late afternoon patrol: 'We covered about six miles. It was a lovely day and the country was looking its best. We walked to Villers-Brûlin, Mingoval and back to Aubigny.'[44] The appeal of the French scenery in Artois was linked to the familiarity of home and the paradox of such golden corn fields and quiet coverts amongst the exhaustive destruction made its subsequent history even harder to bear. As author John Lewis-Stempel noted, 'in the Somme, the British found a second home. One reason the Somme would come to haunt the collective memory of the British soldiery is that its despoilation seemed like original and native sin.'[45] Morris, whose parental home in Carshalton was close to lavender fields and watercress streams, enjoyed the French rural idyll. He was still having a good time the next day, thanks to the continuing sunshine and the indulgence of his commanding officer: 'Have had a very enjoyable day today. The weather was perfect and the Major told me to take an FE that landed here last night to Candas… so Harris got the Major to let him come with me.'[46]

After delivering the aircraft they took a tender to No. 8's aerodrome, La Bellevue, where Harris picked up his letters. A meandering drive took them back to Savy: 'Drove back to Avesnes-le-Comte and on to Estrée where we spent another hour or so getting trout for dinner. There is a hatchery there and we saw the fish caught. An awfully pretty sport.'[47] The RFC officers ate well in comfortable mess rooms in undisturbed French villages, but trout was still a treat. They hadn't had the inconvenience of having to catch it themselves – unlike the Poor Bloody Infantry (or PBI as they were known) who sometimes resorted to detonating small bombs in Somme waterways to perk up their rations the quick way.[48]

An unpleasant surprise awaited Morris and Harris on arrival back at Savy at 7.00 pm: 'Had hardly got out of the tender when I was informed that four of us including myself were to be lent to 23 Squadron for a few days as they were rather overworked, and we were to proceed over there immediately, a nasty blow for No. 23 has the reputation for hard work.'[49]

Morris's dejection was understandable. In his semi-autobiographical novel of the air war, *Winged Victory*, V. M. Yeates captured the agitation of pilots taken out of familiar surroundings:

> 'I don't want to go to this comic squadron,' he orated, 'I'd much rather stay here with you fellows and win the war in good company. The trouble with this squadron is that we're too good. This is only the beginning. You'll find they'll be sending you all away one by one to show other squadrons what to do to the poor Hun when met flipping about miserably in an Albatros that can't catch fish and has to live on bluebottles in summer and bits of Archie.'[50]

In his diary that evening, Morris added sorrowfully: 'Also Harris was to go back to No. 8 at once. So I packed a few things including my bed and was driven over by tender, the same tender taking Harris on to No. 8'[51] Harris was not the only one going to No. 8. After weeks of constant fighting and flying, Albert Ball's tank of youthful energy and drive was in danger of running dry and he had asked Hubbard for a few days off to rest. His trust in the sympathetic commanding officer, if not exactly misplaced, backfired on him when Brigadier-General Higgins was passed the request and decided instead to send him to No. 8 on 17 July.[52]

Higgins may have been motivated by a desire to put Ball in his place and avoid a dangerous precedent: the pilot had voiced frustration with aircraft and equipment quite openly and he could not be given special treatment, despite his increasingly obvious star quality. Artillery cooperation work was barely less dangerous, in slower and more vulnerable machines, and Ball would now have to fly with an observer, unsettling for a man used to taking risks with only his own life to worry about.

Morris's diary gives few clues as to his own response to stress. But in between the fishing trips and the lie-ins, there were hints at the strain and fear that he never wrote about frankly. On 15 July he had an early night after two long patrols, and the following day wrote: 'Was not for patrol today, there not being enough machines and they evidently thinking I needed a rest.'[53] The reality was that he had already experienced the loss of several colleagues in No. 11, and was having to deal with the fear of flying in deeply unreliable aircraft. In France this came with the added danger of a forced landing behind enemy lines. He had learned for the first time the personal nature of warfare, when he and Glover had been attacked at close quarters on 1 July.

In a famous comment, Churchill's doctor Charles Wilson, showed how deeply his experiences on the Western Front had enabled him to see clearly what combat fatigue did to men: 'Courage is will-power, whereof no man has an unlimited stock; and when in war it is used up, he is finished. A man's courage is his capital and he is always spending.'[54] Harold Balfour of No. 60 squadron wrote that summer:

> I can remember my bedroom companion in the farmhouse in which we were billeted, felt as I did, and how each of us lay awake in the darkness, not telling the other that sleep would not come, listening to the incessant roar of the guns, and thinking of the dawn patrol next morning. At last we could bear it no longer, and calling out to each other admitted a mutual feeling of terror and foreboding. We lit the candles to hide the dark, and after that felt a bit better, and somehow got through that night as we had to get through the next day.[55]

The German Air Force had begun to respond to the RFC's success by switching its attention from Verdun and strengthening resources on the Somme. On 30 June, the eve of the battle, enemy aircraft had numbered 129 compared to the RFC's 401, but by 19 July, after the second phase of the battle began, expansion to 164 had been achieved.[56] Most ominously for the fighter squadrons of the RFC, this included two new units drawn, like their own, from single-seater pilots with a proven flair for combat.[57]

The BE bombing squadrons, which had suffered bad losses from flying without observers, needed protection and the enemy's communication targets still had to be pursued, particularly around Bapaume. What had been skirmishes between a couple of pilots were turning into multi-aircraft engagements. As Trenchard stood firm in the face of mounting casualties, the machines themselves were often falling apart around the squadrons who had neither the time nor the specialised skills to fix them. Morris's FB5 Gunbuses were no longer up to the job and the FB9 'stream-lined' version had proved a costly mistake. Lieutenant Colonel Murphy, Officer Commanding Thirteenth Wing, showed his frustration in a blunt report to Third Brigade HQ that accompanied one more broken machine recently delivered from Villacoublay by the now missing Lieutenant MacIntyre: 'Here is another case of structural weakness. The undertaking of a satisfactory repair entails complete dismantling of the nacelle, cleaning of the joints and brazing. This is nothing short of a skilled frame-builders job and is not work that could be undertaken in a squadron by an ordinary fitter or welder.'[58]

*

Morris had good reason to be apprehensive about his move to No. 23, 11's sister army squadron of Third Brigade RFC. Both units provided offensive patrols and escort protection for the frequent bombing raids being done by the BEs of Nos 8, 12 and 13 Squadrons. No. 23's commanding officer, Major Alexander Ross Hume, was a very different individual from the famously kind 'Mother' Hubbard. Ross Hume was a veteran RFC man, but by all accounts his man management was terrible. His unaffectionate nickname in the corps was 'Slippery

Sam': earned for an unbending application of orders which some saw as pointlessly lethal. During the months of the Somme campaign, with the intense pressure of flying hours, the *esprit de corps* at No. 23 was a world away from the relaxed command of Major Hubbard, just a few miles northeast at Savy. Captain Harold Wyllie, a flight commander with No. 23, wrote of the uncomfortable atmosphere at Le Hameau: 'The Squadron has got demoralised and jumpy, simply because officers, in addition to the great strain of the work in the air, have been so hunted and insulted by Ross Hume on the ground that they don't know where they are at.'[59]

Le Hameau was just over ten minutes away by tender. In contrast to the sloping field at Savy, the site on which No. 23's aerodrome buildings were positioned was higher, with long views east to Filescamp Farm. It was a flat and exposed spot compared to the sheltered valley of the Scarpe, and the canvas of billet tents flapped endlessly in the wind. Morris had the company of the three other No. 11 officers transferred with him: Captain Archibald Field and Lieutenants Turk and Scott. He shared a tent for the first night with 'one Firbank',[60] his mission the next day to form part of the escort for a bombing mission to Bapaume. The change from his cheerful tone of the last few days in the diary was abrupt: 'Felt rather fed up at being so summarily shifted for Lord knows how long.'[61] It was a painfully early start the next morning:

> Was called at 4.30 and felt rotten... Field and I were lent to A Flight under Hargreaves. The machines were just getting ready when clouds were seen coming up from the E. and soon the whole sky was covered with stuff at about 1000 feet. The boming [sic] stunt was of course a washout, although we still had to stand by for it. Went back to my tent and washed and shaved and had another breakfast.[62]

'Boming' was a spelling that Albert Ball sometimes shared – illustrating the novelty of new explosive technology employed from aeroplanes.[63]

The blessed relief of dud weather continued on 23 July but Morris's dejection continued: 'played bridge practically all day. Wonder when we shall get back to No. 11 again.'[64] The squadron's reputation for 'hard work' seemed to have been severely compromised by the bad visibility, as there was apparently nothing to do but sit around. But Morris was fretful about having to stay at Le Hameau for good. On Monday, 24 July he wrote: 'Played bridge again. Having really quite a pleasant time except for fear that we shall stay here for some time. Went for a walk with Vernon, an observer and a very decent chap in the evening. I am sharing his tent.'[65] Second Lieutenant Vernon's decency had been tested to the limit by his implacable squadron leader. When his photographs were deemed inadequate by Ross Hume, Vernon and his pilot Captain Ralph Adams risked annihilation by rifle fire on the German side of the lines on a day when no humane commanding officer would have sent his men up. Captain Wyllie had vented his frustration in his diary: 'The General was furious when he heard about it. Ross Hume has the worst eye for weather I have ever come across – he cannot tell whether clouds are at 500 feet or 1,200 feet.'[66]

On Wednesday, 26 July Morris was settling down to yet another game of bridge when there was some good news, bringing his reluctant exile from Savy to an end after five nights: 'Got an order about 11 am to proceed back to No. 11 Squadron. Jumped for joy. Got back in time for lunch.'[67] He was relieved to see the same faces still in the mess; there appeared to have been no empty chairs to fill whilst he had been away, although his colleague the Australian Lyle Buntine wrote to his parents on 1 August: 'We had an awful accident here the other day. A chap went up and stayed for a long time. In fact so long that all his petrol ran out and he couldn't get down and I believe he is still up in the air and has starved to death. Rotten luck ain't it.'[68]

Morris found the ground crews still hard at it: 'Found everyone alright but of course they hadn't done any flying. Practically all machines still out of action through the dud engines.' But his delight at his return to No. 11 was obvious, 'Quite a treat to wake up and find myself in my own room again.' A hint of gleeful irony appeared with the timing of a rare sunny morning: 'Extraordinary to relate the weather turned out quite nice and fine. Bet No. 23 were sorry they didn't keep us another day. However as we only had two machines in working order I didn't get into the air at all today.' His first flight in a week on 28 July came to an abrupt end when tell-tale vibrations signalled more gudgeon pin problems: 'Another machine out of action.' The ground crews worked through a dud day on 29 July whilst Morris 'did nothing very successfully', and he noted on the next; 'Mechanics are working day and night on machines and have already got several into trim.'[69] On 30 July, Foot (now promoted to temporary Captain and in command of C flight) had a bad landing in his Nieuport Scout that sent it to Candas for repairs, putting another machine out of service.[70]

On the last day of July 1916 Morris wrote:

> Lovely morning. Sky cloudless and wind in the N.E. Perhaps it has set in fair for a few days. Went up after lunch with Lt. Rees, a fairly new observer, a Welshman in the Royal Welsh Fusiliers, to take some photos. There were some small clouds about but not sufficient to interfere with us. We took 18 plates altogether, all on this side of the line of course, and more for practice than anything else. Came in about 4 pm. Had hasty tea and went up again with Rees in company with four more machines to do a patrol. The formation having got up to 1100 feet, we crossed the line and strolled about over Achiet for about a quarter of an hour, then came back, having seen no Huns.[71]

With that last business-like entry, Morris's diary ended.

*Chapter 13*

# A Plucky Observer

On 31 July 1916 General Trenchard's world very nearly turned upside down, according to Maurice Baring: 'As we were coming back from the Chief's house, the steering gear of the car broke, and we alighted in the ditch.'[1] Despite this hiccup, the shared feeling amongst the Allied war leaders was one of optimism. Baring's own favoured reading during the first phase of the Battle of the Somme was Dante Alighieri, concentrating on the Paradiso rather than the Inferno, and the Allies were moving forward.[2] Trones Wood and Delville Wood had seethed with tenacious German soldiers but both had eventually fallen. By 17 July, the British Army had partially recovered from the mainly disastrous opening day of the Big Push to take Bazentin Ridge.

The RFC made a crucial reconnaissance discovery on 22 July that changed plans for the next phase of the battle. A major offensive was intended for the strong German position running to the north west of High Wood but a significant new trench full of infantry was discovered by airmen of No. 34 Squadron.[3] Australian troops took the village of Pozières and then received the brunt of a German counter-attack. In a literally uphill struggle the Allies had reached the Albert–Bapaume road, but on the high ground ahead the German Army had the assets of long-held encampments to exploit, with none of the problems of rapid forward expansion. There were new challenges of communication and supply for the Allies to overcome before any wearing down of the enemy could be effective.[4]

In contrast, the German infantry were beleaguered by the energy and commitment of the Royal Flying Corps and bewildered at the apparent invisibility of their own aerial support: 'You have to stay in your hole all day and must not stand up in the trench because there is always a crowd of English over us. Always hiding from aircraft, always with about eight or ten English machines overhead, but no-one sees any of ours.'[5]

Maurice Baring enjoyed hearing reports of exasperated Germans: 'The Germans in the trenches put up a notice the other day saying: "Tell your ___ Flying Corps to leave us alone. We are Saxons."'[6] It was a weaselly tactic that attempted to exploit a recognised history of distrust of militaristic Prussians amongst Saxons – and the British saw through it: 'As it happened, they were Bavarians.'[7]

Baring's easy-going manner contrasted sharply with Trenchard's seriousness. RFC casualties were rising at a deeply worrying rate, and the commander's letters to Brancker were increasingly demanding. Writing on 25 July, he addressed the recent problems at No. 11 that Morris had referred to in his diary just over ten days before:

> When can I count on all 160 hp. Beardmores coming out will have [sic] the proper gudgeon pins and Idler wheels as every engine at present has to be taken down directly the machine arrives to change the gudgeon pins. Result – in No. 11 Squadron there is not a single machine serviceable to fly.'[8]

A piecemeal method of supply was counter-productive: 'What date will all machines be coming out with these new fittings it is no good sending them out without as I have not the men to do it out here.'[9]

The dozens of blank pages at the end of Morris's diary could well have been a reflection on the heightened tempo of his own experience of the war. Fatigue, and the tyranny of a daily entry must surely also have played their part. His friendship with the twenty-one-year-old Welshman who would die with him under Richthofen's guns was one of the stories left untold in the weeks leading up to his death.

*

Tom Rees was born to a farming family in the small village of Deffynog in Breconshire on 18 May 1896, making him just a few months older than Morris.[10] His upbringing was strikingly different from his future pilot, in a quiet and deeply rural environment within sight of the Welsh mountains. He was gifted with four brothers and sisters and spared the zealous application of many middle names. His short and to the point first name was 'the first modest attempt in the Rees family to cease repeating Christian names exactly in every generation', and it marks him out in the records: always Tom, rather than Thomas.[11] In a county which produced no less than twelve Rees children with variants of the same Christian name in the last decade of the nineteenth century, it was a sensible flag.[12]

As the youngest son, his horizons were wider than those of his oldest brother David John, who was actively involved in the running of the farm. The middle boy, William, had joined the Royal Engineers and was serving in Tripoli, attached to the Royal Armoured Car Division.[13] Tom Rees went from the village school to grammar school in Brecon town, becoming a pupil teacher locally in his last year at Brecon Boys School. From there he appears to have passed effortlessly on to the University College of Wales at Aberystwyth in 1913, where he joined the Officers' Training Corps.[14] Rees was the only student to start the honours course in geology in the autumn of 1914 and never returned to finish it.[15] He attested on 2 December 1914 at the college in Aberystwyth, aged eighteen.[16] Like Morris, he joined a local volunteer regiment, the 14th Service Battalion of the Royal Welsh Fusiliers. His attestation document bears the hopeful stamp of 'Welsh Army'. David Lloyd George wanted to form an army corps solely made up of his compatriots – but with insufficient recruitment, it was a title never to be realised. As part of the 38th Welsh Division, the regiment retained a patriotic flavour and Tom's battalion was one of the original Pals units, attempting to draw men mainly from areas of north Wales. Although the principality made up the bulk of its men, it was not an exclusive club. Rees's battalion in particular took twenty-one per cent of its recruits from England.[17] There were rumblings of discontent about its 'political' nature – the 14th's commander was one of two Members of Parliament given divisional leadership by their party leader, David Lloyd George.

Rees's OTC experience and natural ability smoothed his own passage up through the ranks: by 18 December 1914 he was promoted to Corporal, and three days after Christmas became a Sergeant. A commission to Second Lieutenant came through on 21 January 1915.[18] Family legend records that his father, 'on observing the ways of the local gentry', was concerned that his youngest son would not be able to survive on a subaltern's pay and offered to supplement his wages. Rees made it quite clear that he intended to live within his means.[19] He remained in Wales in the spring and early summer of 1915, learning the art of professional soldiering.[20] The local newspaper reported on the activities of both Rees boys in uniform, noting how the war was reaching into the most rural of communities: 'The Congregation Church at Cwmcamlais, situated as it is in a quiet glen, undisturbed by any sound, except the "noise of many waters" is concerned about two of its boys, trained in its Sunday school and active Christian workers. These are two brothers, sons of Mr and Mrs Rees, Cefnbrynich farm.'[21]

Rees's progress with the battalion was a sign of great things to come:

> He has also been doing duty as Acting Assistant Adjutant. At the present time he is on the point of being transferred to the front. He is destined, if spared, to rise still higher, for he is gifted with a good physique, tall, strong and energetic, and he is one who is born to command. May these noble brothers be spared to return to their respective professions, after the Armageddon is past![22]

The 14th Battalion embarked for France in late November after a long march over the downs to the port of Southampton. Four days and 'a hundred hours of rain' later they reached their billets around Richebourg, in the vicinity of Neuve Chapelle.[23]

Escaping the misery of the Picardy mud for the Flying Corps made for a physically less demanding war, but any experience or status Rees gained in the infantry didn't translate to any special perks once he had been accepted into the welcoming arms of the RFC.[24] The career progression of observers was not tempting in late 1915. If a soldier had ostensibly professed a desire to leave the infantry for the Flying Corps, then his parent units had no motivation to promote him. The War Office had officially sanctioned the downgrading of any other non-flying training in their focus on producing pilots, resulting in the unsatisfactory situation of the RFC having to 'beg, steal or borrow' observers.[25] There was no shortage of volunteers, but HQ were too distracted by the casualty lists to pay enough attention to the longer term need for skilled, professional multi-taskers; able to man guns, range artillery, and use wireless, Morse code and maps to a high level of competency.

To mitigate the problem, the RFC offered brief sabbaticals for officers to train as observers, but the numbers persuaded to stay on permanently were low. The inferior status of non-pilot aircrew was reflected in their pay and most attachments were short-lived: men deciding either that they would be better off returning to their parent units to make career progress, or to retrain as higher-status pilots. In December 1915, around seven weeks before Rees left the ranks to become a subaltern, there was an improvement: all observer Second Lieutenants on the General List were made eligible for elevation to Lieutenant, but any further ascents were unlikely.[26] The timing of his promotion may suggest when he actually transferred, but his progress beyond that rank was still far from assured. As a war volunteer who had signed up for short service, this was less galling for Rees than it was for the men who had started the war as professional soldiers. But unlike Morris, who enjoyed a pay rise as soon as his wings were won, observers like Rees had to complete their training, prove themselves on active service, and then wait until there was a job available in a squadron before they could end their period of probation.[27] A half wing badge marked out their distinctive role.

The demand for observers jumped with the arrival of the two-seater 'Fees' – taking over guns, wireless equipment and performing photographic reconnaissance left the pilot able to concentrate on flying. Rees already had an interest in photography, and evocative prints still exist of his family – including his brother-in-law working on a hayrick in preparation for thatching at the Herefordshire farm he shared with Rees's sister Mary.[28]

By the time the Welsh Division met Prussian guards at Mametz Wood on 10 July 1916, dying in their hundreds over five days of (even by Western Front standards) bloody fighting, Rees had left the infantry for good.[29]

\*

A.J. Insall wrote a cameo featuring a young observer on attachment to No. 11 in 1915. It was a fictional account undoubtedly based on an amalgam of all the new observers he had watched clamber eagerly into the nacelle of a Gunbus. He named the officer 'Lieutenant Erebus', a name which classics-educated, public school RFC officers would have recognised for its association with darkness, not to say chaos. Erebus's progress was held up as typical of a new observer, with the caveat of an unfortunate episode where he 'came near to destroying an entirely unaggressive BE2c from a neighbouring squadron.' Later, the hapless Erebus's attempts to retrieve a wind-snatched map provide a comic interlude that must have rung bells with every flying officer compelled to take up a keen but green observer:

> Erebus, in his anxiety to retrieve his lost property and mark on the position of the anti-aircraft gun, forgot all about his heavily-lined Burberry until the wind got in under its tail and whipped it, inside out, over his head. Holding on desperately to the map with one hand, and to the edge of his cockpit with the other, he contrived to turn about in a darkened world and lower himself back into his seat: whereupon the gale got in at the front, bellied out the now unbuttoned waterproof behind him and plastered it smoothly over the aeroplane.

The unlucky pilot, whose daylight has been so unexpectedly removed, is sunk as low into the nacelle as poor Captain Cooper (even with a

Whitgift School's Officers' Training Corps, 1911. (*Courtesy of Whitgift School*)

Second Lieutenant
Lionel Bertram
Frank Morris in
the uniform of the
Queen's Royal West
Surrey Regiment.
(*Courtesy of Phil Evans
Whitgift School*)

*Above left*: Arthur Travers Harris, later 'Bomber Harris', who was in two of Morris's squadrons in 1916. (*Courtesy of The Royal Aero Club Trust*)

*Above right*: Morris's aviator's certificate photograph, 1916. (*Courtesy of The Aero Club Trust*)

*Below*: Albert Ball, No.11 Squadron's greatest gardener. Handy with a Nieuport Scout. (*Courtesy of Greg VanWyngarden James F. Miller*)

SAVY-BERLETTE. - Le Pont de la Scarpe

*Above*: Savy-Berlette, the Artois village that was home to No.11 Squadron in 1916. (*Author's collection*)

*Below left*: General Hugh Trenchard, head of the Royal Flying Corps in France in 1916. (*Courtesy of Greg VanWyngarden James F. Miller*)

*Below right*: Captain David 'Munshi' Gray - economical with the truth when necessary. (*Courtesy of the Royal Aero Club*)

*Above left*: Gray during his brief time with No.60 Squadron in 1916. (*Courtesy of Annette Carson*)

*Above right*: Captain Ernest Leslie Foot, No.11 Squadron's aerial acrobatic wizard and close friend of Albert Ball. (*Courtesy of The Royal Aero Club Trust*)

*Below left*: Second Lieutenant John Wilfred Toone, Morris's Parisian partner-in-pleasure in June 1916. (*Courtesy of The Royal Aero Club*)

*Below right*: Lieutenant Tom Rees, left, Morris's observer, with his brother David John. (*Courtesy of Meriel Jones*)

Oswald Boelcke (in aeroplane), Germany's supreme air tactician, with Jasta 2 in 1916. (*Courtesy of Greg VanWyngarden James F. Miller*)

Manfred von Richthofen.
(*Courtesy of Greg VanWyngarden James F. Miller*)

Alex Hamilton's painting of the dogfight, commissioned by Morris's school, Whitgift, to mark the centenary. (*Courtesy of Whitgift School*)

Morris's FE2b 7018 Punjab Montgomery, shortly after being brought down by Richthofen on 17 September 1916. (*Courtesy of James F. Miller*)

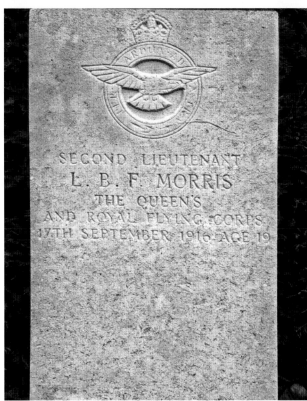

*Above left*: Replica of Richthofen's first victory cup. (*Courtesy of Whitgift School*)

*Above right*: Morris's grave in Porte-de-Paris cemetery in Cambrai. (*Author's collection*)

*Below*: Richthofen's souvenir – the Boulton and Paul plaque from FE2b 7018. It was mounted, amongst several others, on the wall in his room. (*Courtesy of James F. Miller*)

Morris's mother Lil (far right) in the late nineteen-forties.

*Left*: Lionel Reid, Morris's cousin, a Trenchard brat who retrained as a pilot in 1942. (*Courtesy of Terry Reid*)

*Below*: Morris's British War and Victory Medals. (*Courtesy of Phil Evans William Wood*)

cushion) had been and now flies blind, with only the help of a newly fitted lamp that illuminates his compass. Initiative is needed:

> He conceived the idea of leaving the aeroplane to look after itself and joining Erebus in the front seat for a little heart-to-heart talk on matters topical.

This consideration is wisely discarded as impractical in the see-sawing Gunbus. Erebus provides an unwitting solution when his exposed position leaves him in full wind and the draught proves too uncomfortable. He begins to drag the awning back in, but not before an urgent telegram is sent by HQ describing 'a Vickers Fighter executing unorthodox evolutions over Abbeville.' The episode ends safely back at the aerodrome with a not-entirely inappropriate explosion from the pilot:

> Entwhistle's rhetoric, after the machine had landed, broke several distinct records.[30]

Insall's story is an affectionate one, related from the safety of post-war peace, but the authenticity is unnerving. To be an observer in the summer of 1916 demanded enormous reserves of courage (arguably even more so than a pilot). Improvisation rather than solid training practice could be crucial. A bad, inexperienced or reckless pilot, with sole control of an aircraft, could kill an observer without coming anywhere near aerial combat. A good observer not only increased a pilot's chances of survival, but enabled him to concentrate on the business end of flying without the added pressure of having to be constantly on the lookout for trouble. Ground crew called them 'Piccadilly Johnnies', after the popular music hall song about affluent young men about town, but recognised their sacrifice: 'They had some guts… they knew they were going to their deaths. God Almighty.'[31]

The bonds of mutual dependency between a pilot and his observer had to be rock solid and based on absolute trust. Norman Macmillan, a pilot and later wing commander who arrived on the Western Front in 1917, told an anecdote about an observer, nearing the end of his mental and physical tether, whose doctor wanted him to stop flying. It was an unthinkable proposal, even for a sick man: 'And what about my pilot, Doc? Do you think I'd let him go up with anyone but me? How would I feel if I stayed on the ground and one day he didn't come back? No, Doc, I keep on flying as long as he does, unless my warrant comes through for Blighty!'[32]

The first appearance of Tom Rees in the records for No. 11 comes on the evening of 3 August 1916, flying with Captain Rough on an offensive patrol near Gueudecourt. Flying at around 7,000 feet at a speed of seventy to eighty miles an hour, they spotted a solitary Fokker which seemed to Rees to be threatening the formation. The new observer took immediate action, emptying a whole drum at it. The German machine, lacking the courage of its convictions, continued on a downward dive out of the FE's way. Which was just as well: Rees's gun had jammed and he was unable to fire any longer.[33]

Rees would have been aware that for most of the summer so far, this half-hearted engagement was typical, as the RFC pushed to keep the skies their own. Flight Sergeant Joseph Hellingoe of No. 11 summed up the belief that Morris shared: 'If they turned towards you, and you turned towards them, then they'd bugger off.'[34] But there was to be no let up. The squadron's crews were flying day after day to keep up the unrelenting pressure on their German counterparts. Their aircrews were to demonstrate the polar extremes of victory and death that hung in the Somme skies as the summer of 1916 stretched into autumn.

*Chapter 14*

# Cabbages and Kings

I n contrast to the precarious existence of No. 11's crews, the flora of Savy Aerodrome thrived. Albert Ball's peas had reached four foot in late June; a productive part of a garden that continued to give pleasure and sustenance to colleagues in his absence. By mid-August he was missing the pleasure of harvesting but had arranged for a gardener to send over the fruits of his labours.[1] The pastoral compensations of nature were keeping men calm all over war-torn Europe. Most famously, the British civilian internment camp at Ruhleben near Berlin, supplied with its raw materials by the Royal Horticultural Society at home, transformed an old racecourse into acres of productive garden that included a heated greenhouse. Its custodians were better fed than many at home in Britain.

The RFC men were also more fortunate than most. This description of dinner at No. 8 Squadron, where the unhappy Ball had been exiled for the time being, showed that at least the food wasn't bad:

> Starting with a hot soup, we went on to tinned salmon with a yellow sauce followed by hot mutton, mashed potatoes and cabbage. Lime juice and whisky helped wash down the 'dog biscuit' bread once a week. A tinned fruit sweet followed by dessert of nuts and oranges finished a record repast.[2]

Tinned goods today are a host's dirty secret, but they had gone from luxurious novelty to an expedient and cheap food solution during the war. Another of No. 11's new observers, Fred Libby, gave an account of his first Mess dinner that was vague about the food but enthusiastic about the ambiance, and observant of rank protocol:

> The dinner is excellent, everything from soup to nuts or cheese, if you prefer. When the liqueurs are served, the commanding officer says, 'Gentlemen, you may smoke.' This is what many have been waiting for, either his permission to be excused or to light a cigarette. It is a nice custom practiced in all British officers' messes and protects the non-smoker from suffering through a haze of smoke while eating his dinner. When the commanding officer leaves the table, dinner is over, and you may do anything you wish, but during dinner no one leaves the table, unless first going to your ranking officer and asking permission.[3]

Libby was a American who had joined the Canadian Army in search of adventure. After driving a truck on the Western Front he applied for transfer to the RFC in the winter of 1915/16. A former cowboy from Colorado, Libby's skill with horses and guns made him a shoo-in for observer duties. Serving briefly in No. 23 Squadron, by August 1916 he had made the same short journey from Le Hameau to Savy (just as Morris had done so happily a few weeks before) arriving around a month after Tom Rees.[4]

Fred Libby appears to confirm the suspicion that, the hell of war notwithstanding, No. 11 Squadron was a happy band of brothers: 'And here are several fellows playing cards. Everyone wanting to give me a drink, all at the same time. This crowd I am going to like. There is a spirit here which speaks of good fellowship and teamwork so essential to a squadron.'[5]

A rare reminder of No. 11's off-duty pleasures survives at the RAF Museum: the record of a concert party on 7 August, shared with No. 13 Squadron, and featuring an array of tunes and comic interludes for all moods.[6] From the naval clarion of *Larboard Watch* ('But who can speak the joy he feels, While o'er the foam his vessel reels') to the comic spoken word of George Robey's 'I Stopped, I Looked And I Listened', waves of nostalgia can still be heard breaking over the fading sheet of type. The gloom of Cyclist Somerville's *When Other Lips* contrasts with a mandolin-skirled version of *Bonnie Scotland* by Sergeant Mechanic Cullen. Amongst the performers there is barely a subaltern to shake a tuning fork at, but if it was a show of the lowest rank (Air Mechanics Kerr, Low and Woodhouse contributed *Hello Little Girlies*) the programme details give no hint of what anarchic twists popular songs were often given by the men of the Flying Corps. Air Mechanic Diamond's *When I Lay Down My Tools*, described as a 'Monologue' sounds inoffensive enough, but what may have been done to *Asleep in the Deep* by Air Mechanic Rigby is revealed by aviation historian Peter Cooksley, who identified its tune with this RFC version of the words:

> Hark how the passenger's startled cry
> Rings as he clutches the side.
> There in the cockpit the pilot lays,
> Cursing his ballast who weakly prays.
> Tho' death be near, he knows no fear,
> For at his side are a dozen beer.[7]

Libby devoted almost a whole chapter of his memoir to an epic drinking episode involving a dinner with an artillery unit, which ended in ignominy amongst pigs and vomit before the main course, after too many cocktails: 'Socially, Price and I are not such a success.' Alcohol was an acceptable anaesthetic for the stress of combat: 'This damn war is just one thing after another. You don't only have to fight Fritz, but you might die with the hiccups, or an overdose of alcohol.'[8] But the contrast of cheerful, slightly manic, abandonment with the punctiliousness of authority, revealed the illusory nature of their high jinks.

*

The first days of August 1916 brought a little-known Western Front phenomenon to the skies of Artois. Hot sunshine beat down from the usually leaden skies, peaking at eighty-eight degrees on 2 August.[9]

For those not detailed for flying that day, lying around the aerodrome and enjoying the heat was a welcome diversion; for others, the lurch from leisure to life-threatening action was as usual, unsettling. Guthrie Anderson with Second Lieutenant Geoffrey Allen dropped two bombs on Le Sars on an offensive patrol, before having to make an emergency landing at Le Hameau after their FE2b developed engine trouble,[10] and Lieutenant William Bowman and Air Mechanic Bernard Mills's FE2b dropped out of the sky sixty feet earlier than anticipated when returning from a test flight.[11] Two of the squadron's NCO fliers, Sergeants Thompson (whose officer namesake in the squadron Second Lieutenant Hector Thompson may well have caused the same kind of confusion that having two Morrises sometimes did) and Clarkson, were on the early afternoon patrol and met a hostile machine over the lines.[12] The combat made the RFC Communique, but despite the German having been seen to fall suddenly, with no definitive evidence of its destruction available, Thompson and Clarkson were denied a victory.[13]

It was Morris's turn again on 3 August. He was reunited with Glover on an offensive patrol that turned into a horribly familiar scenario – a gang of eight German aircraft they were obliged to meet head on. Glover's combat report stated: 'Upon our approaching to within 300 yards, half a drum was fired at the nearest hostile machine, but without effect.'[14] Morris and Glover were not alone – the FE2bs were most effective as pack aircraft – but the numbers of enemy planes were increasing, and the odds were shortening. With a survivor's hindsight, William Fry wrote after the war:

> [The] flight commander was nearly always an efficient leader, otherwise he would not have survived or been in that position. His deputy leader and perhaps one other pilot were experienced and reliable fighters and maybe there were one or two who had survived the dangerous early days and were getting to know their way about. The rest were beginners who had to be protected…The Flight Commander led, with his deputy on one side and another experienced pilot on the other. The difficulty was that enemy formations

and machines naturally attacked the planes at the rear, in the belief that the pilots were the least experienced... [Sometimes] an experienced pilot was detailed to fly in the rear of the formation, weaving to and fro, keeping on the alert... The trouble was that the pilot weaving to and fro soon found himself dropping behind.[15]

Compelled as they were to cross over the lines, those pilots unlucky enough to fall behind had far fewer options than their enemies. The prevailing west wind was in their faces, slowing down homeward journeys and putting them at risk of anti-aircraft fire. Some pilots attacked over enemy territory believed that the success of the Flying Corps in harrying the troops on the ground would carry a dangerous penalty. Heading as far away as possible from the long-suffering German soldiers in their trenches was a priority for any stricken RFC machine.[16]

The archetype of chivalrous air combat faded as the struggle for the skies intensified. On 5 August, one of No. 11's scout pilots, Second Lieutenant John Drysdale, had his engine shot up by a hostile aircraft, and was pursued to land at Berles-au-Bois. Ground crew risked their lives under continuing fire to salvage what they could of the Nieuport's instruments, guns, engine and petrol tank.[17] Drysdale had a nightmarish week; his escape on the 5th was lucky but two more aeroplane casualty reports, on two consecutive days, had his name on them.[18] Yet another of the squadron's scouts was broken on 10 August, although the pilot in this case, Second Lieutenant Brian Toms, despite suffering the horror of half of the propellor of his Bristol Scout breaking off in mid air, managed to bring the plane to land without injury to himself.[19] Still Morris remained absent from the aeroplane (and personnel) casualty lists throughout August.

The King arrived on the Western Front on 9 August, creating additional security duties for the RFC. His visit to the Third Army's trench mortar school at Ligny-Saint Flochel was behind the lines, within the parish of No. 11.[20] Nearby St Pol, home to the Third Army HQ, had already suffered a raid on 22 June. As Allied aviation effort concentrated on the build up to the first day of the Somme, German bombers had evaded the notice of the RFC and killed several Royal Engineers as well as refugees from Arras, who had thought they were safe further back from the fighting.[21] Nothing could be left to chance with the monarch's visit. Guthrie Anderson's logbook for 9 August included the entry: 'St Pol patrol. Guarding the King.'[22] Fred Libby was apparently kept in the dark as to why B Flight spent four days flying backwards and forwards for fifteen miles behind the lines; he then allegedly drew the long straw and shook the King's hand.[23]

As well as transportation and billet sites, German aerodromes were key objectives. HQ squadrons saw the thickest of the fighting on the Fourth Army front, whilst the Third Brigade's air support was utilised in a provocative bombing offensive. Physical targets successfully attacked, struck at the heart of the enemy's own capabilities – and the resultant collateral aggravation also proved a useful stick to beat down German morale. A reconnaissance patrol report for Morris and Rees on 17 August illustrated the meticulous observation of enemy comings and goings: in a hour and a half in the air, twenty-five tense minutes were spent flying over the railway systems around occupied Douai. At 7.15 am, Rees recorded: 'Two trains going towards Douai from E. consisting of about forty trucks each. Trucks were open and seemed to be greyish-white – probably wooden cases.'[24]

The RFC Communique of 11 August reported raids on railway targets that No. 11 had taken part in – only one train near St Leger was actually hit, but for the enemy, the incident was typical of a persistent and disquieting nuisance.[25] The developmental nature of bombing at the time could appear chaotic; especially when the FEs were acting as escort to the vulnerable bomb-carrying BE2s or BE12s, (sometimes joined in the event of a scrap by the expert scouts of No. 60 Squadron). William Fry explained this haphazard approach: 'There was considerable confusion and crowding, machines from all three squadrons mingling together.' Once the target had been reached, it was every man for himself: '[They] then joined up with the nearest machine or group and made for the lines, sorting themselves out after crossing and making their way home to the squadrons individually. I cannot recall squadron machines ever coming home together in formation.'[26]

This disarray was inevitable as bombing formations attracted intense attention from the enemy; other variables including problems with engines, and deteriorating weather conditions, could also develop at the worst possible moment for attacking crews. In those circumstances it was always a good time to have Albert Ball around. Happily for No. 11, Ball was now back where he felt he belonged, after his enforced absence on artillery and bombing, which he admitted to his parents had been a useful experience: 'I think it is has done me good being here, for I now know artillery work and bombing. All this helps to make a good flying officer.'[27] A phone call from Major Hubbard on his birthday, 14 August, recalled him to Savy and included the news that a brand new Nieuport Scout was waiting for him.[28] As always, professional pleasures were mixed with the culinary and horticultural advantages Ball was generous enough to share with his colleagues: 'I received your topping pudding a few days ago. It was O.K. All the chaps thought so, and you bet I did... My hut and garden are very topping just now. I am writing this letter in my hut with the door wide open.'[29] It was business as usual for Ball. Almost straight away he was back in the game: two 'driven down' aircraft accepted at Thirteenth Wing HQ for 16 August marked a spectacular return to success.[30]

As the war on the ground continued, the pounding artillery of the Somme was at its most insistent around the Thiepval Ridge, both sides pushing for the crucial high ground. In the air the cost of the RFC's offensive policy was questioned. Trenchard had warned Haig that the German Air Service was increasing in strength and organisational effectiveness, but an infamous episode illustrated the RFC chief's bloody-minded commitment to the Army and the strain of battle that had provoked it. Disagreements with Hugh Dowding, commander of No. 60 Squadron (and future Fighter Command chief in the Second World War) had been papered over; but Trenchard could not forgive Dowding's priorities. The unit had suffered appalling decimation at the hands of the enemy, but their commander's humane actions to relieve them, together with his implied challenge to the wisdom of Trenchard's offensive strategy, were too much for the RFC Commander. Brancker received a letter from Trenchard on 19 August that showed not only his intransigence, but also the strain that did much to create it. A note of exhausted defiance was given its own subheading: '3. I have been a year now in command and I have not been ungummed during that time, but I do not expect to last another year.' He went on to demand: '6. I want to know that if I decide to tell Dowding that he is too much of a 'dismal Jimmy' for active service conditions and does not give me that amount of assistance I expect from a Wing Commander, whether you are prepared to take him home and send me another commander.'[31] Dowding was removed from operations in France and Trenchard's subsequent reputation suffered from his inability to express the complicated and stress-ridden motivation behind his tactless behaviour.

The motivation for the behaviour of the aircrews on active service with the RFC was similarly complex. War subverted the old-fashioned chivalry bred in the classrooms of the nation's public schools. The individuals on the front lines on the ground, and in the air, whose job it was to kill Germans, also shared their daily hardships: Albert Ball's victory scores suggested a complete lack of ambivalence towards his foes, but in private, his letters home identified mixed feelings which could have been construed as dismal Jimm-ery in the most alarming quarters. Two days before his death, Ball wrote to his father: 'Oh! I do get tired of always living to kill, and am really beginning to feel like a murderer. Shall be so pleased when I have finished.'[32]

*

At Savy, the members of Nos.11 and 13 Squadrons gathered together on the evening of 20 August for another concert party. Air Mechanics Carpenter and Rigby duetted on *The Moon Hath Raised Her Lamp*, a hit of the (eighteen) sixties originating from an opera *The Lily of Killarney*, long forgotten by all but a few James Joyce scholars combing *Ulysses* for musical notes. Sergeant Mechanic Cullen – clearly something of a star instrumentalist – flaunted his mandolin again with a selection of melodies, and *Killarney* by Air Mechanic Taylor kept the wistful Celts gazing mournfully into their glasses. Two unknown 'Cinematographs' punctuated the proceedings and the evening was rounded off with a coyly titled, but no doubt lively, *Quartette* from Carpenter, Rigby, Foster and Magson.[33] Morris's Antipodean colleague Lyle Buntine wrote of one of these musical evenings:

> It is just after 10.00 pm and a glorious evening. A real Australian night. There is not a breath of wind. The air is quite warm and all is still except for the distant rumble of guns and the sound of the dynamo supplying light for the work-shops. I have just come from a concert which we got up. There was quite a lot of very good talent there too. After the concert I went for a stroll and watched the continual flicker of the star shells all along the line turning night into day. It is a wonderful sight like a gigantic fire-work display.[34]

The following day Morris and Rees were detailed for a reconnaissance patrol, west to the enemy-occupied Valenciennes on the border of Belgium, and then circling southwards via the railway town of Solesmes, towards Cambrai. As they flew in decreasing circles around the area, Rees's attention was drawn to grounded kite balloons near the village of Hamblain-les-Pres and a few solitary trains running. Closer inspection of Valenciennes and Cambrai centres revealed something more interesting: two aerodromes, neither with any aircraft visible. The Cambrai aerodrome, 'a landing T and a white circle near PETIT FONTAINE [sic]' in Rees's words, was Proville, near the Saint Quentin canal.[35] Already very familiar with the territory east of the lines around Cambrai, Morris and Rees flew over an area swarming with renewed German aviation effort.

The signs that a shift in the aerial war was coming were increasing. On the following day, Morris and Rees fired an opening salvo for the RFC in a day of tremendous dogfights involving dozens of aircraft. Albert Ball would miss dinner and a concert party at a neighbouring unit and Captain Foot, deputising for Major Hubbard, (who was on leave), faced a flood of paperwork in the Commanding Officer's absence.[36] No less than ten combat reports for No. 11 arrived in the squadron office before sunset on 22 August.

*Chapter 15*

# Follow the Leader

On the evening of 22 August 1916, strong solar disturbances were picked up by the astronomers of Kew Observatory in London and dramatic auroral displays were seen all over Europe.[1] One hundred and fifty miles away from London on the Western Front, the men of No. 11 Squadron had seen enough tumult in the skies for one day.

Morris and Rees had taken off for an offensive patrol at 5.00 pm, in advance of two bombing raids leaving Savy not long after them.[2] As they flew south the ground beneath them cracked into trench lines; landmarks were few, but the incongruous chalky mound of the Butte de Warlencourt stuck out, an ants' nest of German resistance. It was only 250 foot high but it may as well have been a mountain to the British troops in 1916, built on top of an ancient burial ground riddled with dugouts and laced with barbed wire.[3] Morris and Rees's role, along with the other patrol aircraft was to divert as many enemy planes from the area as possible whilst the bombers did their work either side of the Butte at Irles and Thilloy. In the patrol formation with Morris and Rees were Captain Gray and his observer Lieutenant Leonard Helder, plus Captain Stephen Price and Fred Libby, the expert drinkers of No. 11. Ball was nearby in his Nieuport scout, on hand in case of trouble.[4]

As they headed on towards the battered city of Bapaume, a group of fifteen to twenty hostile aircraft appeared below: LVG reconnaissance/artillery machines accompanied by faster Roland scouts. The crews of No. 11 dispersed, then each chose a target. The strange dance of dogfighting, this time on a bigger scale than anything the British squadron had previously experienced, began. Aircraft sprang and surged in all directions like dragonflies. Gray and Helder took on their nearest five enemy planes but were thwarted when their gun jammed. Price and Libby closed to within 250 feet of another that appeared to nosedive away out of control after receiving half a drum of bullets from the FE2b. Wheeling to face another of the enemy, Libby let loose a further drum and a half and a German plane fell away, apparently out of control.[5] Morris and Rees's part in the mêlée was equally dramatic:

> A number of hostile machines were observed at about 7,000 ft. The nearest was engaged at 300 yards, it was apparently hit and spiralled to earth under control. Another formation of about 4 hostile machines were observed South of Bapaume. Nearest was engaged and fire first opened at 200 yards. It was apparently hit and was observed to side slip then nose dive to earth out of control. This machine was seen on the ground later in wrecked condition at M.36 B approx. sheet 57c. Another 4 hostile machines were engaged in turn, one of which dived to earth apparently under control. Hostile machine fired white puffs of smoke apparently to show their identity to Anti Aircraft.[6]

Hubbard's men battled their way east of Bapaume, and Price and Libby again seized the initiative: 'A ROLAND scout was engaged ½ a drum being fired. It was seen to go down out of control smoking profusely. Seven other hostile machines were engaged but the actions were indecisive.'[7]

Despite the efforts of their patrol colleagues, the bombers en-route to Irles and Thilloy also met trouble at around 7.00 pm. For the observing German defenders of the Butte de Warlencourt, it was an evening of great spectacle; dozens of aircraft pivoting in all directions over their heads, the sound of machine gun fire punctuated by the stutter and acceleration of engines as aeroplanes on both sides circled, charged and dived. How No. 11 had responded to perhaps their most powerful challenge yet was reported unambiguously in the RFC Communique, and the map co-ordinates for the plane that had been seen on the ground appear to have validated Rees and Morris's victory claim in the eyes of Thirteenth Wing:

> On the front of the Third Brigade, an offensive patrol of 11 Squadron encountered a formation of about fifteen German machines, chiefly Rolands and LVGSs. These were engaged by our FEs, assisted by one Nieuport Scout. The engagement became of a general nature, all of our machines being engaged. Second Lieutenant Morris, pilot, and Lieutenant Rees, observer, singled out one machine which was seen to side-slip and plunge to earth out of control, and was seen on the ground in wrecked condition. Three others were driven down by the combined attacks of our machines and appeared to be completely out of control, although lost to view before hitting the ground. Of these, one, a Roland Scout, was seen emitting clouds of smoke, as though on fire. This latter machine had been engaged by Captain Price, pilot, and Lieutenant Libby, observer. Three other machines were seen to land under control and the whole hostile formation was completely broken up.[8]

The ringleader of No. 11's hit squad later wrote with brevity to his parents of the events that evening:

> Met 12 Huns. No. 1 fight. I attacked and fired two drums, bringing the machine down just outside a village. All crashed up. No. 2 fight. I attacked and got under machine, putting in two drums. Hun went down in flames. No. 3 fight. I attacked and put in one drum. Machine went down and crashed on a housetop. All these fights were seen and reported by other machines that saw them go down. I only got hit 11 times in the planes.

Ball's choice of the adverb 'only' was typical:

> I returned and got more ammunition. This time luck was not all on the spot. I was met by about 14 Huns, about 15 miles

over their side. My windscreen was hit in four places, mirror broken, the spar of the left plane broken, also engine ran out of petrol. But I had good sport and good luck, but only just, for I was brought down about one mile over our side.[9]

Landing near the village of Senlis-le-Sec was another stroke of luck as he didn't have to go far to get a message sent back to Savy. The ground crews of No. 11 had a southwards journey of around thirty miles to reach Ball and his broken aeroplane. They worked through the night to repair it as the pilot slept 'near the machine'; either too exhausted, or enervated by the need to get back into the Nieuport, to seek a more comfortable bed.[10] B Flight NCO, Sergeant Crisford, recalled the squadron's reaction when Ball finally returned to Savy at 8.30 the following morning: 'Everyone was keen to inspect the machine, and when eyes were directed towards the windscreen it helped explain the nature of the scrap.'[11]

Third Brigade's War Diary reported thirty-three combats for 22 August; four German planes seen to crash, three more stated to have been sent down out of control and less specifically, 'numerous other machines' which were 'driven down under control and compelled to abandon their formations'.[12] Just three of No. 11's men were named in the Brigade's intelligence report after this day of intense fighting – Ball, with his remarkable hat-trick of success, and Morris and Rees, their claim validated by the map co-ordinates for the downed plane that Rees had been so careful to note. But just as with the 1 July episode, eyewitness evidence from excited crews is difficult to confirm in a dispassionate – albeit still incomplete – historical appraisal. There were five recorded German air service casualties that day, but matching their final locations on the ground to a combat in the air remains an inexact science when dogfights drifted over wide geographical areas. What happened to the airmen Rees and Libby saw falling to earth that day remains unknown but Morris and Rees were credited with their first victory, which was included in Third Brigade's War Diary and the RFC Communique.[13]

For all the morale-raising curtain of victory scores, the men of No. 11 Squadron had little more than survival on their minds in those moments and their immediate concerns in the heat of combat were to do with endurance, not competition. The French had started applying the word 'l'as' to fighter pilots like Adolphe Pegoud; in translation the term 'ace' began to lend a sporting glamour to the air services of the Great War that has been seductive ever since. Those dogged enough to establish the hard facts (and to state just how much difference the debatable victory lists made to the outcome of the war) risk denting national pride and shattering imaginative illusions. Iconoclasm is just as irresistible but honest reappraisals of the aggregate nature of what the RFC was trying to achieve show that their war was resolutely unglamorous. It was all about killing the enemy aircrews and smashing up their assets.

The raiders of No. 11 had certainly done their work. Nearly thirty bombs were dropped on what appeared to be a battery (or a dump, according the Intelligence report) as well as huts nearby. A second party hit the village of Thilloy, reporting 'several explosions' after releasing nine bombs.[14] The gumption of the British crews, breaking up a formation of around twenty German machines, was rewarded by the sight of most of the enemy heading for home, two shot down and one reeling away out of control.[15] The Communique claimed a total triumph for this impressive performance: 'the enemy force was routed, and the description of aircraft landing in all directions suggests a state of near panic.'[16]

In the midst of the celebrations following No. 11's success that evening, there was an edge of regret. Ball's performances in the squadron whilst Morris had been with them had turned him from a talented journeyman into an extraordinarily focused fighter pilot whose fame within the Corps was growing. The RFC now needed him in a new unit where he could be even more effective. With the final flourish the following day of an acrobatics display alongside Captain Foot for the benefit of his No. 11 colleagues, Ball was gone; albeit only across the fields to Le Hameau.[17] His departure confirmed the rumours that No. 60 Squadron was collecting the finest scout pilots, including the one who during that summer had begun, as the unit's historian, Captain A.J.L. Scott, wrote: 'to show the Flying Corps what fighting in the air really meant.'[18] Beyond the portentous history, little questions tease: what happened to Ball's garden? And was Morris one of those astonished colleagues crowding around the windscreen of the Nieuport on the morning of 23 August 1916, looking for the holes left by bullets so urgently searching for the pilot's head?

\*

For the minions at RFC HQ on the receiving end of the most deafening of his booms, the indefatigable nature of the General Officer Commanding was less easy to admire than Ball's gallantry, but Trenchard's obduracy also said much about how he got through such a terrible war. His grim determination to sort out intractable details was often at the expense of his loyal but long-suffering staff, as Maurice Baring reflected generously: 'He would find out if Squadron B had received its split pin, or what Mr A. from England has answered when asked for it. This did not conduce to our repose, but it did further the efficiency of the RFC.'[19] Baring had an endearing ability to take the sting out of the worst of Trenchard's bellicose behaviour, devising various 'Field Punishments' for the General when he felt he had gone too far. Quaking pilots who had been on the sharp end of a blast of discipline from the GOC were given a conspiratorial smile and wink from Baring, who imposed minor irritants, such as hiding Trenchard's pipe, or developing inappropriately timed fascinations for birds.[20] The General's brain, whirring as it was with endless detail and initiative, rarely worked in effective concert with his powers of articulate speech, and it was Baring's skills of diplomacy and comprehension, not to mention empathy, that made them a dauntless (and daunting) team. Trenchard acknowledged Baring's patience and intelligence, describing his junior as his mentor and guide, an extraordinary compliment from a man to whom humility did not come naturally. Optimism, in contrast, was an importunate character trait that was vital to any First World War commander. Its value, as applied to the overall Somme campaign, and in relation to realistic outcomes of trench warfare, has been questioned, but Trenchard, as a late Victorian, knew its importance to a service so prone to everyday disaster. It was a mask that rarely slipped: the death in 1917 of Major Hubert Harvey-Kelly, the first RFC man to land in France in 1914, showed a side of the GOC that was almost always kept stringently under control, as Archibald James, observed: '[It was] one of the very few occasions when I ever saw Boom relax into gloom and sorrow. Normally he was incredibly level all the time.'[21]

Trenchard's demands on his airmen reflected his own high standards. No. 11's workload continued to increase as the entire RFC strained with the pressure of battle. On 25 August Price and Libby, on escort duty for a repeat bombing raid on the Warlencourt/Irles Valley, claimed a German Aviatik near Bapaume.[22] Another of the day's twenty-one combats had Tom Rees's name on the report, flying as observer to Captain Gray. Their diving attack on one of three hostile machines which Rees said 'was seen going down at great speed', doesn't appear on any victory list. There was no let up for the bombers of Third Brigade and their No. 11 escorts. The Bois de Loupart was their destination on the morning of 27 August, and the village of Grevillers, on the slopes of a well-defended hill, doomed to be tugged bloodily between the opposing armies for much of the war, took the force of eleven 112 pound bombs in the afternoon: 'Several pilots reported that practically the whole centre of the village had collapsed in a state of ruin'.[23] A repeat visit was paid the following day to both targets.[24]

On 29 August, as the engine of another battle-scarred No. 11 machine (belonging to Second Lieutenant Turk and Lieutenant Scott, who had forced down a Roland the previous day) was taken to Candas for repairs,[25] there was a shake up at the head of the German Army. It was to have profound consequences for the RFC. Changes in the enemy's air service followed, quickly reaping successful rewards. German Chief of Staff General Falkenhayn was replaced by General Paul von Hindenburg. A crucial appointment in the new pecking order was his deputy, Eric Ludendorff, whose belief in the aeroplane as a war-winning tool changed the way the Germans fought in the air; taking them away from the torpidly defensive approach that had been exploited so ruthlessly by the RFC. Efforts were now swung decisively away from Verdun and focused on the battlefields of northern France.[26]

Faster and more versatile aircraft were almost ready to be deployed –
the Albatros D series with not one but two synchronised machine guns.
Three were spotted by DH2s of No. 24 Squadron on 31 August and
proved within half an hour to the British pilots that an alarmingly
efficient new answer to the Nieuport Scouts and DH2s had arrived.[27]
At Bertincourt aerodrome, around twenty miles from Cambrai, the
most gifted tactician of the German air service and its leading ace,
twenty-five-year-old Oswald Boelcke, was assembling a group of handpicked airmen to fly the new machines. Amongst them, arriving on
1 September, was a Polish-born Prussian cavalry officer turned pilot:
Manfred von Richthofen.[28]

*

On the same day, No. 11 were on the move. It was not a tiring journey
and within hours they found themselves at the other end of the same
very large field from which Ball and No. 60 were flying.[29] With the
single-seater scout planes now gone, No. 11 was operating solely on
FE2bs, and had reached its full establishment of eighteen aircraft.[30]
The huge expanse of flat grass between the hamlet of Le Hameau
in the west, and Filescamp Farm (used by No. 60) in the east, was
perfect for landing grounds, and livestock were kept tied up to avoid
collisions.[31] No. 11 were nearer the village of Izel-lès-Hameau, with
its pretty white-washed cottages. The scouts of No. 60 Squadron
occupied the side of the 'half farm, half château' with its orchard,
recalled lovingly by Arthur Gould Lee as 'that paradise of a wartime
billet.'[32] The farm was big enough to accommodate both squadrons:
FE2bs, DH2s and Nieuports arrived and departed from different ends
of the field.[33]

   The nearby village inspired a few cheeky lines of a Tommy
marching song:

> We don't want a girl from Izel-lez-Hameau,
> From Izel-lez-Hameau,
> From Izel-lez-Hameau,

> She may be all right, but we don't care a dammo,
> So we don't want a girl from Izel-lez-Hameau.[34]

The men of No. 11, well-used to appearing to not give a dammo, were also tested by the mobility of their living arrangements. The Australian Buntine, who had changed his billet no less than three times (moving from farmhouse to tent, on to a boys' schools and then back to a tent in woods, and finally back to a farmhouse again) since arriving with No. 11 in early July, was distracted from the upheaval by the background din of war: 'The guns are making a big noise this morning. It sounds louder because the wind is that way. At present we are in rather a muddle and working hard to get things straightened out. It is no joke for a whole squadron to move.'[35]

The extra hassle of moving aerodromes had to be done on top of unremittingly exhausting patrol duties as Buntine explained:

> I have been absolutely as full as I can stick of work and when the evening comes we are usually too tired to write letters. I got up at 3 o'clock this morning and have been on the go ever since. We do this about every second day and the other days we get up late, i.e. at 6 o'clock. It's usually past eleven before we can get to bed so you can understand that I'll be ready for leave when I get it.[36]

As the men settled in to their new base, they had no knowledge that the zenith of the RFC's achievement on the Somme was already behind them. Seven new German fighting squadrons (*Jagdstaffeln* Nos. 1–7) had been formed in the month of August to counter the success that the FE2bs, Nieuports and Sopwiths had enjoyed.[37] But as far as the aircrew of No. 11 Squadron could see, the general way of the war, with Romania entering the conflict on the Allied side, and the British and French armies about to cooperate in another effort to straighten the lines and force the enemy back, seemed to be steadily improving. Despite losses sustained, the squadron's successes gave no suggestion of catastrophe ahead for No. 11.

*Chapter 16*

# Broken Birds

By the beginning of September 1916, Morris had been on active service in France for over four months. He may have qualified for home leave after three of those: perhaps another explanation for his characteristic absence from squadron records for the first two weeks of August. To be still alive and in one piece, despite the quickening odds as the air war on the Western Front intensified, was remarkable. The RFC as a whole appeared to be surprisingly resilient. Like a fighter who gets knocked down, and just keeps getting up again, the stamina of the Corps to withstand the damage that was evidently being done was miraculous.

Running through Trenchard's correspondence of that period was an urgent insistence on perseverance over panic. He emphasised the reasons for optimism such as the comparative absence of German aircraft crossing the lines into Allied territory. The potential of the enemy to return to levels of aerial domination that created the 'Fokker fodder' in 1915 and early 1916 was never far from his thoughts, and whilst inadequate aircraft supply remained damaging to the RFC, it was again the aircrew that were most sorely needed. Trenchard continued to press Brancker for more pilots than the Deputy Director of Military Aeronautics could provide:

> I have nothing more urgent than pilots. I know I have been very heavy on you for pilots just lately, but I cannot help it as just at present I want to get all the pilots I can. I wish my demands would go down but at present they can't. The Bosche seldom comes over our side of the lines still, and that is the main thing.[1]

His recognition of the difficulty this presented was obvious but nothing would distract him from the end result he believed was achievable: the same 'wearing down' of the enemy that Haig was committed to.

A lurch in RFC casualties for the Battle of the Somme did nothing to change this determination. In July 1916 the numbers jumped from the previous month's 34 to 134.[2] This fits into the legend of the futility and waste of the campaign, but provides no measurement of the morale-sapping effect on the enemy of the RFC's dominance of the skies for most of the summer. British pilots were dying in their hundreds, but in keeping the Germans behind the lines, there was little opportunity for the enemy to gather intelligence.

Statistics have an addictive quality that can lead to compassion fatigue. For the men facing death on a daily basis the pitiless burden of stress was greater than any of the physical demands of war. Even the greatest of aces struggled – pilots courageous enough to shoot down enemy aircraft weren't automatically able to cope with the consequences of what they had to do. The peculiar nature of air combat created its own 'flying sickness', the slow-burning effect of pernicious stress that by stages destroyed the crew's mental and physical health until either it was too late, and they were killed, along with others, or if they were lucky, an experienced commanding officer would notice: 'The airmen seem to go more slowly. In the infantry type, a man breaks down through an explosion and develops the thing suddenly, but in the Flying Corps they get more and more nervous until somebody sends them on leave or they crash.'[3] Although an experienced commanding officer could spot the signs of combat fatigue, no such thing had been recognised officially. Neither had there been clinical recognition of the particular environmental burdens that were placed on airmen: general good health, good eyesight and hearing, and an affinity with horses were presumed to be adequate qualifications.[4] The effects of altitude were not a secret amongst the airmen: severe headaches due to the lack of oxygen and sudden descents causing bleeding ears, nausea and light-headness followed by severe pain as blood pressure returned to normal. In March 1916, the physical demands of flying were acknowledged: however, a discreet moral judgement still lurked in assessments that the French were making, as reported in *Flight*: 'They recognise that a great deal depends on the physical condition of the man sent up. If he is the wrong type the strain imposed on him by altitude alone may well defeat his utility. If he is the right type his value must needs be very much greater.'[5]

But the psychological strain on airmen was becoming impossible to ignore, with increasing numbers succumbing to nervous conditions. A recent study of the RFC's Medical Board record cards by Dr. Lindsay Shaw Cobden found two-thirds were suffering from either 'neurasthenia' or 'nervous debility', both enigmatic terms which covered a wide spectrum of psychological horrors.[6]

A fortunate few benefitted from far-sighted therapeutic help of the type made famous at Craiglockhart Hospital in Edinburgh, where Siegfried Sassoon and Wilfred Owen were treated; for the remainder, a rest was prescribed, with varying results. It was not until after the war that Air Vice Marshal John Salmond was able to admit publicly that 'all war pilots would inevitably break down', although this was then qualified with: 'if not relieved.'[7] Signs of nerves weren't difficult to spot: extreme irritability without warning, stomach problems, shaking hands, restlessness and recklessness in the air and on the ground. In that most euphemistic of modern terms, they self-medicated, covering anxiety and trauma with displays of high spirits. The classic symptom was nightmares; in one case a terror of anti-aircraft fire was translated into surreal hallucinations by a pilot who had been shot down:

> It was a condition which started in a dream, waking him up, and then continued after he had waked. He had a curious idea of white birds of peculiar, ill-defined form that were first in the extreme distance and then gradually came closer and closer to him. This woke him up screaming and then spoilt his sleep.'[8]

Naturally awkward personalities could become insufferable under the strain of war. One armament officer with No. 60 Squadron had a particularly toxic effect on the men working for him:

> He seems to be incapable of managing the NCOs and men under him. I have already had to reduce a quite excellent sergeant, who was previously a first-class workman and extremely keen, but was found by Mr W to be inefficient and insubordinate. The Offence Reports from No. 60 Squadron are largely concerned with disputes between this officer and the NCOs. Possibly the strain of active service re-acts on this officer's nerves, that he bothers the men until such matters are brought to such a pass, that a serious charge has to be brought against them.[9]

In 1917 an officer of No. 11 was admitted to hospital in a distraught state, afraid he was about to cut his own throat. As a veteran of three years in the infantry, the neurosis was put down purely to his previous service in the trenches, and a rest cure was prescribed.[10]

Away from the war, a thin veneer of control could crack amongst family and friends. Some of the most famous fighters demonstrated clearly when their capital was spent by dying in accidents unaccountable for fliers of such skill and experience. The seemingly unbreakable Edward 'Mick' Mannock, the highest scoring British ace of the war, was revered for his pluck and patience, but the depth of his anxiety and fear was revealed in terrible bouts of weeping whilst on leave. Repression was the most acceptable remedy in the Flying Corps – together with an application of black humour: Mannock's favoured description of sending an enemy down in flames was 'Sizzle, sizzle, wonk!'[11] He himself was burnt to death: his plane hit by ground fire and bursting into flames whilst flying dangerously low *after* shooting down a German LVG. It was a basic error of judgement that appalled his colleagues and a death that fitted his own macabre mantra.

As one of Whitgift's suffering conquerors (*Vincit qui patitur*), Morris, like many others so proudly bred at the nation's public schools, was one of those most at risk. According to Sassoon and Owen's doctor at Craiglockhart, they were habituated to stoicism and fearful of showing open emotion.[12] The succinct tone of Morris's diary demonstrates this ingrained self constraint. When in 1922 the War Office published the findings of a Committee of Enquiry into Shell Shock, the Flying Corps was singled out for their success in dealing with the problem more quickly than the Army. Their competency was attributed to the smaller size of the service, with relatively fewer men engaged in combat, and communication between commanding officers and medical officers more easily facilitated. But the report also recognised that there were never enough medical officers for a service with such a chronically high turnover.[13] Humanity had to be balanced with the glorification of suffering, in order that men, naturally eager to give of their best, should continue to do so. The official war correspondent Philip Gibbs wrote of the results:

> Some young flying men complained to me, bitterly, that they were expected to fly or die over the German lines, whatever the weather, or whatever the risks. Many of them, after repeated escapes from anti-aircraft shells and hostile craft, lost their nerve, shirked another journey, found themselves crying in their tents, and were sent back home for a spell, by squadron commanders, with quick observation for the breaking point; or made a few more flights, and fell to earth like broken birds.[14]

Between his arrival with No. 11 on 19 May and the day before he died, Morris had seen nine squadron members disappear from the mess; seven of whom were dead. Another three had been wounded in action and one (Captain Cooper) killed in an accident. September 1916 was to be a deadly month for No. 11. For the full four months from 1 May to 31 August, ten men had been killed or gone missing. For the month of September *alone* the squadron lost seventeen men.[15] Their sister unit, No. 23, had been moved south west to Fienvillers, replaced by No. 60 Squadron, returning from the rest break that Trenchard had fallen out with Dowding about. Despite the concentration of some of the best scout pilots in the RFC, there was little No. 60 could do to stop the blow that No. 11 was about to suffer.

*

The objective of Bapaume, at the apex of chalk-scored roads leading to Arras, Cambrai, Péronne and Albert, lay like a mirage for the Allies in 1916; huddled safely well behind German lines and as distant as the Eastern Front for the infantrymen inching backwards and forwards on the Somme. For the RFC, flying over many shell-savaged towns, the nearness of Bapaume was a taunt that the Corps could answer indirectly. Despite its impregnable nature, the town's roads and railways were threads that were vulnerable in the face of a few well-aimed bombs. And if the bombs didn't hit the targets, the element of cage-rattling was a useful distraction that the Third Army squadrons had come to specialise in.

Like Arras, Bapaume had been marked by conflict for centuries, and was to change hands more than once before the end of the war. In 1916 it was the strategic objective of the next stage of the Somme offensive, the Battle of Flers-Courcelette. Every RFC airman in the northern sector of the Western Front was familiar with the simple web of highways that led from the town. The Fourth Army would try to push forward to the south east of Bapaume, occupying a string of villages (Gueudecourt, Lesboeufs and Morval) on high ground overlooking the road to Péronne. As the days shortened in September 1916, the bombing campaign intensified. Joseph Hellingoe, of No. 11, described the very basic technique he employed to drop bombs from an FE2b: 'You just pull the cord out and drop them over the side. Hung them on the gun rail and dropped these six bombs. Pip! From a couple of thousand feet.'[16]

On 2 September, another three of the No. 11's officers were lost over Bapaume. Guthrie Anderson and his observer Second Lieutenant Allen met a Roland on a late afternoon offensive patrol. Their gun jammed and the engine of their FE2b was hit; Allen was shot dead and Anderson's right arm wounded. Crossing over the lines, Anderson brought the aeroplane down with no further injury to himself but the aircraft was written off: 'presumed total wreck'. Again the components of the machinge were heroically retrieved despite its precarious landing so near to the danger of further enemy attention.[17] Later that evening Second Lieutenants Eric Burton and Frederick Griffiths were outgunned by seven hostile machines. Seeing the FE2b going down, two of their fellow No. 11 crews went to their aid: Captain John Quested and his observer Lieutenant William Wyatt attacked a pursuing Roland with a burst of tracer fire, sending the German aeroplane diving swiftly away. Second Lieutenants Henry Turk and George Welsford engaged a further two. Quested and Wyatt then found themselves with enemy aircraft on three sides; Wyatt instantly turned his gun on one of them at a bracing twenty yards range, sending it over into a full cartwheel on its right wing tip and off earthwards, apparently out of control. They used up one more drum; half at the falling plane for good measure, and half emptied into one of the other hostile aircraft. When their engine began to choke, they made for the lines, chased by a still-firing Roland. Both crews who had gone to Burton and Griffiths's aid arrived safely back at Le Hameau.[18] A casualty report was filed for Burton and Griffiths: it was, as was the custom, short: 'The machine left the aerodrome at 6.15 pm on 2 September. No further information has been received since concerning it.'[19] A French pilot was later to report their safe landing, but it was on the wrong side of the lines.[20]

It was obvious to the men of No. 11 that the flashes of organised aggression from the German Air Service were becoming more and more frequent. A corresponding increase in the numbers of combat reports Hubbard had to read confirmed the growing threat. Third Brigade were in action on 3 September dropping bombs on railheads; the following day they were blessed with forty-eight hours of rain and a much-needed rest before being sent out again in force on 5 September to escort bombers targeting Achiet-le-Grand.[21]

On 7 September mechanics arrived in Arras to rescue Sergeant Thompson and Flight Sergeant Drudge from an unusual location. Whilst on photographic duties, the engine of their FE had shuddered dangerously close to the nacelle, and they were forced to land on the racecourse, escaping serious injury.[22] Returning to Achiet-le-Grand on 8 September, three of the FE2b crews including Captain Foot were still able to intimidate a group of German aircraft away from the main show as a dump near a railway was bombed. Foot and his observer Second Lieutenant Welsford claimed two victories the following day when Irles was once again the target, and Second Lieutenant Thomas Molloy and Sergeant Allan drove off an LVG that appeared to go out of control.[23]

Buntine, flying on the same day with his observer Sergeant Godfrey Morton, was attacked by three German aircraft. A burst of euphoria at seeing one of them head nose-first for the ground, was short-lived when, despite reaching the relative safety of the formation, their FE2b was attacked from behind. Buntine wrote from hospital to his family in Australia:

> I did quite a lot of dodging for a while, at the same time climbing and making for the lines. Soon the shells suddenly stopped. Then there came a whistle of bullets from behind and I felt as if somebody had hit my arm with a hammer and it fell to my side useless. I grabbed the joystick with my left hand and swung around to see what was there. I saw two German aeroplanes diving at me, firing as they came. We went for one and drove him off. Then we went for the other; but before he went he fired several shots at us which cut all the control wires. The engine was also hit and stopped.[24]

What Buntine hadn't mentioned, was how he saved Morton's life with a frantic wrench as he pulled the FE2b violently away from the gunfire. He continued not to mention it for the rest of his life but his presence of mind was recorded in a recommendation for the Military Cross awarded to him in October 1916.[25] 'The machine dived so suddenly that the observer nearly fell out, but the pilot lent forward and pulled him back.'[26] In the combat the FE2b's engine had stopped, half of the propellor had been lost, and Buntine was shot in the arm. He still managed to cross the lines and bring the plane to land before further disaster: 'Then I sent a man for a doctor and lay down on the ground as my arm was pretty painful and I was feeling faint.'[27] Buntine was visited in hospital at Le Havre by Hubbard and three of his No. 11 comrades, bearing the squadron's good wishes and pride at his 'gorgeous scrap'.[28] The wound was a Blighty, troublesome enough for him to be sent all the way back to Australia. Morton, unhurt despite the challenging descent he had suffered, was awarded the Military Medal.[29]

A new aeroplane arrived at Le Hameau on 9 September to replace Buntine and Morton's beaten-up machine.[30] FE2b 7018 *Punjab 32 Montgomery* had been paid for from a fund raised in the district of Montgomery, in what was (until Partition) the Indian state of Punjab. It was allotted to Morris and destined for an active service life of just over one week.

*Chapter 17*

# Bombs Over Bapaume

On 11 September 1916, five FE2b night bombers of No. 12 Squadron got lost in the darkened clouds on their way to Achiet-le-Grand.[1] Their targets were no surprise for the Germans, but the increased nocturnal scheduling of the raids was significant for another, more clandestine reason, as Lieutenant Robin Rowell of No.12 Squadron observed:

> Why are all the FE2bs learning to night-fly so suddenly? Nobody knows. But within a week or so all the FE2b squadrons were night flying, and then they started to drop an occasional 20lb bomb on some wretched village just over the lines. Why are the FEs flying tonight? They don't even know themselves, except that they were told to go and fly up and down the lines from Arras to Albert; and when one machine came back another went out to drop a bomb that could do no-one any harm.[2]

A new weapon was under wraps. For the first time in the history of warfare, the tank was going into action. The RFC were buzzing up and down the lines at night to drown out the noise of the tanks being driven to their jumping off points for the third stage of the Somme campaign. The Flers-Courcelette offensive, to begin on 15 September, was planned to create a breakthrough in the enemy's third line of defence.[3] The cavalry would then stream through to high ground beyond. The use of the word 'breakthrough' (always having some wishful thought behind it in 1916) was still a misnomer in the face of a slow war of attrition, and German kite balloons had already spotted an unusual new kind of armoured vehicle behind Allied lines.

But hopes were high, and Trenchard wrote to Brancker on 9 September, telling him confidently that the RFC's night bombing was becoming more successful.[4] A much-needed surge of momentum was created by the French Sixth Army on 12 September; an opportunity for the British to push ahead three days later.[5] But bad weather on the next two days kept the RFC on the ground, and the lack of reconnaissance held up progress: the hiatus between the French and British Army's attacks created a breathing space for the Germans and allowed them to bring in their own reinforcements for a battle already very clearly signposted to them. The preceding bombardment was better concentrated and effective, but it left the already pulverised ground in an impossibly mired state. One hundred yard-wide strips of land were spared the assault of artillery to assist the tanks in getting ahead, but in many places the shell holes were full of water, creating often insurmountable obstacles for the large but untried machines.[6]

The crews of No. 11 returned yet again to the arteries of the German Army around Bapaume on 14 September. At 9.30 am Morris and Rees were in a reconnaissance formation over the town led by Captain Gray, and including Price and Libby. Gray's observer Lieutenant Helder reported attacking three German LVGs which then dived away.[7] Rees's account told of how he and Morris had broken away to attack eight hostile machines:

> We dived towards them and first opened fire at about 500 yards. Engaged four who manoeuvred round us, one was heavily engaged and after about half a drum of Tracer had been fired at it, it turned away leaving a trail of smoke. The other three machines withdrew, and we came on to rejoin the formation.[8]

Fred Libby's version was bullish and oblique:

> Seven machines seen, two on the ground, five in the air, three Aviatiks, two LVGs. Three engaged – two and a half drum tracer ammunition used. One hostile machine brought

down in smoke, other two driven down. Tracer ammunition could easily be seen going into hostile machine.[9]

The last line of Rees's report confirmed Libby's confident assertion of victory: 'The machine engaged by Captain Price was also seen to go down smoking.'[10]

In the end the RFC Communique listed both crews as having driven down one enemy plane each; victory or not, they had undoubtedly seen them off, at least for one day.[11] Three of No. 11's other FE2bs, this time escorting a bombing raid, also drove away German machines threatening BE2cs raiding a railway dump.[12] The clouds closed in later on in the afternoon, preventing effective reconnaissance, but Lieutenant John Quested and Sergeant Morton had the satisfaction of reporting a large fire in the vicinity of Achiet-le-Grand.[13] No losses were suffered by the squadron despite the intensity of the fighting; a lucky and unsustainable result.

*

No one was left in any doubt as to the desperate effort now needed. Early in the morning of 15 September, a car passed Le Hameau on its way to No.60 Squadron's officers' mess at the other end of the field, where a familiar tall man got out. Trenchard's physical presence at the aerodromes again created a powerful focus. For those given responsibility for the supremely dangerous job of destroying German kite balloons, his arrival and famously frank admission 'it's far more important to get that balloon than to fail and come back'[14] had a sombre and tangible effect on the men, as Lieutenant Alan Bott of No.70 Squadron (who had also received a visit from Trenchard) described: 'It was as if the electricity had been withdrawn from the atmosphere and condensed for use when required.'[15] By 6.20 am the third and final phase of the Battle of the Somme had begun, and the men of nine divisions went over the top.[16]

The RFC were given the historic privilege of watching the first tanks in action. There were some stunning successes: by midday the north and west of the village of Flers had been taken by Fifteenth Corps; the observers of No.3 Squadron spotting a flock of soldiers with an accompanying tank marching down the main street of the village.[17] This picturesque snapshot in the history of tank warfare was embroidered by British newspapers, but in many cases the vehicles got stuck in the mud, leaving them an irresistible target for enemy artillery. The villages of Flers, Courcelette and Martinpuich *had* all been taken, what was left of High Wood surrendered, and the German Army had been further weakened. But with no definitive breakthrough, the losses of over 20,000 were as dreadful as 1 July. As the casualty telegrams began to find their way back to Britain, triumphant headlines suggesting that the worst was over looked increasingly facile. Rarely had so little been achieved at the cost of so many lives, (around 8,000 of both German and Allies has been estimated) but the final surrender after such slaughter drew an essential line under an episode that haunted the Allies long after the trees had grown back on the ridge of High Wood.

The fighter squadrons had endured a day of brutal struggle on 15 September, the RFC holding back at great cost a bigger challenge than they had ever dealt with before. The fatigued British crews' immediate need to deal with the present threat in front of them was joined by a sense of anxiety about how they could continue to wrestle an enemy in such numbers. A bewildering array of surviving combat reports attest to a sense of the continuing pressure on the pilots and observers of No. 11. Accuracy of reconnaissance was crucial to the planning of the day's bombing attacks: Morris and Rees were in the air by 5.30 am, along with Lieutenant Frederick Sargood and Captain Field, noting the movements of German trains north-east of Arras and then south to the village of Croisilles. By 9.00 am another FE2b flight escorting the bombers of No.12 were on their way to Bapaume station but they met opposition in strength. The chaos caused by the burgeoning numbers of hostile aircraft comes across in the wildly varying estimates of their numbers from the FE2b crews having to deal with them: Foot, with Welsford, reported as many as twenty at various heights. Quested changed his report of 'several' to 'a great deal' within the same combat report, no doubt distracted when empty bullet cases thrown out of the deflector bag and 'back into the breech', caused a gun jam – his observer Corporal Monk, equally busy, was faced with another jam when he was 'unable to keep the gun in cocked position.' The crews brought down four of the attackers and then pushed doggedly back over the lines.

Lieutenant Bowman saw a German observer 'apparently killed or badly wounded' as his plane disappeared towards Bertincourt, but his own observer, Sergeant David Walker, had been hit in the stomach and was unable to protect them any further. The bombing leader of No. 12 Squadron was wounded in the arm as he flew low over Bapaume station, but the BEs were able to finish their work without serious casualty. Thirty-eight bombs had been dropped, and according to the Communiques, four German planes had been seen to crash with another two driven down.[18] It was a good tally for a morning's work but there was much more to come. Just after 11.00 am, Morris and Rees were again in the air over German aerodromes. Rees's detailed report of observations took in the village of Mouevres where all was quiet on the ground; no troop movements were seen on the roads or canals but he would have been worried by other developments of 'pronounced hostile aerial activity.' Thirty-five minutes later they reached Vélu, where Oswald Boelcke's new squadron had started life in a few administrative buildings. Rees took four photographs, and they dropped two bombs from the FE2b as a parting gift. Their cheek was not appreciated by the aerodrome's inhabitants and Rees wrote with typical RFC understatement that they had not been able to observe any explosions: 'It was impossible to locate them accurately owing to being engaged with EA [enemy aircraft].' His report confirmed their dilemma:

> Several Hostile Aircraft were seen N. of VELU flying S.E. They were followed, and made for the aerodrome at VELU. Here there were 4 other hostile machines above us. We first of all opened fire at long range and made for the aerodrome, and there dropped our bombs and took photographs of the aerodrome; then continued the fight.

There was little chance of a quick exit as more German aircraft suddenly appeared:

> The 4 HA were now re-inforced by about 6 or 7 more, and attacked all four of our machines. A machine was singled out and we flew towards it and fired about half a drum at it and it turned away and then the others were engaged in quick succession and by circling around one another our formation were able to keep all HA engaged and prevent them from getting behind anyone. During the fight 2 HA were seen to retire, and one dived in smoke, the other went down so steeply that it must have been out of control. Owing to all our ammunition, except part of one drum, being used up we were compelled to come home.[19]

Rees's account showed how the 'bristling hedgehogs' worked, and why their unorthodox formation was so necessary. Their route home took them over the epicentre of the day's events. The speed of the British progress had made aerial communication with the ground forces patchy. Rees wrote that at 12 noon: 'no infantry flares were seen but shrapnel barrage was well to the front of Flers.'[20]

The pages of Third Brigade's War Diary for 15 September tell a story of continuing ferocious effort: No. 11's late afternoon offensive patrol was met by yet another formation of uncertain numbers of enemy aircraft, some of them of a type that the British crews had not seen before and couldn't identify on their combat reports. The new machines were aggressive but failed to intimidate: two were seen by Lieutenant George Clayton to veer away, apparently out of control. Second Lieutenant Archibald Cathie reported eight combats with no decisive results, but the squadron's blood was up and an impassive note of expedience crept into his report: 'On crossing line at 1500 feet we emptied three drums on German front line trench where men were observed working.'[21]

At RFC HQ, Maurice Baring's memories of 15 September hinted at the sense that a watershed had been reached by the RFC: 'It was a terrific day in the air. It was not before a year had passed that so much flying was done in the air again, 1,308 hours of flying were done; 24 German machines were brought down and two kite balloons.'[22] Captain Foot and Welsford, who had already claimed a German Aviatik on a morning bombing escort,[23] went up on a late afternoon offensive patrol and met fierce opposition: 'Whilst on active patrol numerous hostile aircraft were seen. We dived on two who separated, diving down to about 4,000 feet.'[24]

At a range of around a hundred yards, they then attacked another and chased it down to 3,000 feet where it then disappeared. Another of the FEs was in trouble: 'Hostile aircraft was then seen on another FE's tail. We engaged it at about 150 yards and chased it away.' A Roland was waiting to attack the same FE: 'Roland dived down at FE. Fire was opened with both guns at seventy yards and many tracers hit Roland which went away apparently untouched.' Foot and Welsford had been surrounded by indeterminate numbers of German aircraft: 'About nine hostile machines were engaged altogether but with no definite results. Several hostile machines were seen landing recklessly on Bertincourt aerodrome.'[25]

Foot's combat report made no mention of what had happened to the FE they had attempted to relieve. Confusion was inevitable on a day of such concentrated fighting: Second Lieutenant Frank Hollingsworth and Lieutenant Henry Wells had failed to return from the late afternoon offensive patrol. In the casualty report Foot had stated seeing 'what he took to be an FE landing north east of Frise about 6 pm' but Hollingsworth and Wells had been brought down at Lebucquiére close to the German aerodrome at Vélu.[26] The burial of both men in a joint grave was a grim indication of the fate they had shared in a burning aircraft. Sergeant Walker, who had been shot in the stomach on the morning patrol, was also more seriously wounded than the bare details of the combat report had suggested: he died the following day and was buried at Habarcq, west of Arras.[27]

\*

As the bone weary crews of No. 11 prepared for another return to Bapaume on the following day, *Jasta* 2 were testing the twin guns of their sixteen new single-seater Albatros D1s. Their commanding officer, Oswald Boelcke, who had his own prototype of the even more advanced Albatros DII to fly, wrote of them:

> Our new machines likewise border on marvellous. They are far improved over the single-seaters that we flew at Verdun. Their climb rate and manoeuvrability are astounding. It is as if they were living, feeling beings that understand what their master wishes. With them, one can dare and achieve anything.[28]

The RFC had little ready to answer this powerful new aircraft, as men like Fred Libby were only too aware:

> God, we need new and faster ships bad... Everyone knows the folks in England are working as fast as possible to give us new ships, but if they don't hurry, who in hell is going to fly them?[29]

At Bertincourt, Boelcke's new squadron were emboldened by the strategic skills of their leader. 'My pilots are all passionately keen and very competent, but I must first train them to steady team-work – they are at present rather like young puppies in their zeal to achieve something.'[30]

An inconsistent series of combat reports for that day points to an increasingly confrontational German Air Force. Early in the morning of 16 September, Captain Horace Davey and Lieutenant Clayton reported leading a reconnaissance west of Marcoing. They were attacked by six hostile aircraft ('mostly biplanes, but Fokkers were also seen close behind') as well as 'an uncounted number exceeding a dozen' which were seen 'hanging about a thousand feet lower down.' Davey and Clayton went to the aid of an FE targeted at close range by a Roland, but it was too late: 'the attacked FE disappeared into clouds under control but with the engine smoking very badly. It has not returned.' The report was clearly marked 7.00 *am*, but there is no corresponding loss recorded for that time.[31]

Twelve hours later one of 'Boelcke's boys', *Leutnant* Otto Höhne, opened *Jasta* 2's account and brought down the fourth of No. 11's FEs that week.[32] Lieutenant Robert Harvey and Second Lieutenant Archibald Cathie drove off two Rolands, returning safely from a reconnaissance patrol around Cambrai, and Quested and Welsford also fought off six enemy aircraft all the way back from Cambrai to the lines, reporting one Albatros, three Rolands and a Fokker.[33] But Second Lieutenant Lionel Pinkerton and Lieutenant James Sanders strayed a little too far into the territory of the increasingly confident German fighting units. The location of the combat was again near Marcoing, a village not far from Cambrai, and the location of an important railway junction accessing both Peronne in the south and Bapaume in the east – a target the FE2bs were drawn to like flies. Pinkerton and Sanders' plane was seen descending in a controlled way but trails of smoke followed it, and No. 11 were another two men and one aircraft down.[34]

At Le Hameau, Lionel Morris read C Flight's orders for the morning of 17 September. Their mission: to escort the bombers of No.12. The target: Marcoing Station.

*Chapter 18*

# Taken at the Flood

*Before striking, obtain an advantageous position and keep the sun behind you.*

*Don't stop an attack once you've started it.*

*Get as close to your opponent before firing and make sure you can see him properly.*

*Don't be fooled by trick strategies and never take your eye off your opponent.*

*Go straight for your opponent if he dives at you.*

*In enemy territory, keep your line of retreat clear.*

*There is safety in numbers; attack in groups of four or six and don't all go for the same opponent.*

*Always strike from behind.*

*Dicta Boelcke*

'A gloriously fine day', remembered Manfred von Richthofen of the morning of 17 September 1916. At Bertincourt, *Jasta* 2 received a thorough briefing from Boelcke and left for their first hunt.[1]

No. 11's C Flight rose early to shepherd the station bombers of No.12 Squadron. Twenty-three-year old Lieutenant Raymond Money from Lincolnshire was flying one of No. 12's escorted BE2s without an observer:

> We started at 6 am and by 7 am we had reached our necessary height of six thousand feet. A thin ground mist partially

obscured vision, and I was congratulating myself that we should get over and back again before the sun had time to dispel it, when, to my amazement and annoyance, the leader fired a green light (the 'Abandon' signal) and went down again. He was followed by the rest of the patrol.[2]

It was obvious to Money, if not his flight leader, that the weather would change for the better; and by 9.05 am the first of No. 11's escort aeroplanes, with its squadron marking of a white triangle on its nose, was airborne for the second time. As leader, Captain Gray's aircraft FE2b 7019 flew with two streamers attached to the wing struts. Five minutes after Gray's take off, Morris was up with Rees, trailing one streamer as deputy leader. Eight BE2s of No.12, shadowed by six FE2bs, crossed the lines by 10.30 am; flying eastwards through clear skies.[3] Two more of No. 11's aircraft carrying Second Lieutenant Thompson with Glover, and Turk with Scott joined the formation.[4]

Before the BE2s had reached their targets, they and their escorts had been spotted by the leader of *Jasta* 2. Boelcke's perception of every black speck on the horizon was beyond his new recruits, who saw nothing until they were much closer to the British squadrons. Boelcke's 'pups' took their cues from their leader, who held back, and held back, for endless minutes at a height of 10,000 feet.

The British bombers arrived at Marcoing and quickly let loose their explosives on the station buildings. Money struggled to keep up as his petrol pump had failed, and the others finished the job without him. Smoke and fire billowed from the ground, distracting the British crews eager to see what damage they had done, but their moment of gratification did not last long. Money became aware something was going very wrong: 'I saw the leader turn back for home with three others with him. The fifth machine had disappeared.'[5] As the aircraft of both No.12 and No. 11 headed west for home, *Jasta* 2 closed in, trapping and confronting them between the front line and Marcoing, where anti-aircraft guns were now awake and ready. The tension for the desperately keen German squadron was unbearable as Boelcke continued to hold his fire, waiting for the optimum opportunity of close combat. Finally, he made his move, choosing Gray and Helder's FE2b, and all hell appeared to break loose. The British formation splintered as the rest of *Jasta* 2 began to careen into them. In a letter later sent to Albert Morris, his son's reactions as Boelcke struck were described by Captain Gray: 'We were attacked by hostile aircraft near Cambrai… the escort of six or seven machines which I was leading (and your son second leader) engaged them. I was ahead with two other machines and one of them which I believe was your son turned back to assist those in the rear.'[6]

The back of the formation was a dangerous place to be and Morris's swift response to the trailing FE fatally exposed his own machine.[7] Instinct would have led the British pilots to try to form a spinning circle for protection but now the opposition was too fast and their guns too numerous. Money provided a chilling theory of how the Germans had engineered the fight:

> The 'circus' had done its work only too well. It must have come up from behind and below the BE2cs, and gallant No. 11 had dived to the rescue. This would be just what the Germans wanted. It looked to me as though they opened out to let the FEs get among them, and then closed in in bunches of three or four on the tails of the FEs.[8]

Richthofen, behind Boelcke, focused on a 'large machine painted in dark colours' and began firing at FE2b 7018.[9] Rees instantly fired back and a futile exchange of bullets continued for the next few seconds.

Morris and Rees temporarily had the advantage. In his haste, Richthofen had forgotten the commandments Boelcke had so rigorously drummed into the new squadron: he was in full view of the crew of the FE2b, and vulnerable to their wide angle of fire. Morris had learned enough in his few short months as a fighter pilot to know that he had to do everything to avoid Richthofen getting behind him. One of the FE2b's guns was within his reach, but the best chance of survival lay with him concentrating on flying whilst Rees took aim at their attacker.[10] Richthofen was persistent and determined, with a confidence that came from weeks of thorough preparation with Boelcke, and a blue-blooded proficiency with a gun. But Morris's skill in those terrifying minutes was evident to his opponent. The following account, reproduced many times, remains hauntingly detailed:

> Apparently he was no beginner, for he knew exactly that his last hour had arrived at the moment if I got at the back of him. At that time I did not have the conviction 'He must fall' which I have now on such occasions.[11]

But in contrast to the slow and careful build-up of the encounter, paced so expertly by Boelcke, Richthofen now responded to the proximity of his target with an atavistic recklessness:

> My Englishman twisted and turned, flying in zig-zags. I did not think for a moment that the hostile squadron contained other Englishmen who conceivably might come to the aid of their comrades. I was animated by a single thought: 'The man in front of me must come down, whatever happens.'[12]

Richthofen's chances were not good against the double guns of the FE2b and the solid defence of its experienced crew. Exasperated and aware of the risky position he had put himself in, he retreated, disappearing into the clouds. Given a breathing space at this decisive moment, he was able to consider the finer nuances of Boelcke's *Dicta*: from that point on Richthofen held the upper hand in his faster and better-armed machine. There would be only one outcome.

Morris believed the German had conceded defeat and looked around him. The FE2b formation was comprehensively ruptured and each of No. 11's crews had broken off into their own fights. One FE on its own was a sitting duck. Morris's only alternative was to head for home as quickly as possible and hope to rejoin at least one of No. 11's machines. He quickly turned the nose of the plane westwards and flew in a straight line. Below him, out of sight, Richthofen seized his opportunity to strike in the FE's blind spot underneath its tail. In seconds his machine gun fire raked the side of Morris's aeroplane as he closed in at precipitate speed. His relish for the attack nearly backfired: 'I had gone so close that I was afraid I might dash into the Englishman. Suddenly I nearly yelled with joy, for the propellor of the enemy machine had stopped turning. Hurrah!'[13]

As Richthofen stayed close and prepared to fire again, the FE began moving erratically. Morris struggled to keep it under control but a hail of bullets had found their way into the nacelle and hit three of his limbs. In the front of the plane, Rees suddenly stopped firing and disappeared from Morris's view. The observer's gun now abandoned, and the engine of the FE spluttering into silence, Richthofen now saw how devastating Boelcke's strategy of restraint and guile could be.

With a dead engine and a wounded observer no longer able to help him, Morris now had to summon all his skill and strength and try to land, aware that Richthofen could kill him at any moment. A few months of dealing with every kind of mechanical failure in the air gave him the hope of still gliding the plane to earth. But he was bleeding heavily from gunshot wounds to the left leg and both arms. Every shallow breath took him closer to unconsciousness. On the ground, armed German troops were watching and waiting.

In the original combat report, Richthofen described the fight, and the FE's tortuous descent to a dead stick landing on its undercarriage. It also stated that another German plane had joined him as he followed Morris down:

> I singled out the last machine and fired several times at closest range (10 meters). Suddenly the enemy propellor stood stock still. The machine went down gliding and I followed until I had killed the observer who had not stopped shooting until the last moment. Now my opponent went downwards in sharp curves. In approx. 1200 meters a second German machine came along and attacked my victim right down the ground and then landed next to the English plane.[14]

According to this account, Morris had landed the plane under control whilst being hounded by *two* enemy aircraft, coming to a rough but safe landing on farmland near a German aerodrome not far from Flesquieres, about seven miles south-west of Cambrai. But a later version of events in Richthofen's autobiography had a more heroic emphasis that removed any acknowledgement of assistance: 'I was so excited that I landed also, and my eagerness was so great that I nearly smashed up my machine.'[15]

As Richthofen landed close to the FE, German soldiers were approaching the British machine with caution. They quickly realised how little threat its occupants now posed. A Tommy on the ground could sometimes be saved from catastrophic arterial gunshot wounds by the quick and simple application of a tourniquet, but it was too late for Morris and Rees. Blood pooled on the nacelle floor around the feet of the slumped bodies of both the pilot and the observer. A romanticised version exists that described the jubilant but compassionate Richthofen, with the assistance of soldiers who had rushed to the scene, gently removing Rees from the nacelle: 'Rees opened his eyes with a boyish smile and died.'[16] Richthofen himself did not include such magnanimous details; his last sight of Morris was of him being placed on a stretcher and taken to the military hospital in Cambrai.[17] A remarkable series of photographs exists of FE2b 7018 apparently shortly after landing, surrounded by a swarm of curious officers and men. There are no crumpled wings or nose tips buried in the earth, and mercifully no prone figures nearby; the only obvious sign of an unusual landing is the odd sunken appearance of the fuselage and the stained tail, spattered with fuel from the bullet-punctured tank.

*

On the other side of the lines at Le Hameau, the day's events became clear as the waiting mechanics locked their eyes on the sky for the FE2bs of C Flight. The disbelief and sorrow when so many failed to return was captured by Fred Libby:

> I shall never forget the day, September 17, 1916, in Eleven Squadron, when all the ground crew of C Flight were

standing in front of their empty hangars, knowing that their entire flight had 'gone west'. The expression on the faces of these chaps was grief without tears, and was one of the saddest sights during my many months with Eleven. One sergeant said, 'Sir, it don't seem possible. We had such fine officers with perfect ships, and they only left four hours ago. To lose them all in one flight is hell'. All the ground crew of Eleven's C Flight could do was to wait for six new planes and twelve new officers.[18]

Libby's details are poignant, but two of the FEs *had* come back. The sergeants Thompson and Clarkson had driven off their attackers and reported, as Turk and Scott did also, sending one of them down out of control. Their survival was probably due to the timely arrival of at least two of No.60 Squadron's scouts.[19] Major Hubbard collected the assembled casualty reports at Le Hameau – all practically identical bar the personnel and aircraft details. The only real scrap of information was always the same: 'Lieutenant H.H. Turk reports seeing two F.s going down under control west of Marcoing.'[20] Second Lieutenant Hector Thompson and Sergeant John Glover had come to grief under the guns of *Leutnant* Leopold Reimann of *Jasta* 2, coming down behind German lines south-west of Cambrai at Trescault. Glover (who had been with Morris in his very first enemy encounter) was dead; Thompson was seriously wounded and died the following day. The scale of the fighting had attracted *Jasta* 4 who joined in and claimed a fourth of the FEs: Molloy and Sergeant Morton were forced to land at Etricourt south of Cambrai.[21] Morton was wounded in the leg and both were on their way into German custody.[22] Money had also been taken prisoner: drawing the attention of anti-aircraft fire from the ground, he was forced to land on the wrong side of the lines. He had watched as *Jasta* 2 had torn into the FEs and BEs and recalled the events in his memoirs:

Suddenly I heard the rattle of machine gun fire. I looked up and saw one of the escorting FE's from No. 11 Squadron going down in a steep spiral with two Huns on his tail. I cursed in impotent anger, and even let off a few rounds from

my Lewis gun in their direction. Suddenly I saw another FE
going down, and a third going to its assistance, although he
himself was being attacked by two more Huns. Out of harm's
way, bunched together on the horizon, was the little group
of four BEs. Six FEs were holding up thirty or forty Huns,
and I cursed and raged furiously at my impotence to help. It
was a sickening and heartrending sight... All this, as far as I
was concerned, had only occupied about three-quarters of a
minute, and I would not have believed it possible that in so
short a time I could have been filled with so great a desolation
and rage. I could not bear to watch the final fate of the FEs.[23]

Another of No.12's pilots, Second Lieutenant Aubrey Patterson, had
accurately bombed the railway target at Marcoing. But he too had been
shot down, and was to die a prisoner in a Cambrai hospital. Money
described his end:

He had been hit at the base of the spine, and the doctors gave
him up from the start. He had a magnificent constitution,
and as he felt no pain and was in good spirits, they had not
the heart to tell him. I was allowed to go and see him, and
he chattered happily about what we had done, and where
we would go, and when. He lived for ten days, and the last
afternoon was terrible.[24]

The captured survivors were imprisoned together in the old citadel of
Cambrai. Gray's observer, Helder, who had been wounded in the arm
by splinters of bullet casing, voiced their shock to Money: "'Poor old
Eleven" he mourned.'[25] Helder and Gray's FE had gone into a spin
following Boelcke's attack: Gray had managed to bring it under control
before they landed, and they had (as was the obligation for imminently
captive RFC personnel) set fire to the FE to avoid German intelligence
or despoilation.[26]

*

At Bertincourt, there were celebrations. Richthofen was exultant after the scrap that his commander described as a 'thorough house cleaning':[27] Bolecke wrote of *Jasta* 2's first outing:

> With some of my men I attacked a squadron of FE biplanes on the way back from C [Cambrai]. Of these, we shot down six out of eight. Only two escaped. I picked out the leader, and shot up his engine so he had to land. It landed right near one of our kite-balloons. They were hardly down when the whole airplane was ablaze. It seems they have some means of destroying their machine as soon as it lands.[28]

Richthofen's combat report stated (erroneously) 'Pilot: NCO Rees, wounded hospital at Cambrai. Observer: Killed, buried by *Jagdstaffel* 4' and he was awarded his first victory.[29] A party was held that evening to mark the successful debut of *Jasta* 2.[30] It was a remarkable achievement for a previously untested unit in new machines against battle-hardened and resourceful opponents. Richthofen decided on a commemorative souvenir to mark his first victory, paying homage to his aristocratic hunting roots. He wrote to a Berlin jeweller ordering a small silver cup, to be inscribed with the legend: '1. Vickers 2. 17.9.1916', Vickers being the usual name the German aviators gave to the FE pusher aircraft. Sixty cups later he was forced to stop. His winning streak had yet to come to an end, but silver was rare and exorbitantly expensive in a nation struggling to survive economically after three punishing years of war.[31]

*

Other not so dramatic, but still disturbing losses were sustained by the RFC on 17 September. There had been four German aircraft brought down, but it was the Marcoing rout following a week of unprecedented fighting that crystallised the thoughts of the RFC's commander about the nature of the new threat facing his aircrews.[32] In a letter written that day to Brancker, Trenchard took pains to point out that the destruction of precious resources was not simply the result of inexperienced pilots: 'Once or twice it has struck me that you have probably, with the enormous number of machines that have been wrecked lately, put it down to accidents. A lot are, but an enormous number are absolutely shot to pieces.' He went on to refer directly to the events of that morning:

> We have had rather a heavy blow today. We were very active all this morning and knocked several railway stations to pieces etc. and I'm afraid we have lost ten machines up to now and only half the day is gone. Four of these machines are 160 hp FEs and four other 160 hp FEs have had their engines so shot about that it will be a long time before they are repaired.[33]

Despite their inferior aeroplanes, the numerical superiority and sheer force of effort of the RFC had held the line in the skies since the beginning of the Somme campaign, but it was now clear to Trenchard that for all the make do and mend of supply, the new squadrons of more effective DH2 fighters, and the insignificant numbers of Nieuport Scouts begged from the French, the Germans were finally mounting a challenge that would soon be beyond the means of the RFC to hold off. The situation for the Flying Corps was reaching a crisis point. Through the fluent conduit of Maurice Baring (who did more than anyone else to add cohesive persuasion to Trenchard's arguments) and with the full support of the Commander-in-Chief of the Army, a memo was published five days after the events of 17 September. *Future Policy in the Air* was sent to the War Office in London bearing the signature of Haig himself. It was written in the uncomfortable knowledge that Trenchard's prediction of a 'drastic reformer' within the German Air Service had already materialised, and that the RFC were trying to shut the stable door after the horse had bolted.[34] There was no choice in Trenchard's eyes but to continue with a full-blooded offensive strategy despite its cost. His close relationship with the French Air Force convinced him that their successes were down to their aggression, after a painful learning curve of misadventure: 'If we were to adopt a purely defensive policy, or a partially offensive policy, we should be doing what the French have learned by experience to be a failure, and what the rank and file of the enemy, by their own accounts, point to as being one of the main causes of their recent reverses.'[35]

In France, watching the day by day depletion of squadrons and aircraft, he was deeply mindful of the sacrifice his men continued to make. Replacements were out of his control and his anxiety showed through his blunt questioning of commitment to the fight at home: 'It is not a question of difficulty of supplying pilots, it is a question as to whether it can be done or whether it can't be done... If we cannot do it, then we are beaten.'[36]

As the casualty numbers rose sharply in the second half of September, the question in many minds, as Morris's colleague Libby had recognised, was whether there would be much left of the Flying Corps to supply. But Major Hubbard filled the empty chairs again at Le Hameau. In the absence of so many capable aircrew, the commanding officer himself had to help train the new observers, taking two up for short flights to Savy on 19 and 20 September.[37] His other more melancholy duties of contacting the families of all the lost men had been discharged promptly the day after most of C Flight had gone missing. The news made its way quickly across the Channel to England.

## Chapter 19

# Our Brave and Good Friends

A small white envelope was delivered to *Merle Bank* on Wednesday, 20 September 1916. Inside was Army form M.S.3 (Cas). The first line, 'Regret to inform you' was stamped on with little care and the top half of the text was cut off. The rest was hand-written and missed the pre-printed ruled lines: '2nd Lieut. L.B.F. Morris RFC is reported missing September 17 this'. Running out of space, the writer then decided on a new sentence on the next line to emphasise the following message: 'This does not necessarily mean he is wounded or killed.'[1] In this way, the British Army began the process of administration of Morris's death.

All the surviving documents of his War Office file are indeed administrative records, full of abbreviations, numbers and dates. In amongst the standard forms and minute sheets, there are occasionally flashes of human emotion, but in a war that used up as much paper as it did lives, the overwhelming impression given by the mostly transcribed pages is of a focused bureaucracy that had precious little time to spare for the comfort of bereaved families. The enormity of the country's loss did not allow for a hierarchy of grief, or an awareness of how unprepared most families were for the consequences – not just personally, but legally too – of a death in action, especially where no will had been left. The onus was on the families to find out for themselves what needed to be done, and the guarded correspondence between the Morrises and the War Office concerned the universal practicalities of death.

Whilst Albert and Lil were absorbing the shock of the telegram, another letter arrived of a more personal nature. The original does not survive, but what must have been a near identical note was received by Rees's father and reprinted in the *Brecon and Radnor Express* a few weeks later:

> My dear sir, I much regret to have to inform you that your son is, in all probability, a prisoner. He and his pilot Lieutenant [sic] L. B. F. Morris were on escort duty in company with other of my machines yesterday and failed to return. A machine which may have been theirs, was seen to go down under control after a fight, so it is believed that the engine was shot through, compelling them to land. It may be some few weeks before you hear from him, but the Germans always treat RFC officers very well. He was the best observer and is a great loss to the squadron. I had never had a braver or keener officer. I sincerely hope you may soon hear from him. Yours very truly, T. O B. Hubbard, Major No. 11 Squadron, RFC, BEF.[2]

Hubbard's crumb of condolence and its reference to the special status of RFC PoW officers was reassuring, and in many cases accurate. Airmen landing, dead or alive, on the wrong side of the lines could hope with some justification that they would be treated with respect in 1916. The unique experience of aerial combat fostered a mutual regard between aviators of both sides, particularly in the case of casualties. Boelcke himself was well known for visiting, and often entertaining, the men he had brought down, and these good manners were returned by the RFC when he himself was killed a little over a month later. A wreath was dropped over *Jasta* 2's aerodrome bearing the words, 'To the memory of Captain Boelcke, a brave and chivalrous foe.'[3] No. 11 Squadron's Lieutenant Lionel Pinkerton (downed, with his observer Lieutenant James Sanders, the day before his Morris namesake) was able to write to his brother from Osnabrück PoW camp. He reported that the survivors of *Jasta* 2's first attack, along with other captured aircrew, had clubbed together to send the Boelcke family a similar tribute, and had received the thanks of his mourning father. Professor Boelcke was grateful to the camp commandant for 'granting the wish of the interned gentlemen' by arranging for the wreath to be sent and asked him to pass on his thanks to the PoWs for 'their noble display of real chivalrous feeling' which had 'left a splendid impression throughout Germany'. He added: 'Please God that the chivalrous relation that has ever existed between German and British airmen, and that to our delight has often been displayed by our son, might soon move into the relations between the two nations.'[4]

On 29 September the *Carshalton and Wallington Advertiser* listed Morris as Missing in Action.[5] As the weeks past, his parents endured the wait for further news. The War Office were cautious in the absence of their son's name in published lists of the dead from the German authorities. Although the first word seems to have come from Pinkerton at Osnabrück, Lionel's flight leader Captain Gray had also managed to pass on the news by the end of September, as a later note in Morris's War Office file recorded:

> Captain D.B. Gray, RFC, a prisoner of war in Germany, states in a letter dated 30 September 1916, that an aeroplane containing Second Lieutenant Morris and Lieutenant Rees was driven down during an aerial encounter. Lieutenant Rees was killed in the air and Second Lieutenant Morris died of his injuries in hospital at Cambrai. The death of Lieutenant Rees has been accepted for official purposes. The death of Second Lieutenant L.B.F. Morris has been accepted for official purposes. The date of his death has not yet been reported.[6]

The final proof was sent firstly to the American embassy in Berlin, and then on to the Foreign Office in London, where the Official List details (received on 22 November) were definitive: 'died 17.9.1916 of Sht Wds in the L leg and R. and L. Arm in the *Kriegslaz Abt*. 1. Cambrai'.[7]

At the beginning of December, the War Office were still holding back from issuing an official notification of death to the Morrises. But by that time Albert had written to Captain Gray. The reply he received put an end to any hopes he and Lil may have still had.[8]

Having lost his battle with Boelcke, Gray and his observer Lieutenant Helder had been forced to land under machine gun fire from the air and the ground, beside a German kite balloon.[9] Gray's letter, dated 25 November, gave the tragedy of Morris's death all the classic constructs of the fallen hero: a careful mixture of empathy and untruth designed to console a grieving father whilst not giving anything away to enemy intelligence. In it he spoke of his personal friendship with Morris, and acknowledged their shared history at ground school, emphasising that Morris's actions in attempting to protect fellow squadron members had resulted in his death.

Gray spared Albert much of his own traumatic experience, describing an FE2b (that had landed near his own) coming down near trees and houses, on an embankment and surrounded by curious onlookers. The German car that took Gray and Helder away from their own crash site, then stopped by the other aeroplane and Gray gathered from the German officer that whilst Rees had been killed, Morris had been taken away in an ambulance.

On arriving in Cambrai late at night, Gray was given more information:

> There was a pilot named Morris in hospital brought down that morning... We saw no-one again until I think the next afternoon when we were told Morris had died that morning. He had been wounded in the air and injured by the crash... We were told that Morris was conscious most of the time and when admitted into hospital was able to give his name, etc. He was very quiet and I think suffered little pain. I would have liked to have seen him but he was already dead before we knew very much about it and we were somewhat dazed and put out by our own experiences.[10]

Gray passed on news from the hospital gleaned from other officers visiting, asserting that conditions were acceptable and that nothing more could have been done to save Morris. He explicitly stated that the end had been peaceful and without great pain. In praise of his younger colleague, he used a a familiar language of heroism and necessary sacrifice:

> He had done a great deal of work and was one of the most reliable and brave pilots I have met. I say this without exaggeration and not merely through a desire to gratify. As you know, his manner was quiet and unassuming but it covered a very stout heart and steady nerve and I am certain he gave a good account of himself. No officer in the Flying Corps could wish to meet a better end.[11]

Gray ended by referring to an enclosed cutting which has long since been lost; expressing perhaps some homily which he hoped would be a solace, 'as day by day our brave and good friends carry out their last orders.'[12]

Lil Morris kept the letter all her life, a precious relic of her only son and a reassurance that his death had been worthwhile. The language Gray used was echoed in millions of other letters to the families of servicemen killed in the war. Every single dead Flying Corps officer was officially stout-hearted for obvious reasons of morale – the kind of economy of honesty that in Morris's case (considering Gray's remarks) appears to have been unnecessary.

Gray took an understandably less frank approach to details of his own circumstances, signing the letter as Captain D.S. Gray of 15 Squadron. He had falsified not only his second initial but also his squadron number – and he was by no means the only captured RFC officer to do so. Some were impressively creative in their attempts to confuse and mislead the enemy. In one instance, details of a brilliant new aircraft, with Crosse and Blackwell engines made by Huntley and Palmer, were 'leaked' according to the tongue-in-cheek testimony of one captured pilot.[13] Gray had told Albert Morris that he had been unable to provide further details as neither he nor Helder spoke German – a spectacularly false assertion on Gray's part, as an audacious method he used when heading an escape from Holzminden PoW camp in 1918 later proved.[14] But more puzzling are the anomalies about the timing of Morris's death and the crash location. Two years later in his repatriation report, Gray was still stating that Morris survived until the morning of 18 September, and identified (as did Helder in his own report) the crash site as being at 'Nurlie': likely to be Nurlu, a full nine miles south-west of Flesquieres and later the site of another aerodrome used by both German and British squadrons as the front lines shifted.[15] Richthofen wrote in his autobiography that Morris had died on the way to the 'nearest dressing station'.[16] Gray's motive may have been to provide a convincing and sympathetic scenario for the Morrises whilst flattering his captors with evidence of their benevolence. Many details obviously ring true, specifically his friendship with Morris and their shared history. And if it was Gray's assumption that the Morrises would have preferred to think of their son bravely lingering on in a comfortable hospital bed rather than expiring on a painful and frightening journey in a German ambulance, he must have hoped that the details of his letter would have provided a more acceptable narrative. One of Richthofen's biographers, the American journalist Floyd Gibbons, painted a touching picture of Richthofen visiting twin graves in the hospital yard at Cambrai; a version of events that suggested Richthofen walking to Cambrai from Bertincourt – a trek of nearly four hours on foot.[17] In reality Rees and Morris were buried miles apart. The location of Morris's grave – Porte-de-Paris Cemetery in Cambrai itself – seems to be the strongest evidence that he had been nearer to the town than the crash site when he died. Rees was given a funeral by *Jasta* 4 at Villers Plouich, nearer to both Nurlu and Flesquieres.[18] Richthofen apparently paid his own tribute, although subsequent translations of his autobiography have differed in their details of it – the laying of a stone to 'honour the fallen enemy on his beautiful grave' (in the 1918 version) fails to identify *which* of his victims this was done for.[19] Richthofen's later biographer Peter Kilduff's phrasing is less romantic but suggests that the crew were buried together: 'Later I erected a gravestone to the memory of my honourably fallen enemies'.[20]

*

Morris and Rees's bravery was still in Major Hubbard's mind on 5 October when he recommended both for a Mention in Despatches. His proposed citation for Morris read: 'For gallantry and devotion to duty during 19.5.16 to 17.9.16. A most reliable and conscientious officer. Had many aerial combats during that period.'[21] Reliable and conscientious officers were ten-a-penny in the autumn of 1916, and a pencil-marked 'N.E.' next to Hubbard's citation seems to stand for Not Expedited. There was no mention of an award for Morris in the *London Gazette*. This was not to belittle or exaggerate his achievements – but there is a sense that Hubbard was anxious to offer some condolence in posthumous reward when other commanding officers would have considered Morris's efforts to have been no more than what was expected of him.

A memo from General Headquarters, RFC to Third Brigade commander Higgins in the same file, attempted to clarify the system of awards and pointed out that many nominations suggested that the officers concerned were *solely* responsible for bringing down aircraft and such recognition ignored the crucial teamwork that enabled victories. The memo also casts doubts on rewarding observers for having taken over in the air from incapacitated pilots, suggesting this was much easier to do in some machines than it was in others. Officers who had brought down fewer than three or four enemy machines were not yet worthy of rewards and neither were those who had attacked kite balloons – but failed to bring them down. The impossibility of a fixed standard for bravery was recognised, and the desire for consistency in the issuing of awards emphasised. But the appearance of the memo, in the records for a month in which casualties had been so high, does little to improve perceptions of the profligacy with which the RFC leadership appeared to be willing to dispense with men's lives. The insistence on gallantry over an extended period also ignored the fact that many aircrew were simply not surviving long enough to warrant recognition under such rules.[22]

*

On 30 November, *Flight* published a list, released in Germany, of aircraft the enemy claimed to have brought down. The 'formidable appearance' of casualties in September was clear, and the magazine noted the high price of the Flying Service's 'Admiralty of the Air'. It reiterated 'the need for further and yet further sacrifice to maintain what we have secured at the price of the devotion of those whose names are enshrined in the Roll of Honour.' The details were sketchy and inaccurate for FE2b 7018, which continued to be identified as a Vickers machine. The pilot was noted as being 'Cpl. Rees', and a question mark was placed next to 'Observer'.[23] But by that time, enough detail had been received for the War Office to finally confirm the casualties, and for Morris's name to appear amongst those listed as killed in the newspapers.[24]

On 1 December, Albert Morris set about the sad task of untangling his son's affairs. He was not sure what to do:

> The Secretary
> War Office
>
> Dear Sir,
>
> My son Lionel B. F. Morris, RFC died in Cambrai Hospital, and was gazetted last Saturday (Nov 25). I wish to take out letters of administration and I understand that it is necessary to have a death certificate, which is granted by yourself. Should this be correct, will you be good enough to forward same on to me. If this not being correct, perhaps you would be kind enough to inform me how I might proceed.[25]

The War Office's response to Albert's letter gives evidence of the administrative headache caused by the deaths of intestate officers behind enemy lines. A tetchy comment was included on an internal minute sheet, in response to a clerk who clearly had gone into autopilot. A request that the 'usual letter' be sent to Albert in response to Gray's evidence of Morris's death was met with exasperation, when the date of death was not stated clearly in it. A War Office employee by the name of Percy Taylor wrote the next paragraph: 'We can hardly send a Presumption Letter without giving some idea of the date the officer is presumed to have died.' He then thought better of the tone of his remark by amending it with a scribbled 'We think' in front of it and further reminders for a definitive date continue to pop up to the bottom of the sheet. This could reflect the confusion caused by Gray's alternative death date, or more simply the carelessness of an overworked employee.[26]

On 13 December Albert received a frustrating reply: the War Office was not in a position to issue a formal death certificate, but a painfully abstruse paragraph subsequently attempted to tell him what to do next:

> I am to add that the Army Council have, unfortunately, no doubt as to the death of this Officer, and to explain that their action, as set forth above, is notified to those concerned upon application for a certificate of death with a view to assisting them in dealing with the estates of Officers whose deaths have not been reported to this Department in a formal individual written sentence. It is understood that these letters which may be used in place of a formal certificate of death, are, as a rule, accepted for Probate and other purposes.[27]

The legal threads were not tied up until well into the following year – on 2 January 1917 Albert Morris was granted letters of administration, giving him what monies his son had left: £98, 12 shillings and 6 pence.[28] Lionel Morris had served the British Army for 186 days, and was paid for the last two weeks of September that he hadn't lived to see.[29] A further small gratuity was paid to Albert in April 1917.[30]

*

Morris's mortal remains were less settled. When the Imperial War Graves Commission were able to survey the Porte-de-Paris Military Cemetery on the outskirts of Cambrai in 1920, they found it badly damaged and riddled with mines placed to deter the advancing Allies in October 1918. The many nationalities of its silent occupants represented the bloody reach of the war: over 100 French, Russian, Romanian, New Zealand, British and German bodies had all been interred, together with a few unfortunate Belgian civilians.[31] The Morrises were given official notice of the location of their son's grave in Plot 46 in August 1917, information which had been forwarded to the War Office via the neutral Netherlands government.[32] Had they been able to visit in the years directly after the war, it would have been a deeply upsetting experience, not just because of their loss, but because the defeated enemy had not respected the cemetery; desecrating it (like many others in the orbit of the fighting) and, in the words of CWGC historian David Crane, 'promiscuously mingling the living, and the dead' as they withdrew.[33] The original copies of the reports for the Imperial War Grave Commission (IWGC) relating to Porte-de-Paris show the difficulty of their work in a cemetery so ruined by explosive action. There are many crossings out and amendments – Morris's entry starts correctly '3rd Bn', but a further two attempts at the name, both of which seem to suggest the report compiler thought he was an American serviceman, have been rejected and finally replaced with 'West Surrey'. Morris's grave was surrounded by dozens of unnamed German and Russian casualties.[34] In 1928 the IWGC reported to Albert that the bodies had been reinterred following a reorganisation of the cemetery. The process of exhumation was gruesome but simple; this description came from an Australian officer working earlier in the war: 'The grave would be opened and the body uncovered. The body was checked for identity discs, paybooks, papers or anything else that could be used in identification. Then the body was wrapped in a blanket, sewn up and marked with an identifying tag for future occasions.'[35]

Following the reorganisation at Porte-de-Paris, all the German bodies had been removed and Morris's grave was now marked by a 'durable wooden cross with an inscription bearing full particulars.'[36] These were basic: 'Second Lieutenant L.B.F. Morris, The Queens and Royal Flying Corps. 17 September 1916 aged 19.' His parents had not paid for any extra inscriptions (which were optional, at a cost of

3½ d per letter) and the RAF insignia, rather than the swifts' wings of the Flying Corps, is incised at the top of the stone.[37] Morris rests in Plot 1 A 16; one of six Royal Flying Corps officers (and one of three soldiers of the Queen's Royal West Surrey Regiment) in Porte-de-Paris. Located in a double row of around fifty graves, his headstone sits in the centre of the section. It is the only one without a cross: the entry for 'Religious Emblem' in the associated IWGC record states clearly his family's wishes that none was requested. For an Englishman baptised in the same church that his parents were married in, the absence of such a familiar benediction after what was the premature death of an only son is conspicuous.

A personal connection existed between Morris and the man who had been charged with the task of producing design recommendations for the cemeteries handed over to the IWGC by the French government. The Commander of 2nd Company, Inns of Court Officers' Training Corps, when Private L.B.F. Morris had joined it in 1915, was Sir Frederic Kenyon. Now that the war was over, Kenyon had returned to his job as Director of the British Museum and was asked by Fabian Ware of the IWGC to deliver a report on the appropriate architectural approach that the Commission should take with the cemeteries, as their own appointed experts could not agree. His eventual findings, accepted by the IWGC in 1918, were deeply controversial. There were accusations of a 'strange sense of disconnection with the realities' of the millions of bodies now in the IWGC's care, and of what those remains meant to their families.[38] The uniformity of rank, stone, building and discreet horticulture that now marks out a Commonwealth War Grave cemetery, was an affront to many who wanted to create their own personalised displays of remembrance, and the decision not to repatriate bodies (intended to democratise the dead by not favouring those who could afford to bring their loved ones home) meant that in many cases poorer relatives could not pay for the trip abroad.[39]

The cemetery holds the graves of three other men whose lives or deaths also gave them a direct connection to Morris, indicating the town's reputation as the centre of the hunting grounds of the air war's most famous pilot. Richthofen's tenth victim, Lieutenant Gilbert

Hall of No. 18 Squadron, brought down north-west of Thiepval on 20 November 1916, lies in the row in front.[40] Lieutenant Aubrey Patterson, the BE2 pilot of No.12, whose lingering death in Cambrai after the events of 17 September had been so affectingly described by Money, is buried in Plot 1 A 4.

A Whitgift connection followed Morris to Cambrai, first to the military hospital and then to the cemetery at Porte-de-Paris. Lieutenant Ernest Porter, who served with the London Regiment, was a Senior Science Master at the school from September 1914, leaving Croydon to enlist in December 1915. A keen boy scout organiser and cyclist, whose 'whole nature was averse to the military life', Porter had apparently led a platoon over the top in an unsuccessful attack and had to be left behind in a shell hole, with what seemed like a minor thigh wound. According to the school magazine, when Porter's fellow soldiers repeated the attack successfully the following day and tried to rescue him, he was no longer there. After four months, word came from the American Red Cross that he had been taken off the battlefield by the Germans and delivered to the same hospital in Cambrai as Morris. Porter disappeared from the shell hole on 17 September 1916. He survived a few more days and died on 22 September, aged thirty-two.[41] His headstone sits beside Patterson's, a few feet away from Morris.

Given the ubiquitous public school dependencies of the RFC, it is not surprising that the Whitgift links persisted in Richthofen's story also. When Richthofen was finally shot down, former old boy Colonel George Barber was one of the doctors on the Medical Board of the Australian Flying Corps. A second autopsy for the pilot, by then known to the French as '*Le Diable Rouge*' (the Red Devil) was supervised by the Australian Imperial Force (AIF) in April 1918. Barber's evidence included a description of how a piece of fencing wire was used to track the trajectory of a wound through Richthofen's chest and heart – in Barber's opinion, a wound matching a bullet hole in the German's plane, that he believed came from the guns of Australian artillery soldiers on the ground.[42]

*Chapter 20*

# The Forgotten Warriors

Of the men who shared Morris's summer in No. 11, the subsequent stories of the fortunate and the fallen reveal not only the gulf between the immortals, like Albert Ball, and the journeymen flying officers, but also the social divide which obscures the contributions of some of the NCOs in the remaining records.

Ball's courage turned him into one of the quintessential fighter pilots of the First World War. According to Algernon Insall, No. 11 Squadron adjutant in 1916, Ball owed much of his success to three of his No. 11 contemporaries: Captain Cooper, Sergeant Foster, and Major Hubbard, 'who showed him the difference between flying as a means of rapid locomotion and flying as an art.'[1] Ball's dedication and total immersion in the job earned him some ambiguous character references, suggesting an unsociable nature, but his letters attest to frequent off-duty engagement with his colleagues and practical reasons for his absences from squadron bonhomie. Putting his hut so close to the hangars enabled him to be ready for action at a moment's notice.[2]

Ball plummeted to the ground in his SE5 from a dark cloud on 7 May 1917 at Annouellin, apparently having become disoriented (possibly fainting) and flying upside down from a position that put impossible demands on an engine which was probably running out of fuel. Whether the loss of his capital of courage contributed to an accident which some saw as inexplicable for a flier of such skill and experience remains a moot point, but the increasing risks he was prepared to take were recognised by his contemporaries. Major James McCudden, who as flight leader with No.56 Squadron lost only four pilots between August 1917 and March 1918, wrote of the dangers of such bombastic techniques: 'I do not believe in being shot about.

It is bad or careless flying to allow oneself to be shot about when one ought usually to be able to prevent it by properly timed manouevres,'[3] For Ball's family, the psychological toll that the war took on him was difficult to miss, as a letter written at the end of September 1916 had shown: 'I feel so sorry for the chaps I have killed. Just imagine what their poor people must feel like. I must have sent at least forty chaps to their deaths. However, it must be done, or they would kill me, would they not?'[4] By early May of 1917 he had been credited with around forty-four victories. Two days before Ball's death, a near-miss with an Albatros which he believed had intended to deliberately collide with his SE5 left him almost unable to talk, as the squadron's recording officer remembered: 'Flushed in face, his eyes brilliant, his hair blown, and dishevelled, he came to the squadron office to make his report, but for a long time was in so overwrought a state that dictation was an impossibility.'[5] But a benchmark had been set by his example and his place in history was made. Thanks to the French, who couldn't resist holding up the hero that the egalitarian caution of the RFC preferred to keep anonymous, Ball's short life came to epitomise the dash and daring of the Great War in the sky. He left behind a legacy of talismanic proportions; summed up by a fellow officer: 'He was grit and fight, fight and grit, first, last and all the time.'[6]

Captain Ernest Foot had used up as many lives as a cat by the end of the war. Joining his friend Albert Ball in No.60 Squadron in August 1916, he survived a crash in a burning aircraft in October of the same year, after a scrap with Boelcke's *Jasta* 2 that won him the Military Cross. Sent home briefly as an instructor in January 1917, he was then amongst the peerless group of RFC scout pilots chosen for the formation of No. 56 Squadron. Again with Ball, he was posted to London Colney in Hertfordshire in preparation for the unit's debut on the Western Front, but was injured in a car accident the day before they were due to leave and had to be left behind. His skills were too precious to be wasted, but the rest of his war was spent far away from the fighting, passing on his experience at the School of Special Flying in Hampshire, where Major Robert Smith-Barry's training reforms were radically improving the life expectancy of new pilots. An acknowledged expert in stunt flying, Foot took a student up with him in an Avro dual control aircraft in September 1917 and the aircraft crashed, injuring but failing to kill him yet again. After the war he stayed in the skies as a cross-channel civilian pilot, continuing to instruct for the RAF and taking part in several aerial races. In 1923 the wing of his Bristol monoplane came off during the Grosvenor Challenge Cup relay, sending the aircraft to the ground near Chertsey in Surrey, where it burst into flames. It was a swift and brutal end for the twenty-eight-year-old pilot, leaving his new bride a widow after just a few months of marriage.[7]

The laconic observer Fred Libby, whose partnership with his pilot Captain Stephen Price in No. 11 Squadron had resulted in five victories by November 1916, was awarded the Military Cross. Returning to the UK to retrain as a pilot, he flew with No.43 and No. 25 Squadrons until 1917. His tally of victories with the RFC has been estimated between fourteen and twenty-four – his shared status as an observer confusing efforts at consistency. A special request from General Billy Mitchell was made for him to join the Aviation Section of the Signal Corps – a unit which then constituted the United States Army Air Service. Although not lacking in patriotism (he had used the Stars and Stripes flag for the streamers on his aircraft), Libby was nonetheless initially reluctant. The intensity of the camaraderie he had enjoyed in the RFC, together with a lack of confidence in America's commitment to air power and an unfortunate encounter with an officious US major, reinforced his misgivings. But in any case his flying career was nearing its end due to a crippling back injury. Serving as an instructor, and taking part in the Liberty Loans fundraising drive in the States, he was unable to go on active service for his home country and was an invalid by July 1918, unable to cross a street without help. An exchange of letters in his War Office file records his attempts to receive the gratuities that his British friends were awarded. The state of his health and his ignorance (or forgetfulness, according to the War Office, who maintained the RFC *had* informed him of what was due to him) cut no ice with the British government he had served so faithfully. They were seeking an end to such claims; his transfer to American service further complicated matters and eventually, despite the support of the American Red Cross, he was told he had left it too late to apply.[8]

Libby's spine injuries, together with the arthritis that so often accompanies broken bones, continued to plague him but his lust for life remained unaffected. A career in civil aviation with early cargo airlines followed, but the appetite for risky businesses fostered by his wartime flying led him to financial disaster as a 'wildcatter', searching for oil. It was an enterprise which turned out to be much more costly than he could ultimately afford, and he lost a fortune. Despite these setbacks, even in his mid-sixties Libby's buccaneering spirit was still strong: the United States Air Force were celebrating their fiftieth anniversary and invited him to pilot a supersonic jet for the first time. He died at the age of seventy-eight in California.[9]

No. 11's commanding officer, Major Hubbard, left the squadron in October 1916, just weeks after *Jasta* 2's decimation of C Flight, going on to lead the Royal Air Force's Martlesham Heath Experimental Aircraft Station, as well as serving as a squadron commander in Egypt, Palestine, and Iraq.[10] His ongoing involvement with the Royal Aeronautical Society continued until well after the war, including a creditable performance in the 1920 Aerial Derby race around London amongst much younger pilots.[11] Retiring from the Royal Air Force as a Wing Commander in 1931, his gentler pursuits then occupied him for the best part of thirty years. Living in Cyprus, he developed a great interest in collecting antiques, amassing nearly 800 items; in 1957 he delighted local museum curators in Nicosia by presenting them with a magnificent eighth century BCE vase which he had rescued from unscrupulous local gold-diggers. Export regulations forced him to leave much of his collection behind when he returned to England by the end of the 1950s. Many pieces were donated to Cypriot museums and some are in the care of the British Museum.[12] This most unwarlike of men, who had nurtured perhaps the RFC's first true fighting squadron, died in Surrey in 1962 at the age of 79.

One of the saddest of stories was that of the courageous Sergeant John Glover, who, according to Morris's diary, had faced off eleven enemy planes on the opening day of the Battle of the Somme. Glover has a named grave at Fins, half way between Cambrai and Péronne to the south, but the details lodged with the Commonwealth War Graves Commission for him are bald – nothing of any family who mourned him, no home address and no birth date to identify how old he was when he died. An observer of such grit could well have gone on to earn his commission on ability, but his anonymity and absence from the records is not unusual. Christian names for such men can be hard to trace. Like most squadrons No. 11 knew the value of their mechanics and NCOs – Ball wrote of buying a football for the men whose appetite for hard work he admired, and officers chipped in to buy Flight Sergeant Joseph Hellingoe a uniform when he earned his commission – but it was still a lonely no-man's land for many of the men from the ranks, who were expected to know their place.[13]

Of all the little-known warriors of Morris's final squadron, it is Captain David 'Munshi' Gray, whose post-No. 11 history is perhaps the most remarkable. Gray's experiences as a PoW provides dangerously fertile grounds for wishful suppositions about what could have happened to his younger colleague, had Morris survived the dogfight on 17 September 1916. Gray's first bitter winter of imprisonment was spent at Osnabrück, where he was photographed alongside about seventy or so other PoWs. As a senior officer, he is seated, looking tense and gaunt next to the Camp Commandant, whose whole body has been erased by persistent pen hatching, making him look grotesquely like someone covered in netting – appropriately, as the motive of the defacement may have been to render him unrecognisable in the event of reprisals at the end of the war.

Gray's character emerges powerfully in the first account of the Holzminden prison camp breakout, published in 1920 by fellow captive Hugh Durnford. This first great escape has been the subject of many books and television documentaries; a blue-print for future generations of British PoWs and one that gave them the reputation (amongst the various nationalities of incarcerated men) as the cohort most likely to dig their way to freedom. According to Durnford, Gray was a natural leader, whose role in the escape earned him another nickname, 'The Father of the Tunnel' and whose bitter intolerance of lice earned him the sympathy of his camp comrades.[14]

Gray put up a spirited challenge to the camp's unbending regime, enduring solitary confinement after suspiciously trumped-up charges of attempted homicide were made against him. His alleged victim, one of the camp postmen, was so unreliable a witness that not even the Germans believed him. Gray had tried once previously to escape, and that failure sharpened his appetite for liberty. Barry Winchester's 1972 book *Beyond the Tumult* tells a riveting story of invention and guile which may or may not have been embellished in the telling, but Gray was certainly one of twenty-nine men who dug their way out of Holzminden in July 1918; and one of ten who managed to make their way back home.[15] He was pictured in shabby, oversized civilian disguise immediately upon reaching safety, his malnourished and filthy state failing to hide a triumphant glint of freedom in his eyes.

Gray returned to instruct with 30 TDS (Training Depot Station) in December 1918 and after the war he picked up a Military Cross, along with other fellow Holzminden escapees.[16] Their story was the subject of a little-known British film of 1938, *Who Goes Next*, starring Jack Hawkins.[17] He relinquished his RAF commission in 1919 and returned to the Indian Army, reaching the rank of Lieutenant Colonel in 1928. By 1933, when he had resigned from the Indian Army, he had collected an OBE, and although he had retired from the reserve of officers in 1939, two months later the Second World War brought him back to the air force. Joining the Administrative and Special Duties Branch of the RAF Volunteer Reserve, his ability and experience were recognised with a promotion to Squadron Leader in 1941. Reaching his fifty-seventh birthday that year, he was gazetted as having finally resigned his commission in November 1942, bringing to an end a long life of military service.[18] There is some evidence that even then Gray refused to stay idle, and joined the Home Guard in his home county of Hampshire. He was killed in a mundane traffic accident in December 1942 and is buried in the village of Wonston.[19] Gray's widow, having lost their only son in a climbing accident, had no family to clear her house after her death in the late 1990s – amongst the belongings given away to a museum was a Crème de Menthe tin in which items of her husband's escape kit had been kept as mementoes.[20]

A photograph of Tom Rees's grave was printed in the *Illustrated Sunday News* in December 1917, showing it bedecked with flowers from the enemy. A full seventeen years later, the Rees family were forwarded a letter from an Ernst Beichter of Württemberg in Germany, containing a similar photograph and a letter:

> After many years I decided to send this snapshot of the grave of the late Captain Tom Rees to his relatives. I shall be only too pleased to give you any particulars you might wish to know about his death. I was detailed for the funeral service, which was carried out in a very impressive manner, from the snapshot you see how many tokens of respect were offered.[21]

The family had suffered a double tragedy in 1916: news of Rees's death reached them on the day they buried his brother. A persistent story exists that David John Rees was killed by lightning – the truth was more prosaic but equally distressing; his death occurred due to an accident whilst he was helping his father fell a tree on the farm. They had miscalculated which way the branches would fall and David John was fatally injured when one of them struck him on the head.[22] In the small Congregational chapel of Sardis in the Cwmcamlais valley near the old Rees family home at Cefn Brynich, a memorial chair with a simple inscription commemorates the brothers.

*

Remembrances of Lionel Morris himself were mostly confined to his immediate family for many years. Whitgift and Croydon included him in their Rolls of Honour, and he is in the long list of names of officers lost in action in the official history of the Inns of Court's OTC. Carshalton, where he lived for only a short time, omitted him from the War Memorial. Tracking war dead after the conflict was a complicated business, often dependent on the active cooperation of the families of the lost men, some of whom may have found the enquiries too painful. Mistakes of attribution were made in Morris's case: Cranleigh School in Surrey compiled a Roll of Honour in 1921 and again in 1949 which listed him; his name is also inscribed in a memorial panel at the school, where the error was only discovered as late as 2016. Another Queen's Royal West Surrey officer, Francis Morris, is still pictured alongside the entry on an old webpage.[23] Richmond, to where Morris's parents moved after the war, has a memorial with a 'B. Morris' – but this also seems to have been a mistake, as the only casualty from the town officially recorded was a soldier called Bob Morris.[24]

These anomalies may have arisen when Morris's story became more widely known in the 1920s, thanks to the interest in the man who shot him down. Richthofen's success whilst he was alive brought him native fame which was eagerly exploited: James McCudden wrote of hearing on German radio that the victory tally of the greatest enemy ace had struck sixty.[25] By the end of April 1918 Richthofen had fallen, and by the time his pallbearers had staggered over the mounds of excavated chalk to deposit his coffin in the earth, the mythologising was well underway. The funeral provided a public opportunity for a magnanimous and respectful response from the Allies: in more private settings the German's aeroplane and clothing had already been comprehensively looted.

In 1927 Gibbons's biography of Richthofen identified Morris publicly as the Red Baron's first victim.[26] Richthofen remains a divisive figure – one man's war hero is another man's unfeeling killer, particularly in Germany, where his autobiography was distorted by propaganda and he was enthusiastically appropriated by the Nazis. On the winning side of the war, the British allowed themselves the favour of cultural superiority on an individual scale, contrasting the homely horticultural pursuits of Albert Ball with the game-bagging, gun-wielding Richthofen. The comparison worked even down to the aircraft – Richthofen's all-scarlet machine was a vulgar display of contempt, while the cheeky red nose of Ball's aircraft was modestly appealing. British fascination with the German kept his memory alive: Richthofen too was a victim of the war and had got his just desserts. The Allies could afford to remember him in a nostalgic way, in keeping with the 'chivalrous' paradigm of the air war. Barely a memoir was written by an old aviator that did not tell of an encounter with the Red Baron. To have met the Richthofen Flying Circus in the skies was a badge of honour that many claimed, in the same tradition that allows most of the oldest oak trees in England to have hosted Charles II on the run. The legend became bigger than the sum of its parts, fighting on, as the famous saying popularly attributed to Richthofen goes, 'to the last drop of blood, to the last drop of fuel.' Even this sanguinary quote can be understood in two different ways, depending on your view – as a reinforcement of the cold-blooded Prussian officer, or (as the full quote, finishing: 'a toast for his fellows, friend and foe' and its context is revealed in Floyd Gibbons's book) as a tribute to two British airmen who had fallen victim to *Jasta* 2.[27] Like all good legends, Richthofen's gathered conspiracy theories: his biographer Peter Kilduff unearthed a 1932 article in a German magazine which claimed the Red Baron had survived his final crash and was then stabbed to death by vengeful British troops.[28]

But as Richthofen's fame grew, Morris disappeared in his own family history. It wasn't a glorious legacy for his parents; grief led to silence and an understandable reluctance to talk about the dead. Compounding this in Albert and Lil's case was the fact that Morris had been their only child – there were few family members of his own generation to keep his memory alive. Albert and Lil chose to return to Weymouth in retirement, where Albert died in 1935. Within a few years, Lil's other closest family members had also died – her brother William succumbing to tuberculosis in 1938 and the much-married Nellie dying in a mental asylum in Essex in 1939.[29]

One link with the past was alive – William had named his second son in remembrance of his dead nephew. In 1934, at the age of fifteen, Lionel Reid joined the Royal Air Force as one of Trenchard's Brats – one of a generation of boys apprenticed to become highly trained aircraft fitters. When war came again in 1939, Reid went to Finland in mysterious circumstances. He was asked to resign from the Air Force and work in a team of four civilian technicians on Hurricane fighters that the Finns had bought from Britain: aircraft that were needed to hold off the Soviet invasion that kicked off the Winter War between the two nations. Britain's negotiations for an alliance with the USSR made it an unpropitious time to be helping the Finns and secrecy was vital. The economic benefit of the Hurricane sale was compromised when the buyers insisted on having trained ground crew to look after them. Two years of high adventure followed: in April 1940 Reid and his 'civilian' colleagues left Helsinki to avoid the advancing Soviets (as well as the Nazis) who were approaching through Norway and Denmark. Flying to neutral Sweden, an encounter with bungling secret agents, attempting to blow up Swedish iron ore destined for Germany, led to the group's arrest and internment for the summer. On arrival back in Britain, Reid rejoined the RAF and then retrained as a pilot in Canada. Echoes of his Morris cousin came in the legend recorded in the family of a bare eight hours tuition in the air before he took his first solo in a de Havilland Tiger Moth in October 1942.[30]

Whilst Lionel Reid continued the family link with the air force that had begun in 1915 (including a brief spell with Ball's old squadron, No. 56, and a distinguished career as a VIP pilot, ferrying the Royal Family on many occasions) his widowed Aunt Lil soldiered on until the late forties. Her great-nephew Michael Reid remembers her as a formidable woman with a no-nonsense attitude and an embarrassing habit of marching to the top of the ration queue – for no other reason than a sense of entitlement. No one else recognised her self-appointed privilege, and she was usually sent back to the end, spluttering with indignation as she went. Lionel Reid, together with Michael's father Alec, had looked out for their mother (also named Lily) when William died, and decided to buy her an expensive flat in Richmond, Surrey. Too expensive, in fact, for their combined financial efforts. Lily Reid was persuaded, reluctantly, to invite her sister-in-law Lil Morris to share the cost and move in with her. Other family members recall the gentle Lily Reid's role was as a housekeeper in all but name to Lil Morris.

Until her death at the age of eighty in 1949, the subject of Lil's dead son was taboo. Michael Reid recalls her intimidating presence in the late forties: 'Lil was a difficult character, no time for little boys. I used to sneak into her room – she had some kind of plaque on her desk with

"The Red Baron" written on it. I knew of the Red Baron of course, but nobody ever talked about Lionel.'[31] Despite the conscientious efforts of her Reid nephews to keep her in the manner to which she was accustomed, Lil turned to the family of her sister Nellie in her final wishes, giving the responsibility of executing her will to Nellie's son Terence Spurling, and leaving him the few items associated with her son that still existed.[32]

Those items gradually left the family. In 1951, Spurling wrote to a Mr Vosper in a letter kept today with Morris's diary, at the RAF Museum:

> Further to our conversation this morning, I hope the enclosed are of interest to you. The diary is of my cousin and when shot down he was only some nineteen years of age. These came into my possession as Executor of my late aunt's estate. Naturally, publicity is not desirable in the accepted sense of the word. But no doubt they will be of general interest to you as museum pieces.[33]

With all members of Morris's immediate family now dead, and Spurling himself barely a toddler when his cousin died in 1916, the desire for discretion over publicity didn't come from an intense and present grief. Morris's extended family were separated from Albert and Lil's intimate loss: Spurling's actions in passing on the diary marked the progress made towards 'second order memory' as well as his awareness that the items held a certain historical *cachet*.[34]

The notebook diary and accompanying letter stayed in the archives of the RAF Museum, and for well over sixty years Morris was little known to all but a small group of aviation historians and enthusiasts. By 2013, no one in his own remaining family knew or remembered much about him.

# Epilogue

In late 2013 I began looking for Lionel Morris. My father Michael's war-time memories of his aunt Lil led to some half-hearted Googling around the name of Manfred von Richthofen. I found short biographical details of Morris in Mike O'Connor's book *Airfields and Airmen: Cambrai*, which mentioned he had been educated at Whitgift, and I contacted the school's archivist, William Wood. Morris's story was unknown to Whitgift, and I passed on to them the basic information I had gathered. Not long afterwards, the Headmaster Dr Christopher Barnett (now retired) invited me to the school to tell me about a First World War exhibition they were planning for the spring of 2016 and told me of their plans to include Lionel Morris.

As an old boy, his story, placed at the heart of the exhibition, held a poignancy as well as a historical interest that touched thousands of visitors when 'Remembering 1916' opened; and the connection with Richthofen resulted in a surprising amount of publicity. The exhibition gave Morris a modest kind of fame and demonstrated the compelling conjunction of world and family history. Whitgift organised a dinner to commemorate the centenary of the events of 17 September, inviting myself, Rees's great niece Dr Meriel Jones (whom I had been able to track down via the internet), and Donat von Richthofen, as well as others who had worked on or helped with the exhibition. There was attention from the national press, including articles in the *Times*, *Telegraph*, *Express*, the BBC News website, and a piece on the *Today* programme on Radio Four. Later that evening, when the Headmaster asked us to drink a toast (in copies of the first victory cup specially commissioned by the school) to 'Lionel, Tom and Manfred', his choice of first names for such distant figures was both slightly awkward and yet appropriate. The Red Baron of such robust legend was remembered by all of us as simply a young man taken by the war, still mourned (like his first victims) by his family.

It was these quiet and personal moments of reflection and discovery, coming about thanks to the exhibition, that were the most moving. Morris was the catalyst for the first reunion in twenty-five years of three generations of his Reid family, gathering at Whitgift to 'meet' the cousin who had been forgotten. In August 2016, militaria collector Phil Evans visited Whitgift and revealed to exhibition staff that he owned a set of Morris's original wings, as well as his two posthumous medals – the Victory Medal, with its appropriate representation of Winged Victory, and the British War Medal. Evans had bought the items in 1986 from a military dealer Jeremy Tenniswood, who remembered little about their provenance, bar the fact that they had come from a house sale in Sutton, Surrey. The medals were issued in their millions to servicemen who had taken part in the Great War, and although both they and the wings were in good condition, they were not in themselves rarities. But on the back of the mounted photograph of Morris that accompanied the wings, there had been a note, 'Shot down by Richthofen', which intrigued Evans. Realising that the items were of historical significance, he did some homework, checking for Morris on the Army lists and reading up on the RFC. Thirteen years later, the family of Tom Rees decided to sell his medals and they had been bought by a bidder who remains anonymous, for £4,500. Subsequently it appears that the medals went missing when their new owner's house was burgled. We were glad to learn Lionel Morris's wings and medals not only still existed, (as so few physical items that link us to him do) but were in safe and respectful hands.

\*

Lionel Morris spent just ten months with the Royal Flying Corps. His ill-timed cameo in Richthofen's rise has leant him a curious distinction in the century since his death. Although his flying was skilful enough to keep him alive longer than many, it was not exceptional and there were no medals for gallantry or tallies of victories that distinguished him. And yet his footnoted exit from the war said nothing of how close he had been to so many defining moments of the air service – the creation of London's defences against airborne attack for the first time in the nation's history, the development of the use of aerial bombing as a strategic war-winning tool, and the beginning of the specialisation of fighter squadrons.

Morris's coming of age in the summer of 1916 also put him in the epicentre of a battle which provided a new measurement for the horrors of war, not just in its awful consequences, but in the judgement of its martials. No ground was ever so incessantly raked over. The initial disasters spoke for themselves: political and military sensitivities thwarted harmonious planning, and an over-reliance on an ineffective bombardment led to the survival of too many Germans in deep dugouts. Communications were lethally chaotic and security carelessly compromised. Above all, the colossal and incomprehensible numbers of the dead replay as an inescapable historical penumbra (often without nuance or analysis), suggesting clear markers for a final damnation of the generals. Despite the careful efforts of historians like Gary Sheffield and William Philpott to show us the unique difficulties of the campaign, the notorious mud of the Somme has shown a persistent ability to stick to the reputations of Haig and his colleagues, who have been only partially forgiven. Many have argued that the slaughter was necessary, allowing the Allies to learn the lessons that eventually led to victory, but retellings of First World War stories in popular culture echoed the concentration on tragedy and grief that was shared by the writers and the artists. They still touch raw nerves today for anyone with an ancestor like Lionel Morris. The RFC's losses were horrifying, and the controversy surrounding Trenchard's determination to press on regardless will, and should, (as a responsibility of civilised nations is to question the methodology of war) continue. The doctrine of offensive airpower, codified in *Future Policy in the Air* (described by Dr David Jordan of King's College London as a 'blunt, unsophisticated instrument' that nonetheless 'did its job') laid down the Royal Air Force's function for the Second World War.[1]

Recent historiography has moved away from an emphasis on the aces and the intimate details of each aircraft, and the study of how the RFC developed as a whole is now being addressed more effectively.[2] But the stories of young men like Morris continue to cast a powerful spell today. It is easy to revere them, but less easy to understand their unquestioning bravery and dedication, and to enter, albeit vicariously, into their world is still a strange experience. Why it is such an affecting leap of empathy is also difficult to explain without descending into *schadenfreude*, or sentimentality. There was little romance about the way they fought and died, or about the risks they took flying in such primitive machines with so little margin for error. The state of war creates uniquely tender moments for men amongst men, and for the those born under Victorian rule, the adjustment to peace-time sometimes created a questionable nostalgia, as one RFC survivor insisted: 'When you get peace, every rotten little man is out for his own.'[3]

But recognising the novelty of the air war, the camaraderie and the joy those men took in the 'great vacancy of the skies'[4] is a less complicated way of relating to those lives so far and yet so near to us. It is only a century away, a blink in historical terms, but one in which the world has transformed itself so utterly that 1916 will always remain unknown to us. Powered flight, that most extraordinary of modern phenomena, was driven through the technological crossroads of the First World War and developed in ways that few could have imagined, in an astonishingly short period of time. The narratives of men like Morris also provide an alternative to the overwhelming sadness and horror that other more well-known versions of the war, particularly in the trenches, bring. We will always be drawn to heroes and measurably great achievements. But it is the quietly diligent, and occasionally circumspect existences that most of us can relate to.

Lionel Morris had something of both lives.

# Acknowledgements

The story of *Lionel Morris and the Red Baron* would never have been unearthed had it not been for the inspiration of Whitgift School in Croydon. Their conviction that Morris's story was worth bringing to a wider audience has inspired me and changed my life. My first thanks must go to Headmaster Dr Christopher Barnett, (now retired), whose immediate and passionate interest in my first cousin twice-removed not only took me aback, but gave me the nudge I needed to take my family history to another level. The school's archivist, William Wood, became a mischievous correspondent with a good line in This Is Your (Cousin's) Life moments of discovery, and remains on perpetual standby for undiscovered gems. I'd like to thank *Remembering 1916*'s researcher, Zapryan Dumbalski, for his work in discovering Lieutenant Porter's proximity to Morris at Porte-de-Paris, as well as alerting me to Richthofen's connection with Colonel Barber. Lionel Morris has made me many friends in unexpected areas: Meriel Jones, Tom Rees's great-niece, has shared so many of her family's memories and mementoes with me and I'm particularly happy that Morris and Rees's friendship continues to inspire ours.

James F. Miller, whose book *FE 2b/d vs Albatros Scouts: Western Front 1916–17* was a discovery that opened many doors. Jim's generous help and consistently entertaining emails have sustained me for several years now, and without him and Greg VanWyngarden, this would probably be a book without pictures. Andy Arnold, whose work on Carshalton's war dead piqued my curiosity, is also a positive spirit who helped me put the word out that the book was on its way. Trevor Henshaw has been an amazing mentor. Trevor's encyclopedic knowledge of, and love for, early aviation history makes his book *The Sky Their Battlefield II* something of a sacred text in the field. I am privileged to have had his tireless help. Nothing has been too much trouble for him, and his encouragement and attention to detail was crucial in enabling me to get past the awkward stage of the first draft.

Hubert Heintz, Caroline Podgorsek and Laurent Grislain in France gave me a unique and unforgettable opportunity to walk in Morris's footsteps. The afternoon I spent with them in the fields and farmyards of Artois gave me local knowledge that I could not have hoped to get from a hundred books, as well as transport when a train strike threatened to jeopardise the *raison d'etre* of my trip.

The Great War Forum (www.1914-1918.invisionzone.com) is an online community of dedicated historians, amateur and professional: I could not have come close to doing Morris's story justice without them. Mike Meech in particular took great pains to answer my obscure questions, and Graham Neale helped me wade through the many combat reports for 22 August 1916 to make sense of them. Harry Brook found me some of Captain Gray's *Gazette* appearances, and Andrew Pentland's website www.airhistory.co.uk is a treasure trove of fully-sourced detail that is invaluable to anyone interested in tracing RFC members. I have benefitted from the help of all of the following: the National Archives, Sutton Archives, Inspire Nottingham Archives, the Research Room at the Imperial War Museum, the Museum of Croydon, Tates Lisoire, Annette Carson, Peter Stone, Heather Godwin, Antony Wyatt, Daryl Moran, Caulfield Grammar School in Melbourne, Phil Evans, Vanda and Gordon Day, Andrew Dawrant of the Royal Aero Club Trust, Neal Bascomb, Sarah Hobhouse, and Jane Gray.

Any first-time biographer takes a crash course in copyright regulations and many of the sources I have used have very opaque origins. Every effort has been made to trace copyright holders: please contact the publishers for any inadvertant omissions or errors. When enquiries about terms of use go unanswered, I have assumed that there is no objection to such material being used.

Excerpts from Lionel Morris's diary are courtesy of the RAF Museum, Hendon; I have made some very minor changes to the diary for the sake of consistency and clarity. Many thanks to Gordon Leith and Nina Hadaway at the Museum and to Lord Trenchard for allowing me to quote from the Trenchard Papers. Excerpts from Albert Ball's letters are courtesy of Inspire Nottingham Archives, and Lyle Buntine's letters are courtesy of Caulfield Grammar School Archives and The Walter Murray Buntine Collection (Headmaster Caulfield Grammar 1896–1931). Excerpts from Frederick Libby's *Horses Don't Fly* are courtesy of Arcade Publishing, an imprint of Skyhorse Publishing, Inc., and those from Peter Hart's *Somme Success: The Royal Flying Corps and The Battle of the Somme* are courtesy of Pen and Sword. Extracts from *The Red Air Fighter* by Manfred von Richthofen are also courtesy of Pen and Sword and Greenhill Books.

For indispensable hospitality and transport, gratitude and love to Carole McLaughlin and Helen and Will Green. Without Gordon Brown's help, many of the research trips I undertook would not have been possible. Rachel Gosling spent precious hours away from her own work to teach me how to use social media without self-loathing. Chris and Liz Rolfe are my literary rocks, providing enthusiasm, levity, essential critical analysis and pointing out the evils of flamboyant adjectives. At Pen and Sword, my thanks to Claire Hopkins, Lori Jones and Janet Brookes.

Finally, to my family, all my love to all of you.

Jill Bush
Seaford, East Sussex
June 2018

# Notes

## Introduction

1. Philpott, William, *Bloody Victory*. p.218 (London: Abacus 2009).

## Chapter 1: South to North End

1. England & Wales Civil Registration Birth Index 1837–1915.

2. UK Royal Navy Registers of Seamen's Services 1853–1928.

3. Census Returns of England and Wales 1881.

4. The National Archives, (TNA) J 77/2161/7682 & J 77/880/6717, Divorce Court Files. See also England Select Dorset Church of England Registers 1538–1999.

5. General Register Office Birth Certificate.

6. England Select Dorset Church of England Registers 1538–1999.

7. National Schools Admission Registers and Log-Books 1870–1914.

8. Ibid.

9. Whitgift School admissions records.

10. Whitgift Foundation Schools Committee Meeting Minutes 29 July 1897.

11. Ibid.

12. 1911 England and Wales Census.

13. Percy, F.H.G., *Whitgift School A History*. p.174 (Croydon: The Whitgift Foundation 1991).

14. Ibid.

15. Ibid.

16. Kipling, Rudyard, *The Complete Stalky and Co.* p.187 (Oxford University Press 1999).

17. *The Whitgiftian*, December 1911.

18. Whitgift School admissions records.

19. 1911 England and Wales Census.

20. Moore, Henry Keatley Sayers, *Croydon and the Great War: The Official History of the War Work of the Borough and its Citizens from 1914 to 1919, Together with the Croydon Roll of Honour.* p.152 (Croydon: 1920).

21. Malden, H.E., *The Victoria History of the County of Surrey: Volume 4.* p.178–88 (London: 1912).

22. Ibid.

23. *Piles Directory*, Carshalton: 1915.

24. www.database.theatrestrust.org.uk/resources/theatres/show/3108-the-cryer

25. Arnold, Andrew, *Their Name Liveth For Evermore.* p.22 (Stroud: The History Press 2014). See also: Sutton School Magazine, Autumn Term 1914 www.worldwar1schoolarchives.org/wpcontent/uploads/2013/09/1914_Autumn1.pdf

26. Moore, op.cit. p.27.

27. Ibid.

## Chapter 2: Goodbye, Good Luck, God Bless You

1. Moore, op.cit. p.26.

2. Arnold, op.cit. pp.36–7.

3. *Daily Sketch,* 13 May 1915.

4. *Croydon Times,* 15 May 1915 and 19 May 1915.

5. *Essex Newsman,* 15 May 1915.

6. Errington, Colonel Francis Launcelot, *The Inns of Court Officers Training Corps During The Great War.* p.20 (London: Printing Craft 1922).

7. Campbell, Baron John, *The Lives of the Lord Chancellors and Keepers of the Great Seal of England: From the Earliest Times Till the Reign of King George IV. Vol. 6.* p.547 (London: John Murray 1846).

8. Spiers, Edward M., *University Officers' Training Corps and the First World War.* p.12 (Reading: Council of Military Education Committees Occasional Paper No.4 2014).

9. Errington, op.cit. pp.21–22.

10. TNA, WO 339/39180, Second Lieutenant Lionel Bertram Frank Morris Royal Flying Corps.

11. Errington, op.cit. p.24.

12. Ibid. p.62.

13. Ibid. p.15.

14. Ibid. p. 22–23.

15. *The Whitgiftian* Vol 33 No 3. June 1915. p.99.

16. Errington, op.cit. Appendix II. p.263.

17. Letter from Second Lieutenant O.C. Pearson 70 Squadron 10 October 1916. https://www.flickr.com/photos/29051501@N08/3009509809/in/photostream/

18. Errington, op.cit. p.25.

19. Wynne, Lieutenant T.S., Quoted in Macdonald, Lynn, *1916 The Death of Innocence.* p.165 (London: Penguin 1987).

20. Errington, op.cit. p.23.

21. TNA, WO 339/39180, Statement of Services.

22. Errington, op.cit. p.23. See also Messenger, Charles, *Call to Arms: The British Army 1914–18*. p.306 (London: Cassell 2005).

23. Errington, op.cit. p.61.

24. Ibid. p.51.

25. Ibid.

26. Ibid. p.17.

27. Ibid. p.50.

28. TNA, WO 339/39180, Application for Appointment to a Temporary Commision, 14 August 1915.

29. *London Gazette,* Supplement 19 August 1915.

## Chapter 3: The Mutton Lancers

1. www.queensroyalsurreys.org.uk/new_music/02.shtml

2. Ibid.

3. www.queensroyalsurreys.org.uk/1661to1966/ww1queens/ww1queens. shtml

4. Imperial War Museum (IWM), 19, Private Papers of Lieutenant D. S. C. Macaskie Special Reserve Certificate October 1915.

5. Regular, Harrison *Customs of the Army: Guide for Cadets and Young Officers 1917*. Quoted in Beckett, Ian T.W, Simpson, Keith, Keegan, John, *A Nation in Arms: A Social Study of the British Army in the First World War*. p.77 (Barnsley: Pen and Sword 2014).

6. TNA, WO 339/39180, Appointment of Commission Instruction Letter from War Office, 19 August 1915.

7. Wylly, Col. C.B. *History of the Queen's Royal Regiment*. p.281 (Uckfield: Naval and Military Press 2009).

8. Moore, op.cit. p.30.

9. Ibid. p.31.

10. *Flight*, 2 July 1915.

11. Moore, op.cit. p.34.

12. Ibid. p.39.

13. White, Jerry, *Zeppelin Nights*. p.159 (London: Vintage 2015).

14. TNA, WO 339/39180, Appointment of Commission Instruction Letter from War Office, 19 August 1915.

15. Macdonald, op.cit. p.155.

16. TNA, WO 339/39180, Letter from L.B.F. Morris to Adjutant, 3rd Queens, 24 September 1915.

17. Ibid. Medical Certificate 24 September 1915.

18. Ibid.

19. Ibid. Letter from L.B.F. Morris to Adjutant, 3rd Queens, 24 September 1915.

20. Mackersey, Ian, *No Empty Chairs*. p.62 (London: Phoenix 2012).

21. *Flight*, 23 May 1916.

22. TNA, WO 339/39180, Appointment of Commission Instruction Letter from War Office, 19 August 1915.

23. *The Whitgiftian* noted on 5 November 1915 that 2nd Lieutenant L.B.F. Morris had been appointed to the 3rd Battalion Queen's Royal West Surrey, noting only much later, in his obituary, that he was 'transferred immediately' to the Royal Flying Corps.

## Chapter 4: This Flying Business

1. Miller, Russell, *Boom: The Life of Viscount Trenchard*. p.92 (London: Weidenfeld and Nicolson 2016).

2. Trenchard Family Archive. Quoted in Miller, op.cit. p.108.

3. Baring, Maurice, *Flying Corps Headquarters 1914–1918*. p.86 (London: Endeavour Press: 2016).

4. Sheffield, Gary, *The Chief: Douglas Haig and the British Army*. p.151 (London: Aurum Press 2011).

5. *Flight*, 16 January 1916.

6. MacDonagh, Michael, *In London During the Great War: The Diary Of A Journalist*. Quoted in White, Jerry, *Zeppelin Nights: London In the First World War*. p.112 (London: Vintage 2014).

7. Boyle, Andrew, *Trenchard: Man of Vision*. p.109 (London: Collins 1962).

8. TNA, AIR 1/997/204/5/1241, Training of Pilots and Observers, 27 January 1915.

9. Jefford, C.G., *Observers and Navigators: And Other Non-pilot Aircrew in the RFC, RNAS and RAF.* p.108 (London: Weidenfeld and Nicolson 2016).

10. Jefford, op.cit. p.44.

11. TNA, AIR 1/138/15/40/281/1a, Pilots and Observers under instruction at Home, 1 November 1915.

12. Ibid. 2b, 6 December 1915.

13. TNA, AIR 1/138/15/40/281, 20 March 1916.

14. Ibid. 18 March 1916.

15. Brew, Alec, *Boulton Paul Aircraft*. p.9 (Stroud: Tempus 2001).

16. Summary of email correspondence with Les Whitehouse, Boulton and Paul Association. Also: ffiske, W.H., *Boulton and Paul in the Great War*. p.43 (Norwich: Private Circulation 1919).

17. Summary of email correspondence with Les Whitehouse.

18. ffiske, op.cit. p.44.

19. Ibid.

20. *Flight*, 8 October 1915.

## Chapter 5: How To Fly A Plane and Other Horror Stories

1. Barker, Ralph, *A Brief History of the Royal Flying Corps in World War 1*. p.300 (London: Robinson 2002).

2. Pengelly, Colin, *Albert Ball V.C.* pp.27, 34–35 (Barnsley: Pen and Sword 2010).

3. Broad, Graham, Meech, Mike etc., *Thoughts on RFC Training Pt. 2*. The Aerodrome Forum 2015.

4. Morley, Robert, *Earning Their Wings: British Pilot Training, 1912–1918*. p.59 (Saskatoon: University of Saskatchewan 2006).

5. Barber, Captain, *How To Fly A Plane*. p.17 (Stroud: Amberley Publishing 2014).

6. Brinkworth. B. J., *On the Early History of Spinning and Spin Research in the UK Part 1: The period 1909–1929*. p.109 *Journal of Aeronautical History Vol 3* 2014. Also: Morley, op.cit. p.88.

7. For a remarkable description of this saga, see Mackersey, Ian, *No Empty Chairs*. pp. 294–299 (London: Phoenix 2012).

8. Lewis, Cecil, *Sagittarius Rising*. p.22 (London: Corgi 1969).

9. Morley, op.cit. p.61.

10. Taylor, Sir Gordon, *Sopwith Scout 7309* (London: Cassell 1968). Quoted in Mackersey, pp. 74–75.

11. Insall, A.J., *Observer*. p.29 (London: Kimber 1970).

12. Mackersey, op.cit. p.75.

13. Skeet, Michael, *RFC Pilot Training*. p.7 (The Aerodrome Forum 1998).

14. Inspire Nottinghamshire Archives (INA), DD/1180/1/49/50, Captain Albert Ball, letter to Ball's parents, 3/6 November 1915.

15. Morley, op.cit. pp.73–75.

16. TNA, AIR 1/1007/204/5/1278, Miscellaneous correspondence on officers, 29 April 1916.

17. Morley, op.cit. pp.75–76.

18. Ibid.

19. *Learning to Fly at Montrose.* p.21 (Ian Macintosh Memorial Trust: Montrose).

20. TNA, AIR 1/997/204/5/241, Memo from Brigadier Ashmore, 13 April 1916.

21. Great Britain Royal Aero Club Aviator's Certificates 1910–1950.

22. Captain Lancelot Prickett, d. 2/6/1916, Acting F/Lt Louis Marcus Basil Weil Royal Naval Air Service, d. 6/4/1917 www. cwgc.org. Lieutenant Geoffrey Lancelot Railton, Royal Naval Air Service, d. 12/9/1916. England and Wales Death Registration Index 1837–2007, also www.hampshireairfields.co.uk/hancrash. html

23. TNA, AIR 76/358/186, Second Lieutenant L.B.F. Morris.

## Chapter 6: Bringing Down the Whales

1. London Screen Archives, *Topical Budget: Army Economy, Hounslow (1916)*, www.londonsscreenarchives.org.uk/public/ details.php?id=19861&searchId=.

2. Cobbett, William, *Vision of Britain Hampshire, Surrey, and Sussex 30 October 1822*, www.visionofbritain.org.uk/travellers/ Cobbett/10.

3. Kingsford, A.R., *Night Raiders of the Air*. p.50 (London: Greenhill 1958).

4. Jones, H.A., *The War in the Air: Being the Story of the Part Played in the Great War by the Royal Air Force Vol III*. p.161 (London: Clarendon Press 1931).

5.  Cole, Christopher, and Cheesman, E.F., *The Air Defence of Great Britain 1914–1918*. p.33 (London: Putnam 1984).

6.  *Hansard,* 6 June 1915.

7.  Jones, H.A., *The War in the Air: Being the Story of the Part Played in the Great War by the Royal Air Force Vol III*, pp.56–7. (London: Clarendon Press 1931).

8.  Castle, Ian, *The First Blitz: Bombing London in the First World War*. p 48 (Oxford: Osprey 2015).

9.  Cole and Cheesman, op.cit. p.37.

10.  Ibid. p.99.

11.  Ibid. p.85.

12.  Sturtivant Ray, Hamlin John and Halley, James J. *Royal Air Force Flying Training and Support Units*. p.298 (Tunbridge Wells: Air-Britain (Historians) Ltd 1997).

13.  Cole and Cheesman, op.cit. p.99.

14.  Ibid. p.85.

15.  Jones, op.cit. p.142. Also: *Yorkshire Times* 2 June 2014. www.yorkshirepost.co.uk/our-yorkshire/heritage/world-war-one/homefront/trawlerman-s-anguished-and-fateful-decision-revisited-1-6648391.

16.  Probert, Henry, *Bomber Harris: His Life and Times*. p.37 (London: Greenhill 2001).

17.  www.gracesguide.co.uk/1915_Aviators_Certificates_-_UK.

18.  Probert, op.cit. p.84.

19.  Cole and Cheeseman, op.cit. p.85.

20.  Letter to Lady Ottoline Morrell, 9 September 1915, quoted in Botting, Douglas, *Dr Eckener's Dream Machine*. p.77 (London: Harper Collins 2001).

21.  Sturtivant et al., p.298. Also Jones, op.cit. p.162.

22.  Saward, Dudley, *Bomber Harris*. p.13 (London: Cassel 1984).

23. Cole and Cheeseman, op.cit. p 45.

24. Ibid. p.96.

25. TNA AIR/1/512/16/3/65/9 2A, Formation of No. 18 Wing, RFC, Memo from Sefton Brancker, 17 March 1916.

26. Poolman, Kenneth, *Zeppelins Over England*. p.127 (London: White Lion Publishers 1975).

27. Morley, op.cit. p.60.

28. RAF Museum, DC71/29/1, Instructions for officers and NCOs joining 19 Reserve Squadron, Royal Flying Corps.

29. Ibid.

30. Cole and Cheesman, op.cit. p.78. See also Jones, op.cit. pp.177–178.

31. Cole and Cheesman, op.cit. p.78. See also *Hansard*, 16 February 1916.

32. www.iancastlezeppelin.co.uk/20-feb-1916/4589874370.

33. Jones, op.cit. p.164. See also Cole and Cheesman, op.cit. p.94.

34. TNA, AIR/1/512/16/3/65/9, Memo from Deputy Director of Military Aeronautics, 26 March 1916.

35. TNA, AIR 1/1799/204/156/7, Report of Pilots on Zeppelin Raid, Report of Lt. Col. Holt to Director of Military Aeronautics, 3 April 1916.

36. Ibid.

37. *The Times*, 3 April 1916.

38. Ibid.

39. TNA, AIR 1/1799/204/156/7.

## Chapter 7: A Torch in the London Night

1. *London Gazette*, 9 May 1915.

2. Cooksley, Peter, *The Royal Flying Corps 1914–1918*. p.32 (Stroud: History Press 2014).

3. Fry, William, *Air of Battle*. p.52 (London: William Kimber 1974).

4. *Flight*, 6 January 1916.

5. Hanson, Neil, *Escape from Germany*. p.209 (London: Corgi 2001).

6. RAF Museum, DC 73/662, Letter from Captain D.B. Gray to Albert Morris, 25 November 1916.

7. Cole and Cheesman, op.cit. p.94.

8. Jones, op.cit. p.164. Also TNA, AIR/1/512/16/3/65/9, Memo from Sefton Brancker 17 March 1916 and TNA, AIR 76/192/96, Gray, David B., and TNA, AIR 1/512/16/3/65 Formation of 18 Wing, Memo from Deputy Director of Military Aeronautics, 26 March 1916.

9. www.iancastlezeppelin.co.uk/1916-aprjul/4590788413.

10. Jones, op.cit. p.244

11. *Punch* quoted in *Flight*, 16 January 1916. p.44.

12. Poolman, op.cit. p.136.

13. Saward, op.cit. p.15.

14. Probert, op.cit. p.38. See also Rimmell, Raymond Laurence, *The Airship V.C. The Life of William Leefe Robinson*. p.50 (Bourne End: Aston 1918).

15. Letter from William Leefe Robinson to his mother, 6 February 1916. Quoted in Rimmell, op.cit. p.38.

16. Letter from William Leefe Robinson to his mother, 21 October 1915. Quoted in Rimmell, op.cit. p.34.

17. *Flight*, 16 January 1916.

18. Jones, op.cit. p.172.

19. Rimmell, op.cit. p.43. Also Cole and Cheesman, op.cit. p.100.

20. Winter, Denis, *The First of the Few*. p.87–8 (London: Allen Lane 1982).

21. Cole and Cheesman, op.cit. pp.88–89.

22. Ibid. pp.127–132. Also www.iancastlezeppelin.co.uk/2425-apr-1916/4590788860. Mrs Fanny Gaze, 79, died of heart failure when nearly fifty bombs landed near her house.

23. Jones, op.cit. pp.203–5. Also: Poolman, op.cit. p.142 and Rimmell, op.cit. p.52.

24. Rimmell, op.cit. pp.52–53.

25. Ibid. p.52.

26. Poolman, op.cit. p.32.

27. Ibid. p.34. See also Rimmell, op.cit. p.53.

28. IWM, Sound Catalogue 24, Archibald William Henry James.

29. Cole and Cheesman, op.cit. p.105.

30. Jones, op.cit. p.167.

31. INA, DD1180/2/29, letter to Ball's brother and sister. The letter may have been written over two days, from May 16 to 17 1916.

32. RAF Museum, DC73/66/1, Notebook of Second Lieutenant L.B.F. Morris.

## Chapter 8: Field Notes from France

1. RAF Museum, DC73/66/1, 18 May 1916.

2. Ibid. 19 May 1916.

3. Shores, Christopher, Norman Franks and Russell Guest, *Above The Trenches: A Complete Record of the Fighter Aces and Units of the British Empire Air Forces 1915–1920.* p.30 (London: Grub Street, 1990).

4. Jones, H., *The War in the Air Vol. III.* p.162. Also Bradbeer, Thomas G., *The Battle for Air Supremacy over the Somme 1 June–30 November 1916.* p.171. Thesis (University of Akron: 2004).

5. TNA, AIR 1/166/15/150/1/1, History of 11 Squadron. p.1. Also TNA, AIR 27/161. Squadron Number: 11 Appendix 1. p. 291.

6. Insall, op.cit. p.106.

7. Bowyer, Chaz, *Albert Ball VC* p.56. (London: William Kimber, 1977).

8. Fry, p.91.

9. Heintz, Hubert, *Sous Le Ciel de Savy 1914–1918* (Chroniqueurs de l'Atrébatie, 2015).

10. Caulfield Grammar School (CGS), Lyle Buntine Archive, letter to his parents, August 1916.

11. www.britishmuseum.org/research/search_the_collection_database/term_details.aspx?bioId=169577.

12. Insall, A.J., 'Cameos of the Air VIII – A.B.' p.204. *Air,* May 1929.

13. Insall, *Observer.* p.113.

14. Ibid. p.114.

15. McCudden, Major James, *Flying Fury: Five Years in the Royal Flying Corps.* p.54–5. (Folkestone: Bailey Brothers and Swinfen 1973).

16. Jones, op.cit. pp.85–6.

17. RAF Museum, DC73/66/1, 19 May 1916.

18. CGS, Lyle Buntine Archive, letter to his parents, August 1916.

19. Insall, *Observer.* p.115.

20. INA, DD/1180/2/29, letter to Ball's parents, 31 May 1916.

21. Ibid. 13 May 1916.

22. RAF Museum, DC73/66/1, 19 May 1916.

23. RAF Museum, X007–2247, Album of the service of Major E. L. Foot.

24. Insall, *Observer.* p.113.

25. Fry, op.cit. pp.105–6.

26. TNA, AIR 27/161, Squadron Number: 11 Appendices: Y. p.296.

27. RAF Museum, DC73/66/1, 20 May 1916.

28. Insall, *Observer.* p.58.

29. Lewis, op.cit. p.51.

30. IWM, 19, Private Papers of Lieutenant D.S.C. Macaskie, letter to his mother, 16 July 1916.

31. RAF Museum. DC73/66/1, 21 May 1916.

32. Ibid. 24 May 1916.

33. INA, DD/1180/2/32, letter to Ball's parents, 24 May 1916. Also RAF Museum, DC73/66/1, 21 May 1916.

34. RAF Museum. DC73/66/1. 25 May 1916.

35. Ibid. 27 May 1916.

36. Ibid.

37. Ibid. 28 May 1916.

38. Ibid. 30 May 1916.

39. Ibid. 31 May 1916.

40. McCudden. p.235.

41. RAF Museum, DC 73/66/1, 31 May 1916.

42. Ibid.

43. Ibid.

44. The exact definition of a victory is still up for discussion, see Chapter 13. Also Briscoe, Walter A, and H. Russell Stannard, *Britain's Forgotten Fighter Ace: Captain Albert Ball VC* p.110 (Stroud: Amberley 2014).

45. RAF Museum, DC 73/661/1, 1 June 1916.

46. Ibid. 2 June 1916.

47. Insall, *Observer*. p.124.

48. *Flying the FE2b* www.thevintageaviator.co.nz/projects/fe-2b/flying-fe-2b.

49. Miller, James F., *FE2b/d vs Albatros Scouts: Western Front 1916–17*. p.25 (Oxford: Osprey 2014).

50. Henshaw, Trevor, *11 Squadron History* (unpublished).

51. Jones, Vol.II. p.196. Also TNA, AIR 27/161. p.299.

52. RAF Museum, DC 73/66/1, 3 June 1916. Morris was flying Vickers FB5 5474.

53. Jones, Vol.II. p.161.

## Chapter 9: Waiting For A Scrap

1. RAF Museum, DC 73/66/1, 26 May 1916.

2. Hart, Peter, *The Somme*. p.74 (London: Weidenfeld and Nicolson 2005).

3. Davis, Richard Harding, *With the French in France and Salonika*. p.44. (New York: Charles Scribner's Sons 1916). www.gutenberg.org/files/30812/30812-h/30812-h.htm.

4. RAF Museum, DC 73/66/1, 3 June 1916.

5. Ibid.

6. Jones, Vol III. pp.188–9.

7. Doyle, Peter, *Disputed Earth: Geology and Trench Warfare on the Western Front 1914–1918*. p.90 (London: Unicorn 2017).

8. *Flight*, 21 November 1916.

9. RAF Museum, DC 73/66/1, 4 June 1916.

10. IWM, Private Papers of Lieutenant Donald Macaskie, letter to Mrs Macaskie 20 July 1916.

11. RAF Museum, DC 73/66/1, 7 June 1916.

12. Ibid.

13. RAF Museum, DC 73/66/1, 8 June 1916.

14. Ibid. 9 June 1916.

15. Ibid. 12 June 1916.

16. Ibid.

17. Ibid.

18. Macmillan, Norman, *Into the Blue*. p.109 (London: Grub Street 2015).

19. RAF Museum, DC 73/66/1, 13 June 1916.

20. Ibid. 14 June 1916.

21. Ibid. 15 June 1916.

22. Ibid. 16 June 1916.

23. Gibbs, Philip, *The Battle of the Somme*. p.27 (Toronto: McClelland, Goodchild and Stewart 1917).

24. RAF Museum, DC 73/66/1, 16 June 1916.

25. TNA, AIR 1/844/204/5/371, Reports of Aeroplane and Personnel Casualties June 1916, 16 June 1916. Lieutenant Gibson was in Bristol Scout 5312.

26. RAF Museum, DC 73/66/1, 16 June 1916.

27. www.airhistory.org.uk/.

28. Cole, op.cit. p.161.

29. RAF Museum, DC 73/66/1, 17 June 1916.

30. Ibid.

31. Ibid. 18 June 1916.

32. Ibid. 19 June 1916.

33. Heintz, p.4. The chateau was destroyed by fire in 1976; only some outbuildings and parkland still remain.

34. RAF Museum, DC 73/66/1, 19 June 1916.

35. Ibid. 20 June 1916.

36. F. Ware to DGR&E, CWGC SDC 60/1 Box 2033. Quoted in Hodgkinson, Peter E. 'Clearing the Dead: The Clearance and Burial of the Remains of British Soldiers from the Great War Battlefields', *Journal of the Centre for First World War Studies 3.1 (2007) 33–60*. University of Birmingham.

37. Farndale, Martin, *History of the Royal Regiment of Artillery*. p.144. (Royal Artillery Institution 1986). Quoted in Bradbeer, op.cit. p.179.

38. Insall, *Observer*. p.88.

39. Farjeon, Eleanor, *Edward Thomas. The Last Four Years*. p.154. Oxford University Press 1958).

## Chapter 10: Up and Down in Paris

1. RAF Museum, DC 63/66/1, 23 June 1916.

2. Jones, Vol II. pp.206–7.

3. *New Zealand Herald*, 27 June 1916.

4. Insall, *Observer*. p.120.

5. Insall, *Cameos of the Air VIII – A.B.* p.205.

6. Ibid.

7. Malinovska, Anna, and Mauriel Joslyn, *Voices in Flight: Conversations with Air Veterans of the Great War*. Location 2352. Flight Sergeant Joseph Lang. (Barnsley: Pen and Sword 2000).

8. Insall, *Observer*. pp.120, 125.

9. RAF Museum, MFC 76/1/7, Trenchard to Brancker, 7 July 1916.

10. RAF Museum, C85/20, Recording of an interview with Mr Joseph Hellingoe.

11. RAF Museum, DC 63/66/1, 21 June 1916.

12. www.thevintageaviator.co.nz/projects/fe-2b/flying-fe-2b.

13. TNA, AIR 1/960/204/5/1043, Reports of RFC Manpower in France. Quoted in Dye, Peter. *Air Power's Midwife: Logistics Support for Royal Flying Corps Operations on the Western Front 1914–1918.* p.160. (University of Birmingham 2013).

14. www.thevintageaviator.co.nz/projects/fe-2b/flying-fe-2b.

15. www.airhistory.org.uk/rfc/aircraft.htm.

16. Holman, Brett, *The Imperial Aircraft Flotilla II*, 15 June 2014. www.airminded.org/2014/06/15/the-imperial-aircraft-flotilla-ii.

17. RAF Museum, DC 63/66/1, 22 June 1916.

18. Ibid.

19. *Daily Telegraph*, 22 June 1916.

20. RAF Museum, DC 73/66/1, 24 June 1916.

21. England and Wales Census 1901

22. RAF Museum, DC 73/66/1, 24 June 1916.

23. Lewis, op.cit. p.59. Also: McCudden, op.cit. p.62.

24. Mitchell, T.J. and Smith, G.M., *Medical Services: Casualties and Medical Statistics of the Great War, History of the Great War, Based on Official Documents.* (London: HMSO 1931). Quoted in Marshall, Richard. *The British Army's Fight against Venereal Disease in the 'Heroic Age of Prostitution'.* ww1centenary.oucs.ox.ac.uk.

25. Hart, Peter, *The Somme.* p.21.

26. Philpott, William, *Bloody Victory: The Sacrifice on the Somme.* op.cit. p.108. (London: Abacus 2009).

27. Fenwick, Jolyon, *Zero Hour. 100 Years On: Views from the Parapet.* p.7. (London: Profile 2016).

28. TNA, AIR 27/161. p.299.

29. RAF Museum, DC 73/66/1, 25 June 1916.

30. RAF Museum, C85/20.

31. Malinovska and Joslyn, op.cit. Location 2358. Ball's biographer Chaz Bowyer says it had been Ball's second attempt that day. Bowyer, op.cit. p.59.

32. Bowyer, op.cit. p.59.

33. Ibid.

34. Due to the weather, 26 June turned out to be W Day – Z Day was 1 July 1916.

35. RAF Museum, DC 73/66/1, 26 June 1916

36. Ibid.

37. TNA, AIR 1/844/204/5/371, Reports on aeroplane and personnel casualties, 26 June 1916. Lietenant Gibson was in Nieuport Scout 5173.

38. RAF Museum, B1963, Log Book of Second Lieutenant G.N. Anderson, 1916–1917, 26 June 1916. Anderson was flying FE2b *Shangai* 6537.

39. INA, DD/1180/2/39, Captain Albert Ball, letter to his parents, 28 June 1916.

40. RAF Museum, DC 73/66/1, 26 June 1916.

41. Ibid. 27 June 1916.

42. Bowyer, op.cit. p.59.

43. Met Office, The, *Remember The Met Office in World War One and World War Two.* 2014. p.5. www.metoffice.gov.uk/media/pdf/r/q/Remember.pdf.

44. RAF Museum, DC 73/66/1, 29 June 1916.

45. TNA, AIR 1/844/204/5/371, 29 June 1916. Anderson and Bibby were in Vickers FB9 7827.

46. RAF Museum, DC 73/66/1, 29 June 1916.

47. Ibid. 30 June 1916.

48. Briscoe and Stannard, op.cit. p.188. Also Jones, Vol II. p.125.

49. Thornton, R.K.R., (ed.), *Ivor Gurney War Letters*. To Marion Scott. 1 July 1916. p.79. (London: Hogarth Press 1983).

50. Lewis, op.cit. p.76.

51. Arnold, Andrew, *Their Name Liveth For Evermore: Carshalton's First World War Roll of Honour*. p.68. (Stroud: The History Press 2014).

## Chapter 11: Z Day

1. RAF Museum, DC 73/66/1, 1 July 1916.

2. Ibid.

3. Ibid.

4. Ibid.

5. Ibid.

6. TNA, AIR 1/2246/209/42/31, Third Brigade War Diary, July 1916.

7. Shores, et al. op.cit. *Above the Trenches: A Complete Record of the Fighter Aces and Units of the British Empire Air Forces 1915–1920*. p.6–7 (London: Grub Street 1990).

8. Schroder, Hans, *An Airman Remembers*. Quoted in Hart, *Somme Success*. p.48.

9. Macdonald, Lynn, *Somme*. p.69 (London: Penguin 2013).

10. Private Arthur Schuman, London Rifle Regiment Memoirs. p. 4–5. Quoted in Hart, *The Somme*. p.130.

11. TNA, AIR 1/2245/209/42/29, 1 July 1916.

12. Shores, et.al. op.cit. p.15.

13. TNA, AIR 1/2245/209/42/29, 1 July 1916.

14.  RAF Museum, MFC 76/1, Trenchard to Brancker 2 July 1916.

15. INA, DD180/2/41, letter to Ball's mother, 1 July 1916.

16. Baring, op.cit. p.153.

17. Lewis, op.cit. p.78.

## Chapter 12: *Hors de Combat*

1. RAF Museum, DC 63/66/1, 2 July 1916.

2. TNA, AIR 1/844/204/5/372, Reports of Aeroplane and Personnel Casualties July 1916, 1 July 1916. Captain Murray and Second Lieutenant Wyatt were in FE2b 6946.

3. Ibid. 3 July 1916. Second Lieutenant Turk and Corporal Parks were in Vickers FB9 7828.

4. Ibid. 5 July 1916. Second Lieutenant Ferguson and Lieutenant Capel in FE2b 6963 landed safely on 5 July, but the machine was found to be so badly damaged that it was sent to Candas two days later.

5. Ibid. Captains Rough and Field were in FE2b 6945.

6. Ibid. 2 July 1916. Lieutenants Toone and Harvey were in FE2b 6537. Also: Henshaw, *The Sky Their Battlefield II*. p.42 (High Barnet: Fetubi 2014).

7. TNA AIR 1/844/204/5/372, 2 July 1916.

8. TNA, AIR 1/1219/ 204/5/2634, Air Combat Reports 11 Squadron July 1916. 2 July 1916. Ball was in Nieuport A134 on both occasions.

9. Ibid. 3 July 1916.

10. Bowyer, op.cit. p.62.

11. RAF Museum, C85/20.

12. RAF Museum, DC 63/662/1, 6 July 1916.

13. AIR 1/844/204/5/372, 6 July 1916. Second Lieutenant Wood and Captain Field were in FE2b 6954.

14. Ibid. 6 July 1916. Lieutenant Foot was in Bristol Scout 2962.

15. Franks, Norman, *Fallen Eagles*. p. 130 (Barnsley: Pen and Sword 2017).

16. RAF Museum, DC 63/66/1, 7 July 1916.

17. TNA, AIR 27/19161. p. 301.

18. INA, DD/1180/2/43, letter to Ball's father, 6 July 1916. Also DD/1180/2/44, letter to his mother 7 July 1916.

19. Boyle, op.cit. p. 201.

20. RAF Museum, MFC 76/1, letter to Brancker, 7 July 1916.

21. RAF Museum, DC 73/622/1, 9 July 1916.

22. TNA, AIR 1/844/204/5/372, 6 July 1916. Captain Rough/ Captain Field were in FE2b 6950.

23. RAF Museum, DC 73/622/1, 9 July 1916.

24. TNA, AIR 1/844/204/5/372, 9 July 1916. Lieutenant Speer and Second Lieutenant Wedgwood were in FE2b 6949.

25. Hughes, Peter, *Visiting the Fallen Arras South*. p. 96. (Barnsley: Pen and Sword 2015).

26. TNA, AIR 1/997/204/5/1241, Training of Pilots and Observers.

27. TNA, AIR 1/2245/209 42/29, Third Brigade Intelligence Diary, 1 July 1916.

28. Henshaw, *The Sky Their Battlefield II*. p. 43.

29. Cole, *RFC Communiques 1915–1916.* p 180. Also: TNA, AIR 1/844/204/5/372, 9 July 1916. Second Lieutenant MacIntyre and Second Lieutenant Floyd were in FE2b 6971. Also: :www.airhistory.org.uk/rfc/people_index.html.

30. INA, DD/1180/2/46, letter to Ball's father, 10 July 1916.

31. Fry, op.cit. p.67.

32. RAF Museum, DC 73/662/1,10 July 1916.

33. A gudgeon pin held a piston rod and a connecting rod together.

34. RAF Museum, DC 73/662/1, 14 July 1916.

35. RAF Museum, DC 73/662/1, 15 July 1916.

36. TNA, AIR 1/844/204/5/372. 15–16 July 1916. Lieutenant Foot was in Bristol Scout 5578. Second Lieutenants Buntine and Wyatt were in FE2b 4279.

37. Ibid. 20 July 1916. Second Lieutenant Fry was in Bristol Scout 5577.

38. *London Gazette* Supplement 4 August 1916. p. 7675.

39. TNA, AIR 1/844/204/5/372, 20 July 1916. Second Lieutenant (J. F.) Morris was in Bristol Scout 5561.

40. RAF Museum, DC 73/662/1, 18 July 1916.

41. Lieutenant John Slessor, 5 Squadron, RFC. Quoted in Hart, *Bloody April.* p 290.

42. RAF Museum, DC 73/622/1, 10 July 1916.

43. Due to the lack of records, it is difficult to identify definitively the Harris that Morris had met, but a likely candidate would be Second Lieutenant Norman Bradford Harris, who can be found in http://airhistory.org.uk/rfc/people.html as having transferred to the air corps via the Royal Fusiliers and looks like an NCO who had re-trained as an observer.

44. RAF Museum, DC 73/622/1, 20 July 1916.

45. Lewis-Stemple, John, *Where Poppies Blow*. p. 22 (London: Weidenfeld and Nicolson 2016).

46. RAF Museum, DC 73/622/1, 21 July 1916.

47. Ibid.

48. Lewis-Stemple, op.cit. p.295.

49. RAF Museum, DC 73/622/1, 21 July 1916.

50. Yeates, V.M., *Winged Victory*. p.133 (London: Grub Street 2004).

51. RAF Museum, DC 73/622/1, 21 July 1916.

52. Bowyer, op.cit. p.64.

53. RAF Museum, DC 73/622/1, 16 July 1916.

54. Moran, Lord, *The Anatomy of Courage* (London: Constable 1945). Quoted in Mackersey, op.cit. p. 262.

55. Balfour, Harold, *An Airman Marches*. p.46 (London: Hutchinson and Co.1993).

56. Jones, Vol III, pp. 201, 471, 105.

57. Ibid. p. 236.

58. TNA, AIR 1/844/204/5/372 17 July 1916.

59. IWM, H Wyllie, Transcript Diary, 19 June 1916. Quoted in Hart, *Somme Success*. p. 69-70.

60. Second Lieutenant Godfrey Firbank was killed in action on 11 September 1916. www.cwgc.org

61. RAF Museum, DC 73/622/1, 21 July 1916.

62. Ibid. 22 July 1916.

63. INA, DD/1180/2/2, letter to Ball's parents, 18 February 1916.

64. RAF Museum, DC 73/622/1, 23 July 1916.

65. Ibid. 24 July 1916. Second Lieutenant Leslie Godfrey Harcourt Vernon was Second Lieutenant Firbank's observer and also died on 11 September 1916.

66. IWM, Captain Harold Wyllie, Transcript Diary, 4 May 1916. Quoted in Hart, Somme Success. p.66.

67. RAF Museum, DC 73/622/1, 26 July 1916.

68. CGS, Lyle Buntine Archives, letter to his parents, 1 August 1916. This could refer to Morris's unfortunate namesake, 2nd Lt. J.F. Morris, who had suffered two bad landings that month. The official history of the squadron lists no other mishaps for the end of the month.

69. RAF Museum, DC 73/622/1, 26–30 July 1916.

70. TNA, AIR 1/844/204/5/372, 30 July 1916. Lieutenant Foot was in Nieuport Scout A126.

71. RAF Museum, DC 73/622/1, 31 July 1916.

## Chapter 13: A Plucky Observer

1. Baring, op.cit. p.86.

2. Ibid. p.127.

3. Jones, Vol III, p.238–9.

4. Philpott, p.254.

5. Anon German soldier, 24 Infantry Division. Quoted in Hart, *Somme Success*. p.28

6. Baring, op.cit. p.127.

7. Ibid.

8. RAF Museum, MFC 76/1, letter to Brancker, 25 July 916.

9. Ibid.

10. England and Wales Birth Registration Index, 1837–2008

11. RAF Museum, AC98/31/2, letter from May Jones to William Evans, 10 November 1988.

12. www.freebmd.org.uk.

13. *Brecon & Radnor Express*, 16 December 1915. National Library of Wales.

14. Ibid.

15. Wall, Anthony, *A Turbid Tale: Geology at Aberystwyth*. p. 23 (Berkely: 2000).

16. TNA, WO 339/23012, Captain Tom Rees, The Royal Welsh Fusiliers.

17. University College of North Wales, Bangor MS 7060. *Nominal Roll of NCOs and Men Who Embarked With the Battalion on 1 December 1915*. Quoted in Beckett and Simpson, p.116.

18. TNA, WO 339/23012.

19. RAF Museum, AC98/31/2, Tom Rees.

20. TNA, WO 339/23012.

21. *Brecon & Radnor Express,* 16 December 1915.

22. Ibid.

23. Griffith, Llewelyn Wyn, *Up to Mametz... and Beyond*. pp.4, 18 (Barnsley: Pen and Sword 2010).

24. Jefford, p.30. The timing of Rees's transfer to the RFC isn't clear in his War Office file and there's no surviving RFC service record that gives a date.

25. Ibid. p.10.

26. Ibid. p.30. Also: TNA, WO 339/23012. Rees was promoted to Second Lieutenant on 21 January 1915.

27. Jefford, op.cit. p.31.

28. Rees Family Archive.

29. TNA, WO 339/23012.

30. Insall, A.J., 'Cameos of the Air III – Poor Visibility'. p.36–8. *Air* May 1929.

31. 1st Air Mechanic William Harris, No. 57 Squadron. Quoted in Joslyn, Mauriel, op.cit. Locations 2947, 2952.

32. Macmillan, op.cit. p.94.

33. TNA, AIR 1/2245/209/42/30, 3 August 1916. Rees and Captain Rough were in FE2b 6965.

34. IWM Sound Archives, Joseph Hellingoe.

## Chapter 14: Cabbages and Kings

1. INA, DD/1180/2/35 and DD/1180/2/60, letters to Ball's family, 5 June, 14 August 1916.

2. RAF Museum, O. B. Rice manuscript letter, 10 May 1917.Quoted in Hart, *Bloody April*, p.295.

3. Libby, Frederick, *Horses Don't Fly*. p.162 (New York, Arcade 2000).

4. TNA, AIR 76 299/102 F. Libby. Libby's service record gives the date of his transfer to No. 11 Squadron as 25 August 1916.

5. Libby, op.cit. p.161.

6. RAF Museum. DC 72/56/27, Programme of Concert by 11 and 13 Squadrons RFC held on 7 August 1916.

7. Cooksley, op.cit. p.193.

8. Libby, op.cit. p.174.

9. Gliddon, Gerald. *When the Barrage Lifts: Topographical History and Commentary on the Battle of the Somme*. Quoted on www.ramsdale.org/timeline.htm

10. RAF Museum, B1963, 1 August 1916. Second Lieutenants Anderson and Allen were in FE2b 6899.

11. TNA, AIR 1/844/204/5/373, Reports on Aeroplane and Personnel Casualties August 1916, 1 August 1916. Lieutenant Bowmand and Air Mechanic Mills were in FE2b 6984.

12. TNA, AIR 1/2245/209/42/30 Third Brigade War Diary August 1916. 1 August 1916. Sergeants Thompson and Clarkson were in FE2b 6983.

13. Cole, *RFC Communiques 1916–1917*. p.205.

14. TNA, AIR 1/2245/209/42/30, 3 August 1916. Morris and Glover were in FE2b 6983.

15. Fry, op.cit. pp.164–5.

16. Ibid. p.168.

17. TNA, AIR 1/844/204/5/373, 5 August 1916. Second Lieutenant Drysdale was in Bristol Scout 5594.

18. Ibid. 11 and 12 August 1916. Drysdale was in Nieuport Scouts A134 and A184 respectively. The 12 August report documented a crash after a special patrol of just 20 minutes. Drysdale may have been on a kite balloon-busting run, although he was not equipped with any Le Prieur rockets.

19. Ibid. 10 August 1916. Second Lieutenant Toms was in Bristol Scout 5572.

20. www.iwm.org.uk/collections/item/object/205072378.

21. MacDonald, Alan, *'A lack of offensive spirit?': The 46th (North Midland) Division at Gommecourt 1st July 1916*. p.183 (Iona Books: 2008).

22. RAF Museum, B1963.

23. Libby, op.cit. p.84. Without specific dates to confirm his recollections, Libby's memoirs weave about as much as a wily FE pilot avoiding enemy fire.

24. TNA, AIR 1/2245/209/42/30, 17 August 1916. Morris and Rees were in FE2b 6973.

25. Cole, *RFC Communiques 1915–1916*. p.219

26. Fry, op.cit. p.68.

27. INA, DD/1180/2/60, letter to Ball's parents 14 August 1916.

28. Bowyer, op.cit. p.72.

29. INA, DD/1180/2/61, letter to Ball's parents 16 August 1916.

30. Franks and Guest, op.cit. p.55. Also: Bowyer, op.cit. p.74.

31. RAF Museum, MFC 76/1/7, letter to Brancker, 19 August 1916.

32. INA, DD/1180/2/106, letter to Ball's father 5 May 1917.

33. RAF Museum DC 72/56/27. Programme of concert by 11 and 13 Squadrons RFC held on 20 August 1916.

34. CGS, Lyle Buntine Archives, undated letter 1916.

35. TNA, AIR 1/2245/209/42/30, 21 August 1916.Morris and Rees were in FE2b 6983. Also: O'Connor, Michael, Norman Franks, *In the Footsteps of the Red Baron*. p.94. (Barnsley: Pen and Sword 2004).

36. Ball Archives, letter to his parents 22 August 1916.

## Chapter 15: Follow the Leader

1. Chree, C, *The Magnetic Storm of August 22 1916*. (The Royal Society 1917)

2. TNA, AIR 1/2245/209/42/30, 17 August 1916. Morris and Rees were in FE2b 6983.

3. Jones, Vol III. p.238.

4. TNA, AIR 1/2245/209/42/30, 22 August 1916. Other combat reports suggest Lieutenants Davey and Sanders in FE2b 4844 were also involved in the offensive patrol. The sprawling events of the day led to confusion in the records as to who had been involved and on what mission – Sergeant Thompson and Captain Field in FE2b 6982 reported a time of between 7.00 and 7.20 pm and scores out 'escort to bombing patrol' in favour of 'offensive patrol'.

5. Ibid. Price and Libby were in FE2b 6994.

6. Ibid.

7. Ibid.

8. Cole, op.cit. pp. 229–230.

9. INA, DD/1180/2/64, letter to Ball's parents, 26 August 1916.

10. Ibid.

11. Bowyer, op.cit. p. 76.

12. TNA, AIR/1/2246/209/42/30, 22 August 1916.

13. Franks, Norman, Frank Bailey and Rick Duiven, *Casualties of the German Air Service 1914–1920.* p. 192. (London: Grub Street: 1999).

14. TNA, AIR/1/2246/209/42/30, Intelligence Summary, 22 August 1916.

15. Cole, op.cit. p. 228.

16. Ibid.

17. Bowyer, op.cit. p. 77.

18. Scott, Group Captain A.J.L, *Sixty Squadron RAF, A History of the Squadron From Its Formation.* p.16 (London: William Heinemann 1920).

19. Baring, op.cit. p.89.

20. Miller, op.cit. pp.122–3.

21. IWM, Sound Catalogue 24, Archibald William Henry James.

22. Cole, op.cit. p.233.

23. Ibid. p.234.

24. Ibid. p.236.

25. TNA, AIR 1/844/204/5/373, 29 August 1916. Second Lieutenant Turk and Lieutenant Scott were in FE2b 4926.

26. Jones, Vol III. p. 251.

27. Henshaw, *The Sky Their Battlefield II*. p.50.

28. Bowyer, op.cit. p.89.

29. O'Connor, Michael, *Airfields and Airmen: Arras*. p.142 (Barnsley: Pen and Sword 2004).

30. TNA, AIR 1/166/15/150. p.3.

31. Fry, op.cit. p.106.

32. Scott, op.cit. p.24. Also O'Connor, Mike, *Airfields and Airmen: Ypres*. p.94 (Barnsley: Pen and Sword 2008).

33. Fry, p.107.

34. Macdonald, *Somme*, pp.107–8. (London: Penguin 1993).

35. CGS, Lyle Buntine Archives, letter to his parents August 1916.

36. Ibid.

37. Jones, Vol. II. p.470.

## Chapter 16: Broken Birds

1. RAF Museum, MFC 76/1/7, letter to Brancker, 9 September 1916.

2. Henshaw, *The Sky Their Battlefield II*. p.347.

3. *Report of the War Office Committee of Enquiry Into 'Shell-shock' (Cmd. 1734)*. 1922. p.59 (London: Imperial War Museum 2004).

4. Cobden, Lindsay Shaw, 'The Nervous Flyer: Nerves, Flying and the First World War.' p.127. *British Journal of Military History*. Vol.4 Issue 2 2018.

5. *Flight*, 2 March 1916.

6. Cobden, op.cit. p.136.

7. *Report of the War Office Committee of Enquiry Into 'Shell-shock'*. p.84.

8. Ibid, p.69.

9. TNA, AIR 1/1007/204/5/1278, 21 October 1917.

10. Cobden, op.cit. p.127.

11. Mackersey, op.cit. pp.284–285.

12. Ibid. p.263.

13. *Report of the War Office Committee of Enquiry Into 'Shell-shock'* p.152.

14. Gibbs, Philip, *Now It Can Be Told*. p. 387 (New York: Garden City Publishing Company Inc 1920). Quoted in Bradbeer, pp.329–30.

15. TNA, AIR 27/161 Appendices: Y. pp.311–322.

16. RAF Museum, C85/20.

17. TNA, AIR 1/845/204/5/374, 2 September 1916. Anderson and Allen were in FE2b 7008.

18. TNA, AIR 1/2246/209/42/31, Third Brigade War Diary September 1916, 2 September 1916. Second Lieutenants Burton and Griffiths were in FE2b 4290, Captain Quested and Lieutenant Wyatt in FE2b 6965.

19. TNA, AIR 1/845/204/5/374, 2 September 1916.

20. Henshaw, *The Sky Their Battlefield II*. p.50.

21. Cole, op.cit. p.243. Also TNA, AIR 1/2246/209/42/31, Intelligence Summary, 5 September 1916 and Jones, Vol III, p.259.

22. TNA, AIR 1/845/204/5/374. 7 September 1916. Sergeants Thompson and Drudge were in FE2b 6989.

23. Ibid. 9 September 1916. Foot was in FE2b 7016 with Second Lieutenant Welsford, Second Lieutenant Molloy and Sergeant Allan in FE2b 6947.

24. CGS, Lyle Buntine Archives, letter to his mother 17 September 1916.

25. Moran, Daryl, email to the author, 23 March 2017.

26. TNA, AIR 1/845/204/5/374 Third Brigade Recommendations for Honours and Awards March 1916–April 1918. Buntine and Sergeant Morton were in FE2b 6988.

27. Lyle Buntine Archives, letter to his mother 17 September 1916.

28. Moran, Daryl, unpublished manuscript, p.88.

29. TNA, AIR 1/845/204/5/374.

30. www.airhistory.org.uk/rfc/people.html

## Chapter 17: Bombs Over Bapaume

1. TNA, AIR 1/2246/209/42/31, Intelligence Summary, 11 September 1916.

2. Rowell H, quoted in Hart, *Somme Success*. p.166.

3. Jones, Vol III. pp.270, 273.

4. RAF Museum, MFC 76/1/7, letter to Brancker, 7 September 1916.

5. The 'British' attack was made up of the combined efforts of the current and former Empire – the Canadians particularly fighting with great tenacity in the Reserve Army.

6. Philpott, p.364.

7. TNA, AIR 1/2246/209/42/31, 14 September 1916. Morris and Rees were in FE2b 7018, Gray and Lieutenant Helder in FE2b 6947 and Captain Price and Second Lieutenant Libby in FE2b 6994.

8. Ibid.

9. Ibid.

10. Ibid.

11. Cole, *R.F.C. Communiques 1915–1916*. p.254.

12. TNA, AIR 1/2246/209/42/31, 14 September. Molloy and Morton were in FE2b 4844, Foot and Welsford in FE2b 7016 and Captain Davey and Lieutenant Clayton in FE2b 7019.

13. Ibid.

14. Boyle. pp.199–200.

15. Hart, *Somme Success.* p.167.

16. Another two divisions were made up of Canadian and New Zealand troops.

17. Jones, Vol III. p.274.

18. Sources for this and the previous paragraph are from TNA, AIR 1/2246/209/42/31, 15 September, and Cole, pp.257–8. Morris and Rees were in FE2b 7018, Foot and Welsford in FE2b 7016, Lieutenant Sargood and Captain Field in FE2b 6982, Quested and Corporal Monk in FE2b 6965 and Bowman and Sergeant Walker in FE2b 6986.

19. Ibid.

20. Ibid.

21. Ibid.

22. Baring, op.cit. p.140. The Official History gives a total of fourteen crashed German planes. See Jones, Vol III. p.280.

23. TNA, AIR 1/2246/209/42/3/34. 15 September 1916. Foot and Welsford were in FE2b 7016.

24. TNA, AIR 1/2246/209/42/31/62,15 September 1916.

25. Ibid.

26. AIR 1/845/204/5/374, 15 September 1916. Hollingsworth and Wells were in FE2b 6947.

27. The deaths of Hollingsworth, Wells and Walker are all listed on the Commonwealth War Grave Commission's website.

28. Van Wyngarden, Greg, *Jagdstaffel 2 Boelcke: Von Richthofen's Mentor*. p.13. (Oxford: Osprey 2007).

29. Libby, op.cit. p.174.

30. Head, R. G, *Oswald Boelcke*, p.122. (London: Grub Street 2016).

31. TNA, AIR 1/2246/209/42/31/74, 16 September 1916. Davey and Clayton were in FE2b 7019.

32. Henshaw, *The Sky Their Battlefield II*. p.53.

33. TNA, AIR 1/845/204/5/374/72 and 73. 16 September 1916. Harvey and Cathie were in FE2b 6973, Quested and Welsford in FE2b 7016.

34. TNA, AIR 1/845/204/5/374, 16 September 1916. Pinkerton and Sanders were in FE2b 6999.

## Chapter 18: Taken At The Flood

1. Richthofen, Manfred von, *The Red Air Fighter*, transl. Barker, T. Ellis. p.92. (London: Greenhill Press 1990).

2. Money, R.R. *Flying and Soldiering*. p.67 (Auckland: PS Chapman 2012).

3. TNA, AIR 1/845/204/5/374, 17 September 1916. Also RAF Museum, DC 73/66/2, letter to Albert Morris from Captain D.S. Gray 25 November 1916 and Money, op.cit. p.67.

4. Accounts vary between eye witnesses as to whether a seventh FE was also present. Gray said six or seven, Richthofen said seven and Money (and Libby who wrote about the aftermath) said six. The subsequent reports which accounted for the victims and the survivors suggest there were only six. Boelcke also stated that out of eight, 'only two escaped'. The arrival of No. 60 Squadron no doubt confused numbers further. The official German Army version stated 'Boelcke in conjunction with other German flyers attacked a formation of 13 aircraft and brought the enemy leader to crash after hard fighting; five more aircraft were brought down

by other German flyers.' See: RAF Museum, DC 73/66/2. Also Richthofen, op.cit. p. 93, Libby, op.cit. p. 234, Van Wyngarden op.cit. p. 13 and Miller, *Inside the Victories of Manfred von Richthofen.* p.21 (Aeronaut: 2016). Thompson and Glover were in FE2b 6994, Turk and Scott in FE2b 6992. AIR 1/845/204/5/374 and AIR 1/2246/208/4312.

5. Money, op.cit. p.67.

6. RAF Museum, DC 73/66/2.

7. Lieutenant Helder's repatriation report confirmed that 'the formation became broken up on account of one machine dropping behind and others turning to support' TNA AIR 1/1207/204/5/2619. Reports by repatriated or escaped RAF officer prisoners of war.

8. Money, op.cit. p.68.

9. Richthofen, op.cit. p.93.

10. For a discussion of this moot point, see: www.theaerodrome.com/forum/showthread.php?t=40352&page=2 There is no mention in Morris's notebook of him actually using one of the FE2b's guns, in a combat situation or otherwise.

11. Richthofen, op.cit. p.93.

12. Ibid.

13. Ibid. p.94.

14. TNA AIR 1/686/21/13/2250 Translation of original combat report of Manfred von Richthofen 17 September 1916. See also Miller, *Inside the Victories of Manfred von Richthofen Vol 1.* p.23.

15. Richthofen, op.cit. p.94.

16. This dashing touch came from the American war correspondent and author Floyd Gibbons, in an article later expanded into a book, *The Red Knight of Germany*, published in 1927. www.archives.chicagotribune.com/1928/01/22/page/59/article/the-red-knight-of-germany.

17. Richthofen, op.cit.p.94.

18. Libby, Frederick, op.cit. p.234.

19. TNA AIR 1/2246/209/42/31.

20. TNA AIR 1/845/204/5/374.

21. Henshaw, *The Sky Their Battlefield II*. p.53. Molloy and Morton were in FE2b 4844.

22. There is some confusion in Money's account as he had described Molloy as having been Gray's observer – and Helder as having been wounded in the ear, rather than the arm as Gray had reported. Money, op.cit. p.70. Also TNA, AIR1/1206/204/5/2619, Reports by repatriated or escaped RAF officer prisoners of war. *Leutnant* Frankl of *Jasta* 4 was credited with the victory. Henshaw, *The Sky Their Battlefield II*. p.53.

23. Money, p.68. The estimate of the numbers of German aircraft is striking, if inaccurate, and indicates the intensity of the experience.

24. Ibid. p.72. Patterson was in BE2d 5873.

25. Ibid.

26. TNA AIR1/1206/204/5/2619.

27. Boelcke, Oswald, *An Aviator's Field Book*. 17 September 1916. (New York: National Military Publishing Co. 1919).

28. Ibid.

29. TNA AIR 1/686/21/13/2250, Combat reports of Capt. Baron Von Richthofen, 17 September 1916.

30. Van Wyngarden, Greg, *Jagdstaffel 2 Boelcke: Von Richthofen's Mentor*. p.14.

31. Kilduff, Peter, *The Red Baron*. p.53 (London: Cassell 1994).

32. Henshaw, *The Sky Their Battlefield II*. p.53.

33. RAF Museum, MFC 76/1, letter to Brancker 17 September 1916.

34. Jones, Vol III. p.473.

35. Ibid. p.474.

36. RAF Museum, MFC 76/1, letter to Brancker, 21 September 1916.

37. RAF Museum B4221. Photocopy of flying log books of Wing Commander Thomas O'Brien Hubbard. 1912–1931.

## Chapter 19: Our Brave and Good Friends

1. TNA, WO 339/39180.

2. *Brecon and Radnor Express*, 5 October 1916.

3. *Flight*, 23 November 1916.

4. *Auckland Star*, Volume XLVIII Issue 36, 10 December 1917. National Library of New Zealand.

5. *Carshalton and Wallington Advertiser*, 29 September 1916.

6. TNA, WO 339/3910.

7. TNA, AIR 1/967/1204/5/1098 Pilot and observer casualties: RFC France 1916 Sept.–1917 Feb. Also: TNA, WO 339/3910.

8. In Morris's Officer Service Records file, 22 October 1916 is given as the date that official notification of his death was received. This date doesn't appear on any other paperwork in his War Office file. See: AIR 76/358/186.

9. TNA, AIR1/1206/204/5/2619. Gray states that both his and Morris's aircraft came down at 'Nurlie'.

10. RAF Museum, DC 73/66 2.

11. Ibid.

12. Ibid.

13. Van Emden, Richard, *Meeting the Enemy*. p.223 (London: Bloomsbury 2013).

14. Gray's extraordinary story is told in several books, see: Durnford, Hugh, *The Tunnellers of Holzminden* (Penguin: 1943) and Winchester, Barry, *Beyond the Tumult* (London: Corgi 1973).

15. TNA, AIR1/1206/204/5/2619. See also www.anciens-aerodromes.com/?p=13794 The 'Nurlie' location was included on the RAF's Roll of Honour: www.rafmuseumstoryvault.org.uk/archive/7000290825-morris-l.b.f.-Morris-bertram-frank

16. Richthofen, op.cit. p.94.

17. *Chicago Tribune*, 'The Red Knight of Germany' 2 January 1928.

18. TNA, AIR 1/686/21/13/2250.

19. Richthofen, Manfred von, p.94.

20. Richthofen, Manfred von, transl. Kilduff, Peter, *The Red Baron*. p.51 (Folkestone: Bailey Brothers & Swinfen 1974). Villers Plouich was closer to Richthofen's base at Bertincourt than Cambrai. Floyd Gibbons wrote that the placing of a stone was a double tribute to Rees and Morris, carried out at both airmen's graves in the Cambrai hospital yard. Whatever the truth, the ambiguity of the quote has inspired speculation about the possibility of Jewish origins for all three men, as there is a Jewish practice of laying stones on a grave. See www.archives.chicagotribune.com/1928/01/22/page/59/article/the-red-knight-of-germany

21. TNA, AIR 1/1515/204/58/51, 3 Brigade Recommendations for Honours and Awards October 1916.

22. Ibid.

23. *Flight*, 30 November 1916.

24. Morris's name appears in the 1 December edition of the *Carshalton and Wallington Advertiser*.

25. TNA, WO 339/3910.

26. Ibid.

27. Ibid.

28. TNA, WO 339/3910.

29. Ibid.

30. UK Army Registers of Soldiers Effects 1901–1929 (database on-line).

31. www.cwgc.org.

32. TNA, WO 339/3910.

33. Crane, David, *Empires of the Dead.* p.136. (London: William Collins 2013).

34. www.cwgc.org.

35. Crane.op.cit. p.142.

36. TNA WO 339/3910.

37. www.cwgc.org.

38. Crane, op.cit. p.131.

39. Ibid. p.201.

40. Franks, Norman, Giblin, Hal and McCrery, Nigel, *Under the Guns of The Red Baron.* p.35. (London: Grub Street 1995).

41. *The Whitgiftian* February 1917. Also: www.grandeguerre.icrc.org.

42. The identity of Richthofen's nemesis is still debated, but most authorities support Barber's theory. Miller, Dr M. Geoffrey. 'The Death of Manfred von Richthofen: Who fired the fatal shot?' First published in *Sabretache, the Journal and Proceedings of the Military History Society of Australia*, Vol. XXXIX, No. 2, June 1998.

## Chapter 20: The Forgotten Warriors

1. Insall, A.J., 'Cameos of the Air VIII – A.B.', *Flying*, May 1919.

2. INA, DD/1180/2/39, letter to Ball's parents, 28 June 1916.

3. McCudden, op.cit. p.120. For pilot loss, see Revell, *Brief Glory*, p.156.

4. INA, DD/1180/2/77, letter to Ball's mother, 29 September 1916.

5. Pengelly, op.cit. p.182.

6. Briscoe et al, op.cit. p.126.

7. *Flight*, 28 June 1923.

8. TNA, WO 339/69688, Lieutenant Fred Libby, Royal Flying Corps.

9. Libby, op.cit. pp.273–4.

10. *Flight*, 19 October 1919.

11. *Flight*, 20 July 1920.

12. The British Museum, Thomas O'Brien (Biographical details) www.britishmuseum.org/research/search_the_collection_database/term_details.aspx?bioId=169577

13. Briscoe and Stannard, p.111. Also RAF Museum, C85/20.

14. Durnford, Hugh, *The Tunnellers of Holzminden*, p.119 (Cambridge University Press: 1920).

15. Winchester, Barry, *Beyond the Tumult*. pp.196–198. (London: Corgi 1971).

16. TNA, AIR 76/192/96, Gray, David. B.

17. Interest in the story remains high and film rights were sold in early 2018 for the latest retelling, Neale Bascombe's '*The Grand Escape*', before the book manuscript had been handed over to the publishers. www.empireonline.com/movies/room/room-lenny-abrahamson-grand-escape/

18. *London Gazette*, 24 January 1919, 23 July 1928, 24 February 1933, 11 August 1939, 21 November 1939, 24 November 1942.

19. Winchester, op.cit. p.201.

20. Conversation with Jane Gray of Wonston, May 2018.

21. TNA, WO 339/23012. Despite an extensive searches, I have not been able to find evidence of Rees's promotion to Captain; the rank he is most commonly believed to have held.

22. *Brecon and Radnor Express*, 16 November 1916.

23. Email to author from Martin Williamson, Cranleigh School Archivist, 8 August 2016.

24. Richmond Local Studies Department.

25. McCudden, op.cit. p.202.

26. Gibbons, Floyd, *The Red Knight of Germany.* p.69. (New York: Garden City 1927).

27. Ibid. p.76.

28. *Guardian*, 16 March 2008

29. General Record Office Death Certificate, 15 May 1935. Also: England and Wales Death Registration Index 1837–2007.

30. Reid, Terry, *The Best Flying Club in the World.* Family Photobiograpy 2016.

31. Conversation between Michael Reid and author, 2013.

32. England & Wales, National Probate Calendar (Index of Wills and Administrations) 1858–1966, 1973–1995.

33. RAF Museum, DC 73/66.

34. Second order memory' as defined by the historian Jay Winter as the collection, organisation, exhibition and cataloguing of memory. Winter, Jay and Emmanuel Sivan. *War and Remembrance In the Twentieth Century.* p.2. (Cambridge University Press: 1999).

## Epilogue

1. Jordan, David, 'Learning to Fly: The Royal Flying Corps and the Development of Air Power' *British Journal of Military History.* Vol 4 Iss. *2*, 2018. p.22.

2. Ibid. p.2–3.

3. Malinovska and Joslyn, op.cit. Locations 515–516.

4. Hynes, Samuel. *The Unsubstantial Air. American Fliers in World War One.* p.17 (New York: Farrar, Straus and Giroux 2014).

# Index